IP Routing Fundamentals

Mark A. Sportack

Cisco Press
201 West 103rd Street
Indianapolis, IN 46290 USA

IP Routing Fundamentals

Mark A. Sportack

Copyright © 1999 Cisco Press

The Cisco Press logo is a trademark of Cisco Systems, Inc.

Published by:
Cisco Press
201 West 103rd Street
Indianapolis, IN 46290 USA

Printed in the United States of America   4 5 6 7 8 9 0

Library of Congress Cataloging-in-Publication Number: 98-84283

ISBN: 1-57870-071-x

Warning and Disclaimer

This book is designed to provide information about IP Routing. Every effort has been made to make this book as complete and as accurate as possible, but no warranty or fitness is implied.

The information is provided on an "as is" basis. The author, Cisco Press, and Cisco Systems, Inc., shall have neither liability nor responsibility to any person or entity with respect to any loss or damages arising from the information contained in this book or from the use of the discs or programs that may accompany it.

The opinions expressed in this book belong to the author and are not necessarily those of Cisco Systems, Inc.

Feedback Information

At Cisco Press, our goal is to create in-depth technical books of the highest quality and value. Each book is crafted with care and precision, undergoing rigorous development that involves the unique expertise of members from the professional technical community.

Readers' feedback is a natural continuation of this process. If you have any comments regarding how we could improve the quality of this book, or otherwise alter it to better suit your needs, you can contact us through e-mail at ciscopress@mcp.com. Please make sure to include the book title and ISBN in your message.

We greatly appreciate your assistance.

Publisher	J. Carter Shanklin
Executive Editor	Alicia Buckley
Cisco Systems Program Manager	Jim LeValley
Managing Editor	Patrick Kanouse
Acquisitions Editor	Brett Bartow
Development Editor	Kitty Wilson Jarrett
Project Editor	Jen Nuckles
Copy Editor	Keith Cline
Technical Editors	Matthew H. Birkner
	David Kurtiak
	Don Slice
	Russ White
Team Coordinator	Amy Lewis
Proofreader	Megan Wade
Book Designer	Trina Wurst
Cover Designer	Karen Ruggles
Production Team	Argosy
Indexer	Kevin Fulcher

CISCO SYSTEMS

CISCO PRESS

Corporate Headquarters
Cisco Systems, Inc.
170 West Tasman Drive
San Jose, CA 95134-1706
USA
http://www.cisco.com
Tel: 408 526-4000
800 553-NETS (6387)
Fax: 408 526-4100

European Headquarters
Cisco Systems Europe s.a.r.l.
Parc Evolic, Batiment L1/L2
16 Avenue du Quebec
Villebon, BP 706
91961 Courtaboeuf Cedex
France
http://www-europe.cisco.com
Tel: 33 1 69 18 61 00
Fax: 33 1 69 28 83 26

Americas Headquarters
Cisco Systems, Inc.
170 West Tasman Drive
San Jose, CA 95134-1706
USA
http://www.cisco.com
Tel: 408 526-7660
Fax: 408 527-0883

Asia Headquarters
Nihon Cisco Systems K.K.
Fuji Building, 9th Floor
3-2-3 Marunouchi
Chiyoda-ku, Tokyo 100
Japan
http://www.cisco.com
Tel: 81 3 5219 6250
Fax: 81 3 5219 6001

Cisco Systems has more than 200 offices in the following countries. Addresses, phone numbers, and fax numbers are listed on the Cisco Connection Online Web site at http://www.cisco.com/offices.

Argentina • Australia • Austria • Belgium • Brazil • Canada • Chile • China • Colombia • Costa Rica • Croatia • Czech Republic • Denmark • Dubai, UAE Finland • France • Germany • Greece • Hong Kong • Hungary • India • Indonesia • Ireland • Israel • Italy • Japan • Korea • Luxembourg • Malaysia Mexico • The Netherlands • New Zealand • Norway • Peru • Philippines • Poland • Portugal • Puerto Rico • Romania • Russia • Saudi Arabia • Singapore Slovakia • Slovenia • South Africa • Spain • Sweden • Switzerland • Taiwan • Thailand • Turkey • Ukraine • United Kingdom • United States • Venezuela

About the Author

Mark A. Sportack is an information technology architect at AT&T and has more than 15 years' experience planning, using, supporting, and managing both information and information technologies. Mark's present responsibilities include specifying both the architectures and technology base for AT&T's local- and wide-area networks, and developing strategies for new and emerging technologies. Additionally, Mark is the author or co-author of several books on various aspects of networking technology: *High-Performance Networking Unleashed, Windows NT Clustering Blueprints, Teach Yourself MCSE Networking Essentials in 14 Days,* and *Networking Essentials Unleashed.*

About the Technical Reviewers

Matthew H. Birkner, CCIE #3719, has been working in the networking industry for seven years. He has been a network design engineer, a network operations center engineer, and a technical support engineer. Formerly senior networking engineer in MCI's outsourcing unit, he was responsible for the resolution of complex customer networking issues. Currently, he is a network consulting engineer for Cisco Systems, where he works on enterprise network designs and performance analysis. Matt holds a bachelor's degree in electrical engineering from Tufts University.

David Kurtiak is a data communications specialist for AT&T, where he provides the Consumer and Small Business Unit with strategic planning for its data communications infrastructure, which consists of a wide variety of networks, computing platforms, network operating systems, and custom-developed applications. He specializes in end-to-end network analysis, planning, and troubleshooting. David is experienced in many telecommunications technologies, including Ethernet, FDDI, switches, hubs, routers, dialup access, VPN technologies, point-to-point digital facilities, Frame Relay, and premise wiring topologies. He is also recognized as the resident expert in TCP/IP networking. David has a master's degree in telecommunications from the University of Colorado at Boulder and a bachelor's degree in information systems from the University of North Carolina at Greensboro.

Dedications

To my precious wife, Karen; I never realized how wonderful life could be until I met you.

To my children, Adam and Jennifer; you two are my pride and my joy.

Acknowledgments

I would like to express my thanks to Ronald Hagen. Thanks, Ron, for that life-changing lunchtime chat all those years ago. You were right: The future of networking was IP. It still is. Thanks for the advice and guidance.

I would also like to thank David Kurtiak, Matt Birkner, Russ White, and Don Slice. I couldn't have asked for a more talented and capable group of reviewers. Thanks, guys, for all your support, assistance, and knowledge.

Finally, I'd like to thank Brett Bartow, Amy Lewis, Kitty Jarrett, Alicia Buckley, and everyone else at Cisco Press and Macmillan Technical Publishing who helped make this book a reality.

Contents at a Glance

Contents

Introduction

Routing is simultaneously the most complicated function of a network and the most important. Most knowledgeable people agree that networking and routing technologies have been around about 25 years. The concept of routing actually dates back to the late 1950s, when computing was still an arcane science in its infancy. Precious few organizations had a single computer, much less multiple computers that needed to be linked together. Internetworking, the interconnection of multiple computers, was still more of a futuristic vision than a reality. This vision predicted a day when computers would be widely implemented and interconnected via a ubiquitous global internetwork: the Internet.

The challenge in building and using a global internetwork is developing the means to find, access, and communicate with remote hosts. Ostensibly, a global internetwork would offer redundancy. In other words, there could be many different physical paths through a network between any given pair of hosts. Mechanisms would be needed that could discover remote networks and hosts and explore the different possible paths (or routes) through the network to those networks and hosts.

Finally, some way to apply either logic or mathematics would be needed. Logically, if there are many different routes to a specific destination, they can't all be equal. Some routes would likely offer either shorter overall paths or better performance than others. Thus, it would be logical to compare all the possible routes and then select the best route or routes. In time, these mechanisms would become known as *routers*. The process of discovering, calculating, and comparing routes to remote networks and hosts is routing.

This book will help you explore the mechanics of routers and routed and routing protocols, and build internetworks using routing technologies. Although this book was designed primarily for the novice, it contains detailed technical examinations of many of today's leading routing protocols. These examinations are sufficiently detailed to be valuable to technical professionals at all levels of expertise. Consequently, you will find this book an indispensable technical reference long after you have mastered the basic theory and mechanics of routing and routing protocols.

Part I of this book provides an overview of internetworking, including the implications of using routers in both LANs and WANs. This overview is provided using the Internet Protocol (IP), which is the predominant routed protocol in use today. IP has grown substantially since its inception approximately two decades ago. Its once simple addressing architecture has become quite complicated during its life. An entire chapter is devoted to examining IP's addressing. This includes the original class-based address architecture, subnet numbers, and classless interdomain routing (CIDR) addresses. This chapter also provides a glimpse at how IP's addresses will change with the IPv6, the next generation of IP. IP addresses are used extensively throughout the book to present you with specific examples of the various routing concepts that are introduced.

Part II of the book delves into a slightly deeper level of detail. Instead of looking at internetworking from a high level, Part II looks at the inner workings of a router. This includes a side-by-side comparison of the two versions of IP, IPv4 (the current version) and IPv6 (the next generation); the various transmission technologies that a router can use for communications; and the mechanics of routing protocols.

There are different types of routing protocols. Generally speaking, they fall into two categories: those that calculate routes based on some measurement of distance, and those that calculate routes based on some measurement of the state of the links that comprise a route. The first type is known as a distance-vector routing protocol and the second type is a link-state routing protocol. An appreciation of the basic functional differences between these two types of routing protocols will prepare you for Part III of this book.

Part III presents a detailed examination of today's leading routing protocols. You will see exactly how RIP, RIP-2, OSPF, IGRP, and EIGRP operate in an internetwork. Understanding the mechanics of a routing protocol will help you design better networks and more effectively troubleshoot and fine-tune an existing network.

The detailed examination of routers and routing in the first three sections of the book provides the context for the last section. The last section of this book emphasizes the implementation of routing technologies and provides insight into the future of routing.

The first chapter of Part IV focuses on building internetworks. An internetwork must accommodate different types of needs. These needs vary considerably from network to network but encompass some specific attributes. These attributes include scalability, geographic distance between the locations in the network, traffic volumes, performance delays, and monetary costs of operating and maintaining the network. The implications of each of these are explored, along with sample network topologies and guidelines for selecting transmission technologies.

One of the more challenging aspects of building an internetwork is coping with multiple protocols. Precious few networks have the luxury of using a single routed and/or routing protocol. There are many reasons for this, including merger and acquisitions, extranets, and even migrations to new technologies. Regardless of the reason, the challenge lies in overcoming the dissimilarities of the routed and/or routing protocols. Chapter 14 examines the options for internetworking with dissimilar protocols (both routed and routing). This chapter includes a look at the implications of a migration to IPv6 from IPv4 and some strategies for successfully conducting such a migration.

The book concludes with an assessment of the future of routing. This is necessary, as technological advances have created substantial confusion, and even doubts, about routers and routing! For example, Microsoft's Windows NT operating system can enable a client or server-grade computer to function as a router. What does this mean for the future of stand-alone routers?

Additional confusion about the future of routers has been caused by the technological developments that blur the previous distinctions between LANs and WANs. Switching, in particular, is rapidly being implemented for both network types, and it can forward Layer 3 packets as easily as Layer 2 frames. Thus, one of the biggest issues facing IT planners is: What is the future role of routing? Are routers still needed? These questions are probed and answered in the concluding chapter.

PART I

Internetworking Fundamentals

CHAPTER 1

An Introduction to Internetworking

Internetworking is the functional interconnection of two or more networks; the resources of each individual network become available to the users and machines connected to the other networks. Internetworking requires a combination of technologies, addressing, and communications protocols. All these must be understood and adhered to universally throughout the internetwork. Many different devices can be used to build internetworks, including switches, bridges, and routers. Although the boundaries between these devices had historically been very distinct, technological advances have blurred these distinctions. Routers offered the unique capability to discover paths (or *routes*) through large and complex internetworks. More importantly, routers could compare different routes through a network to find the most efficient one between any given points in the network. Routing is still critical to internetworking. Routing is no longer a function of just standalone routers, however. Routing can be performed by computers attached to local area networks (LANs) or even by LAN switches!

This chapter introduces the concept of internetworking, examines the role of the router in an internetwork, and defines some of the more salient terms and concepts that are reinforced throughout this book. Given that internetworking is best understood through the use of a layered model, this chapter begins with an overview of the most common of such models: the Open Systems Interconnect (OSI) reference model. This forms the context for an examination of the mechanics of passing data between internetworked computers, as well as between networks, using the Internet Protocol (IP).

THE OSI REFERENCE MODEL

The International Organization for Standardization (ISO) developed the OSI reference model to facilitate the open interconnection of computer systems. An *open interconnection* is one that can be supported in a multivendor environment. The reference model identifies and stratifies into logically ordered layers all the functions required to establish, use, define, and dismantle a communications session between two computers without regard for those computers' manufacturer or architecture.

Implicit in this definition of the OSI reference model is the assumption that an unknown quantity of distance and networking gear separate the two communicating devices. Consequently, the model defines mechanisms for passing data between two machines that share the same LAN or WAN. More importantly, the model identifies functions that allow two machines that are halfway around the world from each other with no direct network connections to pass data between themselves.

The Dawn of Openness

Today, the OSI reference model is sometimes regarded as logical but trite and not particularly useful. When it was developed almost 20 years ago, however, it was viewed as radical if not outright revolutionary. At that time, computer manufacturers locked customers into proprietary, single-vendor architectures. The price of the convenience of such one-stop shopping was a very long-term commitment to a single supplier. Frequently, this resulted in inflated prices, forced upgrades, and other unpleasantries that consumers had little choice but to endure.

The notion of functional modularity, or *layering*, seemed antithetical to the conventional wisdom of that era. Customers would be able to mix and match components to build their own networked computing infrastructure. Such an approach would enable competitors to steal business away.

Many companies resisted the concept of open networked computing and remained dedicated to tightly integrated proprietary architectures. These companies learned to listen to the marketplace the hard way: They lost business to upstart companies with open products.

The Seven Layers

The OSI model categorizes the various processes needed in a communications session into seven distinct functional layers. The layers are organized based on the natural sequence of events that occur during a communications session.

Figure 1-1 illustrates the OSI reference model. Layers 1–3 provide network access, and Layers 4–7 are dedicated to the logistics of supporting end-to-end communications.

OSI reference model layer description	Layer number
Application	7
Presentation	6
Session	5
Transport	4
Network	3
Data link	2
Physical	1

Figure 1-1

The OSI reference model.

Layer 1: The Physical Layer

The bottom layer, or Layer 1, of the OSI reference model is called the *physical layer*. This layer is responsible for the transmission of the bit stream. It accepts frames of data from Layer 2, the data link layer, and transmits their structure and content serially, one bit at a time.

Layer 1 is also responsible for the reception of incoming streams of data, one bit at a time. These streams are then passed on to the data link layer.

The physical layer, quite literally, operates on only 1s and 0s. It has no mechanism for determining the significance of the bits it transmits or receives. It is solely concerned with the physical characteristics of electrical and/or optical signaling techniques. This includes the voltage of the electrical current used to transport the signal, the media type and impedance characteristics, and even the physical shape of the connector used to terminate the media.

Transmission media includes any means of actually transporting signals generated by the OSI's Layer 1 mechanisms. Some examples of transmission media are coaxial cabling, fiber-optic cabling, and twisted-pair wiring.

Layer 2: The Data Link Layer

Layer 2 of the OSI reference model is called the *data link layer*. As all the layers do, it has two sets of responsibilities: transmit and receive. It is responsible for providing end-to-end validity of the data being transmitted.

On the transmit side, the data link layer is responsible for packing instructions—data—into frames. A *frame* is a structure indigenous to the data link layer that contains enough information to make sure that the data can be successfully sent across a

LAN to its destination. Implicit in this definition is that the data link layer contains its own address architecture. This addressing is only applicable to other networked devices that reside locally on the same data link layer domain.

NOTE

A data link layer domain is all the network components that propagate a data link layer broadcast. Typically, a data link layer domain is regarded as a LAN segment. Not all LAN technologies adhere rigidly to the functionality specified for the data link layer in the OSI model. Some LAN architectures do not support reliable delivery, for example. Their data frames are transmitted, but their status is not tracked. Guaranteeing delivery would then be left to a Layer 4 protocol, such as Transmission Control Protocol (TCP).

Successful delivery means that the frame reaches its intended destination intact. Therefore, the frame must also contain a mechanism to verify the integrity of its contents on delivery.

Two things must happen for a successful delivery to occur:

- The destination node must verify the integrity of that frame's contents before it can acknowledge its receipt.

- The originating node must receive the recipient's acknowledgment that each frame transmitted was received intact by the destination node.

Numerous situations can result in transmitted frames either not reaching the destination or becoming damaged and unusable during transit. It is the data link layer's responsibility for detecting and correcting any and all such errors. The data link layer is also responsible for reassembling the binary streams that are received from the physical layer back into frames.

The physical and data link layers (1 and 2) are required for each and every type of communication regardless of whether the network is a LAN or wide-area network (WAN). Together, these two layers provide all the mechanisms that software applications need to contact and communicate with other devices connected to the same LAN. In Figure 1-2, all the user machines can directly access the local server. Consequently, they do not require the use of network layer protocols or addressing to communicate with each other.

Figure 1-2
The physical and data link layers are adequate for delivering datagrams locally.

These two layers are also highly interrelated and, consequently, come bundled together in products. When you purchase LAN hardware (Ethernet, Token Ring, FDDI, and so on), for example, you have simultaneously selected both a physical layer and a data link layer specification. Figure 1-3 uses the IEEE's reference model for Ethernet LANs to demonstrate the tight coupling between the first two layers of the OSI reference model.

NOTE

The Institute of Electrical and Electronic Engineers (IEEE) is another standards-setting body. One of their more noteworthy efforts has been the standardization of LANs and metropolitan-area networks (MANs) through their Project 802. Project 802 contains hundreds of individual specifications for specific aspects of local and metropolitan-area networking. IEEE-compliant LANs include Ethernet (IEEE 802.3) and Token Ring (802.5). All the specifications in the 802 family of standards are limited to the physical and/or data link layer.

The IEEE's 802 reference model actually breaks the OSI model's data link layer into two separate components: Media Access Control (MAC) and Logical Link Control (LLC). The MAC sublayer is responsible for physically transmitting and receiving data via the transmission media. The LLC is the component that can provide reliable delivery of data frames. In practice, this function is frequently ceded to transport layer protocols rather than implemented in the data link layer.

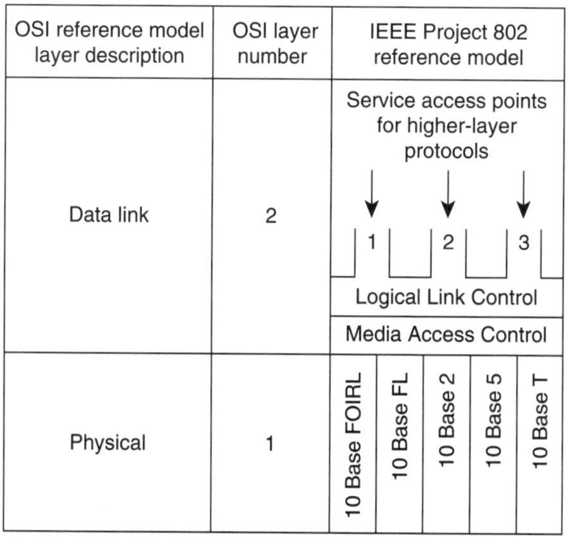

OSI reference model layer description	OSI layer number	IEEE Project 802 reference model
Data link	2	Service access points for higher-layer protocols ↓ ↓ ↓ 1 | 2 | 3 Logical Link Control Media Access Control
Physical	1	10 Base FOIRL | 10 Base FL | 10 Base 2 | 10 Base 5 | 10 Base T

Figure 1-3

Ethernet's physical and data link layers are tightly coupled.

Selection of a LAN architecture, however, does not limit the choice of higher-level protocols. Instead, you should expect that a protocol stack that encompasses Layers 3 and 4 will interoperate with existing standardized data link layer protocols through well-defined open interfaces.

Layer 3: The Network Layer

The *network layer* enables internetworking. The protocols at this layer are responsible for establishing the route to be used between the source and destination computers. This layer lacks any native transmission error detection/correction mechanisms and, consequently, is forced to rely on the end-to-end reliable transmission service of either the data link layer or the transport layer. Although some data link layer technologies support reliable delivery, many others do not. Therefore, Layer 3 protocols (such as IP) assume that Layer 4 protocols (such as TCP) will provide this functionality rather than assume Layer 2 will take care of it.

NOTE

It is important to note that the source and destination computers need not reside within the same data link layer domain. If they were attached to the same LAN, the data link layer mechanisms would be adequate to provide delivery. However, many applications require the services provided by TCP and/or IP to function properly. Therefore, even though a source and destination computer may be capable of communicating perfectly using just physical and data link layer protocols, their applications might require the use of network and transport protocols.

Figure 1-4 illustrates the same network as Figure 1-2. The only difference is that a second network has been connected to it via a router. The router effectively isolates the two data link layer domains. The only way to communicate between these two domains is through the use of network layer addressing.

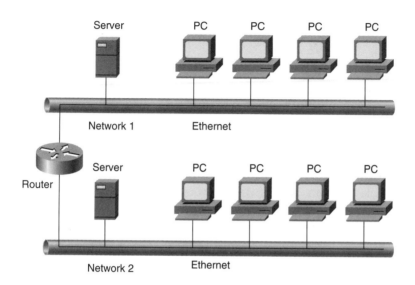

Figure 1-4
The network layer is required for delivering packets between networks.

In this situation, if a user on Network 1 needed to access information stored on the server of Network 2, network layer addressing would be needed. The network layer can perform this intermediary function because it has its own addressing architecture, which is separate and distinct from the data link layer machine addressing.

The network layer mechanisms have been implemented in a series of protocols that can transport application data across LAN segments, or even WANs. These protocols are called *routable protocols* because their datagrams can be forwarded by routers beyond the local network. Routable protocols include IP, Internetwork Packet Exchange (IPX), and AppleTalk. Each of these protocols, as well as the other routable protocols, has its own Layer 3 addressing architecture. This addressing architecture is used to identify machines that are connected to different networks. Routers are needed to calculate the routes and forward the data contained within the routable protocol packets to machines that lie beyond the local link of the transmitting machine.

IP has emerged as the dominant routable protocol. Consequently, this entire book reinforces the fundamentals of routing using only the IP protocol in the examples and illustrations.

Unlike the first two layers, the use of the network layer is optional in data communications. The network layer is required only if the computer systems reside on different networks, or if the communicating applications require its services. In the first case, the different LAN domains would have to be interconnected somehow (as illustrated in Figure 1-4); otherwise, the communications could not occur. Alternatively, application software could require the use of either network or transport layer mechanisms, regardless of how the communicating devices are interconnected.

Layer 4: The Transport Layer

Layer 4, the *transport layer*, provides a similar service to the data link layer, in that it is responsible for the end-to-end integrity of transmissions. Unlike the data link layer, the transport layer can provide this function beyond the local LAN segment. It can detect packets that were either damaged or lost in transit and can automatically generate a retransmit request.

Another significant function of the transport layer is the resequencing of packets that, for a variety of reasons, may have arrived out of order. The packets may have taken different paths through the network, for example, or some may have been damaged in transit. In any case, the transport layer can identify the original sequence of packets and put them back into that sequence before passing their contents up to the session layer.

Much like the interrelationship between the first and second layers, the third layer of the OSI reference model is usually tightly interrelated with the fourth layer. Two specific examples of routable protocol suites that tightly integrate these two layers are open standard TCP/IP and Novell's IPX/SPX (Internetwork Packet Exchange, Sequenced Packet Exchange). This interrelationship is illustrated in Figure 1-5, using the TCP/IP reference model. Together, these layers provide the mechanisms that enable the transfer of information between source and destination machines across a communications network that spans beyond a Layer 2 domain. These layers also provide other functions such as resequencing packets received out of order and retransmitting packets not received or received damaged.

OSI reference model layer description	OSI layer number	TCP/IP equivalent layer description
Application	7	Process/ application
Presentation	6	Process/ application
Session	5	Host-to-host
Transport	4	Host-to-host
Network	3	Internet
Data link	2	Network access
Physical	1	Network access

Figure 1-5

The TCP/IP reference model demonstrates the tight coupling of the network and transport layers.

Layer 5: The Session Layer

Layer 5 of the OSI model is the *session layer*. Many protocols bundle this layer's functionality into their transport layers. Some specific examples of session layer services are Remote Procedure Calls (RPCs) and quality of service protocols such as RSVP—the bandwidth reservation protocol.

Layer 6: The Presentation Layer

Layer 6, the *presentation layer*, is responsible for managing the way that data is encoded. Not every computer system uses the same data encoding scheme, and the presentation layer is responsible for providing the translation between otherwise incompatible data encoding schemes, such as American Standard Code for Information Interchange (ASCII) and Extended Binary Coded Decimal Interchange Code (EBCDIC).

The presentation layer can be used to mediate differences in floating-point formats, as well as to provide encryption and decryption services.

Layer 7: The Application Layer

The top, or seventh, layer in the OSI reference model is the *application layer*. Despite its name, this layer does not include user applications. Instead, it provides the interface between those applications and the network's services.

This layer can be thought of as the reason for initiating the communications session. For example, an email client might generate a request to retrieve new messages from the email server. This client application automatically generates a request to the appropriate Layer 7 protocol(s) and launches a communications session to get the needed files.

NOTE

Note that most of today's networking protocols use their own layered models. These models vary in the degree to which they adhere to the separation of functions demonstrated by the OSI reference model. It is quite common for these models to collapse the seven OSI layers into five or fewer layers. It is also common for higher layers to not correspond perfectly to their OSI-equivalent layers. Additionally, models may not even describe the full spectrum of the OSI's layered functions! The IEEE's layered functional model, for example, is just for LANs and MANs—it does not extend above the data link layer. Ethernet, Token Ring, and even FDDI are compliant with this model.

Misperceptions About the OSI Reference Model

It is important to note that the OSI model has been so successful at achieving its original goals as to almost render itself moot. The previous proprietary, integrated approach has disappeared. Today, open communications are requisite. Curiously, very few products are fully OSI compliant. Instead, the basic layered framework is frequently adapted to new standards often with substantial changes in the boundaries of the higher layers. Nevertheless, the OSI reference model remains a viable mechanism for demonstrating the functional mechanics of a network.

Despite its successes, a few misperceptions about the OSI reference model persist; they are discussed in the following sections.

What's in a Name?

The first misperception is that the OSI reference model was developed by the International Standards Organization. It was not. The OSI reference model was developed by the *International Organization for Standardization*. Some reference sources identify this organization with the acronym *IOS*. Although, technically, this is the correct acronym, that organization eschews its acronym in favor of a mnemonic abbreviation: *ISO*. ISO is derived from the Greek word *isos*, which means equal or, in this case, standard. Unfortunately, this mnemonic lends itself to misinterpretation as an acronym for International Standards Organization. Look it up on the World Wide Web at http://www.iso.org. Further confusion is added by the OSI reference model's name. OSI is an abbreviation of Open Systems Interconnection. Unfortunately, this abbreviation is yet another combination of the letters *I*, *S*, and *O*.

Layer 0

A common misperception is that OSI's Layer 1 includes anything that either generates or carries the data communications signals. This is not true. It is a *functional* model only. As such, Layer 1 (the physical layer) is limited to just the processes and mechanisms needed to place signals onto the transmission media and to receive signals from that media.

Its lower boundary is the description of the physical connector that attaches to the transmission media. *It does not include the transmission media!* Consequently, transmission media are sometimes referred to as *Layer 0*. Obviously, there is no Layer 0, just like techno-politics isn't really Layer 8.

The confusion surrounding the placement of transmission media within the model seems to stem from the fact that the physical layer provides specifications for the media's performance. These are the performance characteristics that are required, and assumed to exist, by the processes and mechanisms defined in the physical layer.

Complete Stacks

A protocol stack is a suite of related communications protocols that offer users the mechanisms and services required to communicate with other network-connected machines. Typically, a stack will encompass two or more of the OSI model's layered functions. From the user's perspective, the protocol stack is what enables two computers to communicate and pass data to each other.

In practice, you will probably never find a single, integrated protocol stack that encompasses all seven layers. There are at least two reasons for this:

- Not every networked computing event will require the functionality of all seven layers.

- Disaggregating networked computing into well-defined and accepted functional layers creates the opportunity for product specialization.

Depending on their mission and market, companies can develop a core competence in just a small subset of the model's functions and can create products that build on that competence. This is the very essence of openness: The innate competitiveness spawned by the model means that it is highly unlikely that any one company can dominate all the layers.

LOGICAL ADJACENCY

The identification and stratification of the sequence of events that support a networked communications session is a tremendously powerful concept. One of the key benefits of this approach is that it enables a concept known as *logical adjacency*, which refers to the apparent capability of peer-layer protocols on source and destination machines to communicate directly with each other. The IP protocols on a source machine are logically adjacent to the IP protocols on the destination machine that they are communicating with, for example.

This isn't, of course, how communication actually occurs. In reality, the vertical orientation of a protocol stack is an acknowledgment of the functional flow of processes and data within each machine. Each layer has interfaces to its physically adjacent layers.

For example, the IP protocols on a source machine are physically adjacent to the TCP or UDP transport layer protocols and to whatever data link layer protocols are also present. As such, it has standard interfaces to both TCP and the LAN's data link layer protocols that are used to pass data to both protocol suites.

The differences between the logical flow of communications and the actual flow of the session are illustrated in Figure 1-6 using the OSI reference model.

Figure 1-6
Actual versus logical flow
of layered
communications.

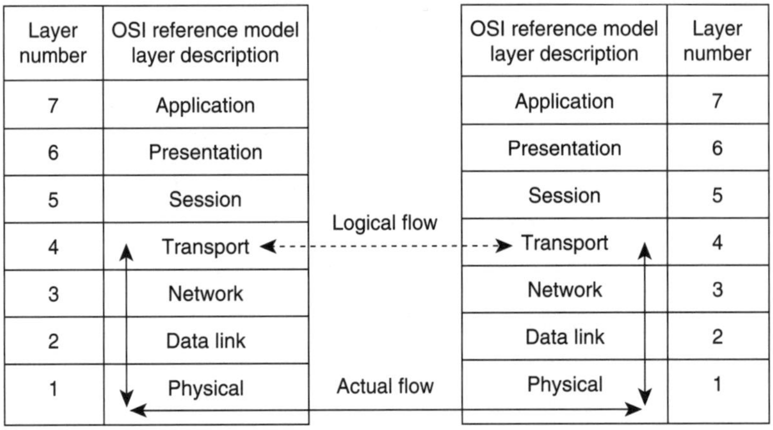

Layer number	OSI reference model layer description			OSI reference model layer description	Layer number
7	Application			Application	7
6	Presentation			Presentation	6
5	Session		Logical flow	Session	5
4	Transport ◄-------------------► Transport				4
3	Network			Network	3
2	Data link			Data link	2
1	Physical	Actual flow		Physical	1

As is evident in Figure 1-6, although communications flow vertically through each protocol stack, each layer perceives itself to be capable of directly communicating with its counterpart layers on remote computers.

The Mechanics of Logical Adjacency

To enable the logical adjacency of layers, each layer of the originating machine's protocol stack adds a header to the data received from the layer above it. This header can be recognized and used by only that layer or its counterparts on other machines. The receiving machine's protocol stack removes the headers, one layer at a time, as the data is passed up to its application. Figure 1-7 illustrates this process. Note that Figure 1-7 presents a theoretical view of layered communications rather than a technically accurate depiction of any single protocol's processes.

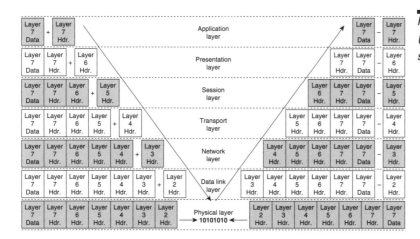

Figure 1-7

Use of layered headers to support logical adjacency.

Given that Layer 3/4 protocol stacks must rely on a Layer 2 and Layer 1 LAN architecture to actually deliver their data, they must have some standardized means of passing data to these layers. The technique that is used is called *wrapping*. The following sections present a highly simplified overview of the way that data is passed between layers in a typical TCP/IP over Ethernet session. Given that routers operate at the first three or four layers (depending on the actual protocol) of the OSI reference model, understanding this process will also provide a glimpse into some of the internal mechanics of a router.

Creating TCP Segments

A communications session begins when TCP (a Layer 4 protocol) receives data from one of the higher-layer protocols and/or applications that it supports for transmission to another networked device. The TCP protocols package the data into *segments*. Ostensibly, applications can forward large quantities of data. TCP, or any transport layer protocol, must begin the process of breaking down a large amount of data into more manageable pieces. Each piece of data is called a *segment*.

Part of the process of segmentation is the population of the TCP header fields. Two of the more important of these fields are the sequence number and the source and destination port numbers of the applications that are sending and receiving the segmented data. The sequence number identifies the order in which the segments were carved from the original data stream. This enables the recipient to reconstruct the data stream without jumbling its contents.

The source and destination ports allow the sending and receiving machines to identify the application responsible for the data via the use of an identification number. This number is referred to as a *socket*. A socket consists of two numbers, the machine's IP address and an application's port number. These two numbers are concatenated into one—the socket. It is a rare machine that only supports a single application. Therefore, it is imperative to be able to forward the data and receipt acknowledgments to the correct applications. These data segments are handed off to the Layer 3 protocol, IP, of the same machine.

Creating IP Packets

IP bundles data received from the TCP into packets (that is, it *packetizes* the segments). Included in the IP packet's header are the source and destination machines' IP addresses. These are the fields that enable routers to forward IP packets to destinations beyond the local network. IP packets that bear application data are also known as *datagrams*.

There will, ideally, be a one-to-one correlation between TCP segments and IP packets. In other words, IP would just wrap a header around each segment and pass it on to the data link layer. It is possible, however, that a segment may not fit entirely within a single packet. When this occurs, the segment's two *fragments* are split between two packets. In such cases, it is possible that just a fragment of a segment arrives at a destination. The IP packet bearing the other fragment can become corrupt, or dropped, in transit. When this happens, it is necessary to retransmit the missing TCP segment data. The IP and TCP protocols must work together to recognize and specifically identify missing data and request a retransmission from the source machine.

The IP packet contains fields in its header that hold both the source and destination machines' IP addresses. Among other things, this is useful in acknowledging successful receipt of a packet and for requesting a retransmission of a garbled packet. After the segments are properly packetized and addressed, IP sends datagrams to its own Ethernet (a data link layer architecture and protocol suite) protocols and the datagrams' network interface card (NIC).

The TCP segment's header includes a sequence number that identifies the specific piece of data that needs to be retransmitted, as well as a socket number that identifies the intended destination application. Together, the IP and TCP headers include all the information needed to successfully engineer a retransmission of the missing data.

Creating Ethernet Frames

Ethernet encases the packets with frames. Given that the origination machine must forward the datagrams through a LAN, regardless of where the datagrams will eventually be delivered, they must be encased in frames. Frames contain addressing that is recognized by the other data link layer devices on the LAN. This addressing is known as Media Address Control (MAC) addressing. Each frame contains the MAC address of both the source and destination machines.

Frames, like packets, may vary in length. Ideally, there will also be a one-to-one correlation between IP packets and LAN frames (Ethernet, in this example). It is possible, however, that some IP packets will be fragmented with each fragment occupying the data field of a different Ethernet frame. When this occurs, it is imperative that the receiving machine's LAN protocols recognize it so that the IP packets can be restored to their original form.

Next, the framed data packets are presented to the physical layer for conversion into a stream of binary digits (bits) that are transmitted to the destination machine's physical layer.

Creating the Bit Stream

The only layered functions that actually are adjacent and can communicate directly are those in the physical layer. Frames received from the physical link layer are converted into the appropriate sequence of 1s and 0s.

The bits may be transmitted as electronic pulses or flashes of light, depending on the transmission media being used. These physical signals are picked off the transmission media by the destination machine or by an intermediary networking device that may lie between the source and destination machines.

The processes that ensue upon reception of the transmitted bit stream vary slightly, depending on whether the recipient is the destination machine or an intermediary networking device.

Receiving the Bit Stream

The mechanics of logical adjacency by a receiving device vary slightly, based on whether the bit stream is received by the destination machine, a bridge, or a router. These scenarios are described in the following sections.

Bit Stream Reception by the Destination Machine

When the bit stream is received by the destination machine, the recipient must convert the seemingly endless stream of 1s and 0s back into a frame of data. Given that both the structure and content of a frame are transmitted in the form of individual bits, the data link layer protocols of the destination machine don't really rebuild a frame. Rather, it is buffering the incoming bits until it has a complete frame. As soon as it recognizes that the incoming bits have formed a complete frame, an error-detection routine is performed to ensure that no errors occurred during transit that would have altered the frame's contents. If the frame is defective, one of two things may happen, depending on the LAN technology. Some LANs, such as FDDI, generate a retransmit request that is sent back to the source machine. Other protocols, such as Ethernet II, just discard the damaged frame and wait for higher-level protocols, such as TCP, to discover the missing data and initiate the retransmission activity.

After a frame is successfully received, the framing is stripped off to reveal the IP packets that were embedded in the frame's data field.

Remember that occasionally there will be no one-to-one correlation between frames and packets. Therefore, the data link layer may find itself with partial IP packets. These are buffered up until all fragments of a packet are received. The fragments are then restored to their original packet structure. Complete IP packets are then passed up the stack to the IP protocols for further processing.

NOTE

As you will see in Part III, "Routing Protocols," some routing protocols share information about MTU sizes. This helps a network fine-tune itself and reduces the likelihood of fragmentation.

The destination machine's IP protocols accept packets from the Ethernet protocols and strip off the packet structure to reveal the embedded data segments. These protocols may have to reconstruct any segments that were fragmented. Completed segments are passed up to the TCP protocols where the segment header is removed and the application data restored to its original state for delivery to the appropriate application or higher-layer protocol. The recipient application, or protocol, is identified by the application port number that was originally set by the source machine's TCP protocol.

Bits transmitted over a network may only be received directly by the destination machine if both the source and destination machines are on the same network. This is typically the case with LAN communications. If the destination machine does not reside locally on the same network as the source machine, however, an intermediary networking device (such as a bridge or router) is needed to forward that bit stream on to its destination.

Bit Stream Reception by a Router

Routers can be used to exchange data between source and destination machines that are not directly connected to the same network, or that for some other reason (such as using different network address ranges) can't directly communicate. As such, they are tasked with accepting bit streams, buffering them until they have a complete frame or packet, and then making a determination about what to do next with that data structure.

To understand how a router can make this next-step determination requires examining the way a router works. First, a router connected to a LAN functions much like any other LAN-attached device. It listens to the transmission media and accepts frames that are either addressed directly to it (that is, the frame's destination address is the router port's MAC address) or have a broadcast address. The router then strips off the framing from the frames that are either directly or indirectly addressed to it and examines the header of the IP packet(s) that were in the frame's data field. This packet is passed to the router's IP protocol stack for further processing.

The router's IP protocol examines the packet's destination address and checks the router's routing tables to see whether it has an entry correlating this address to an interface port. Assuming that it already knows about this destination IP address, the packet is passed to the appropriate interface port. The port, which is really a specialized NIC, applies the logic of its LAN architecture and wraps a new frame around the IP packet. This frame contains the MAC address of the router port rather than the MAC address of the IP session's source machine. The destination MAC address of this frame is the MAC address of the IP packet's destination address. This new frame is placed on the network for delivery.

Figure 1-8 shows a network that better illustrates this process.

Figure 1-8
The router forwards
frames to their destination
on Network 1.

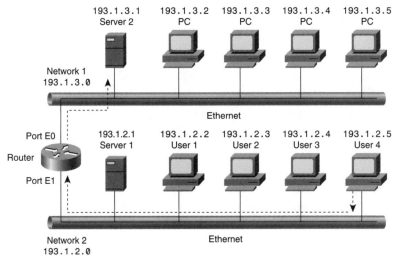

In Figure 1-8, there are two LANs. The first one uses the IP address range 193.1.3.0 through 193.1.3.5. The second network uses the IP address range 193.1.2.0 through 193.1.2.5. In this example, User 4 (source IP address 193.1.2.5) on Network 2 needs to communicate with the server on Network 1 (destination IP address 193.1.3.1). This user's IP protocol stack recognizes that the destination address is inconsistent with the addresses of other local machines, so it passes the data to the NIC along with instructions to deliver it to the router's E1 port. The NIC wraps an Ethernet frame around this IP packet, including source and destination MAC addresses, and transmits the frame.

The router's E1 interface port sees that the frame is addressed to it, so it accepts the frame. The router strips off the frame and discards it. The IP packet that was inside the frame is passed to the router's IP stack for examination. The IP protocol stack sees the destination IP address is 193.1.2.5. This address is already known to the router and is associated with interface port E0. Therefore, the IP packet is passed to that interface port. Port E0 wraps a new frame around the IP packet. This frame contains the MAC address of the server's NIC in the destination MAC address field and the

MAC address of the E0 port in the source MAC address field. This frame is placed on Network 1 for delivery to the server.

Bit Stream Reception by a Bridge

Bridges are relatively unintelligent network devices; they have a limited capability to analyze received frames and make forwarding decisions. Like routers, they buffer incoming bits until they can reconstruct the original frame. They examine that frame and check its destination MAC address. Bridges, like routers, build and maintain a list of devices that are known to exist somewhere beyond each of its ports. This table is called a *bridging table*, and it merely correlates a bridge port with a destination MAC address.

If the bridge determines that the destination MAC address resides on the same network that it came from, it assumes that the destination machine has already received it. Otherwise, the bridge assumes that the source machine needs its assistance in delivering the framed data. Subsequently, the bridge checks its bridging table to see which network (that is, bridge port) that frame should be sent to. If the bridge receives a frame but doesn't have an entry in its bridging table for that frame's destination MAC address, it floods that frame out of all ports except for the one it came from.

As soon as the bridge has determined where to send the frame, it converts the frame back into a bit stream and transmits it on the appropriate bridge port. This stream is, essentially, identical to the stream that was received. The only modification is that the bridge retransmits the bit stream at its original signal strength.

Bridges have two potential uses:

- They can segment a LAN environment into two (or more, depending on how many ports the bridge supports) media access domains.

- They can interconnect adjacent LANs.

In either case, bridging two LANs together results in two separate media access domains within a single data link layer broadcast domain. Figure 1-9 illustrates the use and impacts of a bridge on a LAN. The two LANs enjoy separate media access domains within a single MAC broadcast domain. In other words, competition for each LAN's available bandwidth remains limited to its own directly connected machines. Both LANs, however, can generate Layer 2 broadcasts (MAC broadcasts) that are propagated by the bridge.

Figure 1-9
Bridges segment LAN's
media access domains.

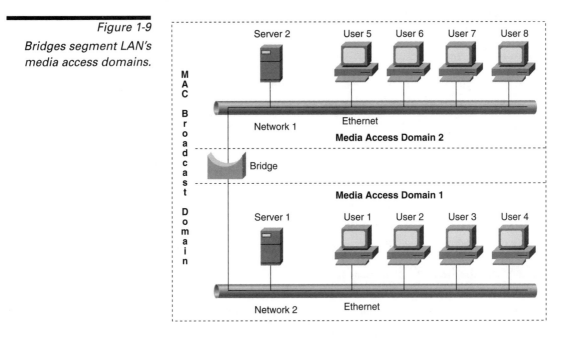

Bridges differ fundamentally from routers in two aspects:

- Bridges are relatively unintelligent devices.

- Bridges operate only at the physical and data link layers. They possess no capacity for network layer packet forwarding.

Given the subtle, but significant, distinctions between the operational mechanics of bridges and routers, it becomes clear that these two devices were designed for different uses. Both can be used to increase the size of networks, but routing is a far more powerful technology than bridging. Bridges are adept at exchanging data between source and destination machines on adjacent LANs. If a source and destination machine pair reside on networks that are not adjacent, they need to route.

THE NEED TO ROUTE

The concept of logical adjacency works just as well between two machines connected to the same LAN as it does between internetworked machines that are thousands of miles apart. Obviously, there are some significant differences between these two extreme examples, but the concept of logical adjacency holds true. The biggest difference lies in establishing the connection between the source and destination machines. On a LAN, the two machines can communicate just by putting their framed data on the transmission media. In an internetwork, the two machines are separated by an unknown quantity of networking hardware and transmission facilities. Flooding the transmission facilities in the hopes of eventually delivering the packets is just not a viable approach.

The only logical solution is to identify a path through the internetwork to the destination. Finding a path, much less the best path, through a potential quagmire of circuits is a daunting task. The next section delves into how the router supports forwarding of packets using network layer addresses, as well as some of the basics of routing and route calculation.

Routers

Unlike most LAN components, routers are intelligent. More importantly, they can operate at all layers of the OSI reference model rather than just the first two. This enables them to internetwork multiple LANs by using Layer 3 addressing.

A router must have two or more physical interfaces for interconnecting LANs and/or WAN transmission facilities. The router learns about the addresses of machines or networks that are somehow connected via each of its interfaces. The list of these addresses is kept in tables that correlate Layer 3 addresses with the port numbers that they are directly or indirectly connected to.

A router uses two types of networking protocols, both of which operate at Layer 3. These are routable protocols and routing protocols. *Routable protocols*, also known as *routed protocols*, are those that encapsulate user information and data into packets. An example of a routed protocol is IP. IP is responsible for encapsulating application data for transport through a network to the appropriate destinations. *Routing protocols* are used between routers to determine available routes, communicate what is known about available routes, and forward routed protocol packets along those routes. The purpose of a routing protocol is to provide the router with all the information it needs about the network to route datagrams.

Routing

Routers are used to forward packets of data between devices that aren't necessarily connected to the same local network. *Routing* is the cumulative processes that discover paths through the network to specific destinations, compare redundant routes mathematically, and build tables that contain routing information.

In the sample internetwork presented in Figure 1-8, the router's task is easy: It has only two interfaces. Any packets received by one of its interfaces was either delivered to the other interface or discarded as undeliverable. In this particular case, the router may well have been replaced by a hub, bridge, switch, or any other Layer 2 device. The router's real value lies in determining routes to destinations on nonadjacent networks. Figure 1-10 illustrates this scenario.

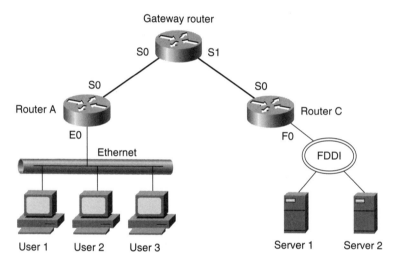

Figure 1-10
Routers can calculate routes through other networks.

In such circumstances, where the destination is not directly reachable, the router can communicate with other routers to learn of the existence of any networks that are not directly connected to it. In the example presented in Figure 1-10, User 1 on a network connected to Router A must access files stored on Server 2. Unfortunately, that server is located on a network that is not directly connected to Network A. This server is two router hops away on the network connected to Router C.

The way that Router A can figure out where to send User 1's packets is rather simple. Upon receiving User 1's data frames, it unwraps the packets that they contain and reads the destination IP address contained in the packet headers. Router A looks up that address in its routing table. The routing table entry tells the router that, although that server is not directly connected to the router, the next step in the path to that server is its S0 (for Serial Port 0) interface.

The S0 interface connects Router A with Router B. Router B accepts the incoming packets (albeit in a stream of bits) from Router A and looks up the destination IP address in its routing table. Router B's table identifies its S1 interface port as the next step, or hop, in the route to Server 2.

Router B forwards all packets addressed to Server 2 through its S1 port, which connects to Router C. Router C can identify the host as residing on its directly connected FDDI network and, therefore, wraps the packets in FDDI frames. These frames bear the MAC address of the router's FDDI port as a source address and the MAC address of Server 2 as the destination address. After the framed data arrives at Server 2, that server's protocols are responsible for checking the validity of the data and forwarding it up through the various layers to the correct application.

This highly simplified overview of a routed connection betrays the complexity of routing and, more importantly, calculating routes through complex networks (which is discussed in the next section). In complex networks, there may be multiple potential paths through a network between any given pair of source and destination machines. Routers are responsible for sharing information among themselves. This information enables them to

- Discover and track the topology of the internetwork

- Discover and track the addresses of subnetworks and hosts

- Discriminate between optimal and suboptimal routes

- Balance loads across redundant optimal routes

These capabilities are examined in much more detail throughout this book.

Calculating Routes

Routers can discriminate among multiple potential paths to select the best one. This process is known as *calculating routes*. Implicit in this description is that there is some logic and mathematics that can be applied in determining routes to far-away destinations. The capability to apply this logic and perform these mathematics is the single most important feature of a router.

The technology that enables routers to calculate routes is known as a *routing protocol*. Actually, there are a wide variety of routing protocols to choose from. Most are widely supported enough to permit the construction of internetworks from routers made by different manufacturers.

Routing protocols enable routers within a network to share information about potential paths to specific hosts within that network. Examples of routing protocols include the following:

- Routing Information Protocol (RIP)

- Open Shortest Path First (OSPF)

- Interior Gateway Routing Protocol (IGRP)

These, and several other routing protocols, are examined in more detail in Part III, "Routing Protocols." Each routing protocol has its own unique blend of features, benefits, and limitations. Many of them are also well targeted to specific functional niches. Consequently, in very large networks such as the Internet or even some large corporate intranets, it is quite likely that you will encounter two or more routing protocols in operation. Therefore, it is a good idea to become as familiar as possible with as many of these protocols as you can. Chapter 14, "Internetworking with Dissimilar Protocols," describes some of the ways that you can get two dissimilar routing protocols to peacefully coexist within the same internetwork.

SUMMARY

The use of IP and routing technologies to create internetworks enables networks to scale up to truly global proportions, provided that they are properly designed and implemented. Internetworks can consist of widely dispersed LANs interconnected with relatively low-speed serial transmission facilities such as leased lines. Alternatively, LANs within a single premises can also be internetworked with routing technologies. Or, you can customize your internetwork to suit your particular combination of requirements.

In short, there is no single, correct way to build an internetwork. Building an internetwork, however, does require an understanding of the fundamentals of routing and IP that relate to your own particular networking requirements. This book is designed to provide you with that fundamental understanding.

CHAPTER 2

Understanding Internetwork Addresses

A critical prerequisite to internetworking is having an efficient address architecture adhered to by all users of that internetwork. Address architectures can take many different forms. Network addresses are always numeric, but they can be expressed in base 2 (binary), base 10 (decimal), or even base 16 (hexadecimal) number systems. They can be proprietary or open for all to see and implement. Address architectures can be highly scalable or intentionally designed to serve just small communities of users.

This chapter examines the address architecture implemented by the Internet Protocol (IP). As IP has evolved substantially over the past 20 years, so has its address architecture. This chapter describes the evolution of the IP address architecture and explains critical concepts, including route summarization, subnetworks, subnetwork addresses or masks, classless interdomain routing (CIDR), and variable-length subnet masking (VLSM).

THE INTERNET'S ADDRESS ARCHITECTURE

The Internet's address architecture is implemented in IP. IP's original addressing scheme dates back to the early days of networked computing. At the time, the Internet itself was little more than a semi-public network that interconnected a few dozen universities, research organizations, and government bodies. Each of these entities that connected to the Internet had limited networked computing infrastructures. Typically, these infrastructures consisted of little more than a mainframe computer or a handful of UNIX-based minicomputers. PCs had yet to coalesce into a usable format, and local-area networks (LANs) were in their infancy. Therefore, an internetwork did not require a robust architecture.

The original Internet was given a relatively simple, but compact, two-level hierarchy. The top level was the Internet itself, and the bottom level was the collection of individual networks that were interconnected via the Internet. This hierarchy is illustrated in Figure 2-1.

Figure 2-1

The Internet used a two-level hierarchy.

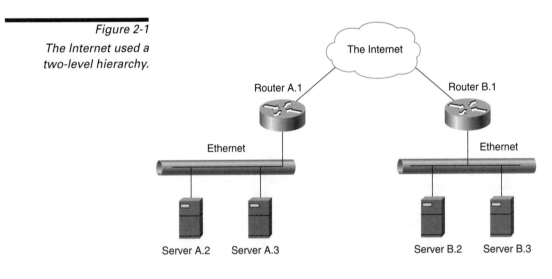

The Internet's simple—but powerful and extensible—architecture served its user community well.

Advertising Network Addresses

Each of the hosts in the Internet needed to be uniquely identifiable. In the Internet's two-level hierarchy, this required an address with two parts:

- Network address

- Host address

Together, these two types of addresses could uniquely identify any and all machines connected via the Internet. It is possible that the needs of a small, networked community could be satisfied with just host addresses, as is the case with LANs. Network addresses, however, are necessary for end systems on different networks to communicate with each other. It is the unique combination of both the host and network addresses that make it possible to access any given host in an internetwork.

The Internet uses this two-level address hierarchy. Rather than calculating and tracking routes to each known host, however, the Internet advertises just the network addresses. End systems that need to access hosts in other networks address their datagrams with the full address, including both network and host numbers, but the routers in the internetwork could assume that the destination network would know how to deliver datagrams to all the end systems within its domain. Therefore, the Internet's routers would only have to track routes to every known network.

To help you better appreciate the concept of advertising network addresses, a fictitious two-level address will be used. These fictitious addresses identify networks with a single alphabetic character and end systems with a single numeric character. These address components follow the familiar convention of IP addresses and separate the components with a dot. Therefore, A.2 uniquely identifies end System 2 in Network A.

A router in the Internet's backbone would quickly become overwhelmed if it tracked paths through the Internet to each end system or host. Instead, the architects of the Internet and IP implemented a two-tiered physical architecture. This was accompanied by a two-tiered network address, consisting of the network's address and a host address. The most practical implication of such a scheme was that routers in the Internet's backbone could greatly reduce their workload by just tracking routes to network addresses.

To understand how network routes are advertised, consider the diagram in Figure 2-2. This diagram shows three networks: A, B, and C. Each has a small number of hosts that are numbered numerically. All the routers have host address 1 in their network number. Therefore, the router that interconnects Network A to the Internet has the address A.1.

The routers that comprise the Internet's backbone could calculate routes through the Internet for each of the hosts in Figure 2-1. Table 2-1 presents their routing tables (in a highly simplified and homogenized form).

Table 2-1 *Routing Table Contents with Host-Based Routing*

Network Address	Host Address	Destination Gateway
A	2	A.1
	3	A.1
B	2	B.1
	3	B.1
C	2	C.1
	3	C.1
	4	C.1

As can be seen in Table 2-1, the destination gateway identified by Internet routers wouldn't vary by host address. Therefore, tracking routes to individual hosts (known as *host-based routing*) would only create unnecessary work for the routers in the internetwork. The destination gateway would, however, vary by network address. Therefore, the Internet's routers can reduce their workload (and increase their efficiency) by not remembering routes to every host. They can advertise routes to network numbers without compromising their ability to deliver datagrams. Table 2-2 demonstrates how network route advertising can reduce the size of routing tables.

Table 2-2   *Routing Table Contents with Network-Based Routing*

Network Address	Forward Datagrams To
A	A.1
B	B.1
C	C.1

The greatly reduced size of the network-based routing tables does not compromise the capability of the Internet routers to forward datagrams to their destinations. Advertising network routes does, however, have numerous other implications. It can improve a router's performance, for example. The more entries exist in a router's routing table, the longer it may take to determine where to forward a datagram. The datagram must be buffered in a router's memory until this determination is made. Consequently, the larger a network's routing tables become, the greater the demands that are placed on the network routers' physical resources. These include random access memory (RAM) and central processing unit (CPU) cycles. Providing increasing amounts of both resources can become expensive.

Closely related to performance, but much more significant, is scalability. Network advertisement enables internetworks to be highly scalable. Proof of this is evident in the mammoth proportions of today's Internet. Without the capability to advertise network routes, the Internet's growth would have been severely constrained.

The Internet was aided in its scalability by its sophisticated address architecture. Its architects foresaw the potential for its growth and developed an addressing architecture that was both flexible and extensible. This architecture was implemented in IP.

IP ADDRESSING

The Internet Engineering Task Force (IETF), architects of both the Internet and IP, elected to use machine-friendly numeric addresses for both networks and hosts. Therefore, each network in the Internet's second tier would have its own unique network number. The administrator(s) of this network would also have to ensure that all the hosts in the network had their own unique host number.

The original version of IP, IP Version 4 (IPv4), uses a 32-bit binary (base 2) address. Each address was organized as four 8-bit numbers separated by dots. Each 8-bit number is called an *octet*. Binary numbers are extremely machine friendly, but are not all user friendly. Therefore, provisions were made to support the use of the more intuitive decimal (base 10) number system for internetwork addressing. The interrelationship between the binary and decimal number systems must be well understood, as literally the entire IP address architecture is based on them. The relationship between binary and decimal numbers is examined in the next section, "Binary Versus Decimal Numbers."

The original 32-bit IPv4 address architecture meant that the Internet could support 4,294,967,296 possible IPv4 addresses—a number originally deemed ridiculously excessive. These addresses were squandered through a number of wasteful practices. Many of the more significant of these practices, and their subsequent fixes, will become more evident as you learn more about the IPv4 address architecture.

NOTE

A new version of IP is nearing completion. This version, IPv6, will feature radically different address architectures. The IPv6 address will be 128 bits long and will use entirely new classifications designed to maximize their efficiency of use. Given that it will likely take several years for this new version of IP to be widely used, this book presents all examples using the IPv4 address architectures. Chapter 5, "Internet Protocols Versions," examines IPv6 in more detail.

Binary Versus Decimal Numbers

In a base 2, or binary, number, the value represented by a 1 is determined by its position. This is not unlike the all too familiar base 10 system, in which the rightmost digit enumerates 1s, the second digit from the right enumerates 10s, the third digit from the right enumerates 100s, ad infinitum. Each digit signifies a ten-fold difference from the digit to the right.

Whereas the base 10 number system provides 10 digits to represent different values (0 through 9), the base 2 number system supports only two valid digits: 0 and 1. Their position, too, determines the value that they signify. The rightmost position, in decimal terms, is equal to 1. The next position to the left is equal to 2. The next position, 4, then 8, and so on. Each position to the left is two times the value of the position to the right.

The decimal value of a binary number is calculated by summing the decimal values of the number's digits that are populated with 1s. Mathematically, each octet of an IPv4 address (there are four of them) can have a maximum value of 255 in the base 10 number system. A binary number equal to 255 consists of 8 bits, or all 1s. Table 2-3 demonstrates this relationship between binary and decimal numbers.

Table 2-3   *Binary (11111111) versus Decimal (255) Values of an Octet*

Digit	8	7	6	5	4	3	2	1
Binary	1	1	1	1	1	1	1	1
Decimal Value of Digit	128	64	32	16	8	4	2	1

As can be seen in Table 2-3, each of the bits in the binary address is populated with a 1. Therefore, calculating the decimal value of this binary number can be done by summing the decimal values of the eight columns: 128 + 64 + 32 + 16 + 8 + 4 + 2 + 1 = 255.

Table 2-4 presents another example of the conversion between binary and decimal numbers. In this example, the fifth digit from the right is a 0. This position represents the decimal value 16. Therefore, this binary number has a decimal value that is 16 less than 255: 128 + 64 + 32 + 8 + 4 + 2 + 1 = 239.

Table 2-4   *Binary (11101111) versus Decimal (239) Values of an Octet*

Position	8	7	6	5	4	3	2	1
Binary	1	1	1	0	1	1	1	1
Decimal	128	64	32	16	8	4	2	1

This relationship between binary and decimal numbers is the foundation for the entire IP address architecture. Remember that there are four binary octets in each IPv4 address. Every other aspect of IP's address architecture, including subnetwork masking, VLSM, and CIDR, is based on these number systems. Therefore, you must understand the relationship between these basic numbering systems, and conversion between them, before you can understand the various ways that IP addressing can be implemented.

IPv4 Address Formats

IP was standardized in September 1981. Its address architecture was as forward looking as could be expected given the state of computing at that time. The basic IP address was a 32-bit binary number that was compartmentalized into four 8-bit binary numbers, or octets.

To facilitate human usage, IP's machine-friendly binary addresses were converted into a more familiar number system: base 10. Each of the four octets in the IP address is represented by a decimal number, from 0 to 255, and separated by dots (.). This is known as a *dotted-decimal* format. Therefore the lowest possible value that can be represented within the framework of an IPv4 address is 0.0.0.0, and the highest possible value is 255.255.255.255. Both of these values, however, are reserved and cannot be assigned to individual end systems. The reason for this requires an examination of the way that the IETF implemented this basic address structure in their protocol.

The dotted-decimal IPv4 address was then broken down into classes to accommodate large-, medium-, and small-sized networks. The differences between the classes were the number of bits allocated to network versus host addresses. There are five classes of IP addresses, identified by a single alphabetic character:

Class A, B, C, D, and E. Each address consists of two parts, a network address and a host address. The five classes represent different compromises between the number of supportable networks and hosts.

Class A Addresses

The Class A IPv4 address was designed to support extremely large networks. As the need for very large-scale networks was perceived to be minimal, an architecture was developed that maximized the possible number of host addresses but severely limited the number of possible Class A networks that could be defined.

A Class A IP address uses only the first octet to indicate the network address. The remaining three octets enumerate host addresses. The first bit of a Class A address is always a 0. This mathematically limits the possible range of the Class A address to ≥ 127, which is the sum of $64 + 32 + 16 + 8 + 4 + 2 + 1$. The leftmost bit's decimal value of 128 is absent from this equation. Therefore, there can only ever be 127 possible Class A IP networks.

The last 24 bits (that is, three dotted-decimal numbers) of a Class A address represent possible host addresses. The range of possible Class A network addresses is from `1.0.0.0` to `126.0.0.0`. Notice that only the first octet bears a network address number. The remaining three are used to create unique host addresses within each network number. As such, they are set to zeroes when describing the range of network numbers.

NOTE

Technically, `127.0.0.0` is also a Class A network address. However, it is reserved for loop-back testing and cannot be assigned to a network.

Each Class A address can support 16,777,214 unique host addresses. This value is calculated by multiplying 2 to the 24th power and then subtracting 2. Subtracting 2 is necessary because IP reserved the *all 0s* address for identifying the network and the *all 1s* address for broadcasting within that network. Figure 2-2 presents the proportion of network to host octets.

	Network portion	Host portion		
Octet	1	2	3	4

Figure 2-2
Class A address architecture.

Class B Addresses

The Class B addresses were designed to support the needs of moderate- to large-sized networks. The range of possible Class B network addresses is from 128.1.0.0 to 191.254.0.0.

The mathematical logic underlying this class is fairly simple. A Class B IP address uses two of the four octets to indicate the network address. The other two octets enumerate host addresses. The first 2 bits of the first octet of a Class B address are 10. The remaining 6 bits may be populated with either 1s or 0s. This mathematically limits the possible range of the Class B address space to 191, which is the sum of 128 + 32 + 16 + 8 + 4 + 2 + 1.

The last 16 bits (two octets) identify potential host addresses. Each Class B address can support 65,534 unique host addresses. This number is calculated by multiplying two to the 16th power and subtracting two (values reserved by IP). Mathematically, there can only be 16,382 Class B networks defined.

Figure 2-3 presents the proportion of network to host octets.

	Network portion		Host portion	
Octet	1	2	3	4

Figure 2-3
Class B address
architecture.

Class C Addresses

The Class C address space is, by far, the most commonly used of the original IPv4 address classes. This address space was intended to support a lot of small networks. This address class can be thought of as the inverse of the Class A address space. Whereas the Class A space uses just one octet for network numbering, and the remaining three for host numbering, the Class C space uses three octets for networking addressing and just one octet for host numbering.

The first 3 bits of the first octet of a Class C address are 110. The first 2 bits sum to a decimal value of 192 (128 + 64). This forms the lower mathematical boundary of the Class C address space. The third bit equates to a decimal value of 32. Forcing this bit to a value of 0 establishes the upper mathematical boundary of the address space. Lacking the capability to use the third digit limits the maximum value of this octet to 255 – 32, which equals 223. Therefore, the range of possible Class C network addresses is from 192.0.1.0 to 223.255.254.0.

The last octet is used for host addressing. Each Class C address can support a theoretical maximum of 256 unique host addresses (0 through 255), but only 254 are usable because 0 and 255 are not valid host numbers. There can be 2,097,150 different Class C network numbers.

NOTE

In the world of IP addressing, 0 and 255 are reserved host address values. IP addresses that have all their host address bits set equal to 0 identify the local network. Similarly, IP addresses that have all their host address bits set equal to 255 are used to broadcast to all end systems within that network number.

Figure 2-4 presents the proportion of network to host octets.

	Network portion			Host portion
Octet	1	2	3	4

Figure 2-4
Class C address architecture.

Class D Addresses

The Class D address class was created to enable multicasting in an IP network. The Class D multicasting mechanisms have seen only limited usage. A multicast address is a unique network address that directs packets with that destination address to predefined groups of IP addresses. Therefore, a single station can simultaneously transmit a single stream of datagrams to multiple recipients. The need to create separate streams of datagrams, one for each destination, is eliminated. Routers that support multicasting would duplicate the datagram and forward as needed to the predetermined end systems. Multicasting has long been deemed a desirable feature in an IP network because it can substantially reduce network traffic.

The Class D address space, much like the other address spaces, is mathematically constrained. The first 4 bits of a Class D address must be 1110. Presetting the first 3 bits of the first octet to 1s means that the address space begins at 128 + 64 + 32, which equals 224. Preventing the fourth bit from being used means that the Class D address is limited to a maximum value of 128 + 64 + 32 + 8 + 4 + 2 + 1, or 239. Therefore, the Class D address space ranges from 224.0.0.0 to 239.255.255.254.

This range may seem odd because the upper boundary is specified with all four octets. Ordinarily, this would mean that the octets for both host and network numbers are being used to signify a network number. There is a reason for this! The Class D address space isn't used for internetworking to individual end systems or networks. Class D addresses are used for delivering multicast datagrams within a private network to groups of IP-addressed end systems. Therefore, there isn't a need to allocate octets or bits of the address to separate network and host addresses. Instead, the entire address space can be used to identify groups of IP addresses (Classes A, B, or C). Today, numerous other proposals are being developed that would allow IP multicasting without the complexity of a Class D address space.

Figure 2-5 presents the proportion of network to host octets.

Figure 2-5
Class D address
architecture.

	Host portion			
Octet	1	2	3	4

Class E Addresses

A Class E address has been defined, but is reserved by the IETF for its own research. Therefore, no Class E addresses have been released for use in the Internet. The first 4 bits of a Class E address are always set to 1s; therefore, the range of valid addresses is from 240.0.0.0 to 255.255.255.255. Given that this class was defined for research purposes, and its use is limited to inside the IETF, it is not necessary to examine it any further.

Inefficiencies in the System

The large gaps between these address classes have wasted a considerable number of potential addresses over the years. Consider, for example, a medium-sized company that requires 300 IP addresses. A single Class C address (254 addresses) is inadequate. Using two Class C addresses provides more than enough addresses but results in two separate domains within the company. This increases the size of the routing tables across the Internet: One table entry is required for each of the address spaces, even though they belong to the same organization.

Alternatively, stepping up to a Class B address provides all the needed addresses within a single domain but wastes 65,234 addresses. Too frequently, a Class B was handed out whenever a network supported more than 254 hosts. Therefore, the Class B address space approached depletion more rapidly than the other classes.

Perhaps the most wasteful practice was that address spaces were handed out on request. Any organization that wanted an address space just requested one. No attempts to verify need were made. Consequently, many organizations locked up substantial portions of the IPv4 address space as a hedge against some unseen, unspecified future need.

Fortunately, this is no longer the case. Numerous extensions to IP have been developed that are specifically designed to improve the efficiency with which the 32-bit address space can be used. Three of the more important of these are the following:

- Subnet masks

- VLSM

- CIDR

These are very different mechanisms that were designed to solve different problems. Subnet masks, both fixed and variable length, were developed to accommodate the multiple logical networks that might exist within a physical site that connects to the Internet. CIDR was developed to eliminate the inefficiency inherent in the original, rigid address classes. This enabled routers in the Internet to more efficiently aggregate many different network addresses into a single routing table entry. It is important to note that these two mechanisms are not mutually exclusive; they can and should be used together.

Managing the Address Space

The Internet's stability directly depends on the uniqueness of publicly used network addresses. Therefore, some mechanism was needed to ensure that addresses were, in fact, unique. This responsibility originally rested within an organization known as the InterNIC (Internet Network Information Center). This organization is now defunct and has been succeeded by the Internet Assigned Numbers Authority (IANA). IANA carefully manages the remaining supply of IPv4 addresses to ensure that duplication of publicly used addresses does not occur. Such duplication would cause instability in the Internet and compromise its capability to deliver datagrams to networks using the duplicated addresses.

Another important goal served by this careful husbandry of the address space is that the rate of depletion of the address space (which fostered the development of IPv6) has slowed considerably. Consequently, the IPv4 address space is expected to remain adequate for many years to come.

Although it is entirely possible for a network administrator to arbitrarily select unregistered IP addresses, this practice should not be condoned. Computers having such spurious IP addresses can only function properly within the confines of their domain. Interconnecting networks with spurious addresses to the Internet incurs the risk of conflicting with an organization that has legitimate claim to that address space. Duplicated addresses will cause routing problems and potentially hinder the Internet's capability to deliver datagrams to the correct network.

THE EMERGENCE OF SUBNETWORKS

The Internet's original two-level hierarchy assumed that each site would have only a single network. Therefore, each site would only need a single connection to the Internet. Initially, these were safe assumptions. Over time, however, networked computing matured and expanded. By 1985, it was no longer safe to assume that an organization would only have a single network, nor would be satisfied with a single connection to the Internet.

As sites began to develop multiple networks, it became obvious to the IETF that some mechanism was needed to differentiate between the multiple logical networks that were emerging within sites of the Internet's second tier. Otherwise, there could be no efficient way to route data to specific end systems in sites with multiple networks. This is illustrated in Figure 2-6.

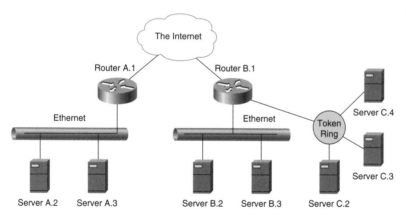

Figure 2-6

The emergence of multiple networks, per site, violated the Internet two-level hierarchy.

One answer was to give each logical network, or subnetwork, its own IP address range. This would work, but would be a tremendously inefficient use of the IP address space. It wouldn't take very long for this approach to threaten to completely consume the remaining, unassigned IP address ranges. More immediate impact would be the expansion of routing tables in the Internet's routers. Each network would require its own routing table entry. Clearly, a better approach needed to be found.

The answer was to organize these logical networks hierarchically and to route between them. Sites with multiple, logical networks should, from the Internet's perspective, be treated as a single network. Therefore, they would share a common IP address range. However, they would need their own, unique range of subnetwork numbers.

Subnetting

In the mid-1980s, RFCs 917 and 950 were released. These documents proposed a means of solving the ever-growing problem posed by the relatively flat, two-level hierarchy of IP addressing. The solution was termed *subnetting*. The concept of subnetting is based on the need for a third level in the Internet's hierarchy. As internetworking technologies matured, their acceptance and use increased dramatically. As a result, it became normal for moderate- and large-sized organizations to have multiple networks. Frequently, these networks were LANs. Each LAN may be treated as a subnet.

In such multiple-network environments, each subnetwork would interconnect to the Internet via a common point: a router. The actual details of the network environment are inconsequential to the Internet. They comprise a private network that is (or should be) capable of delivering its own datagrams. Therefore, the Internet need only concern itself with how to reach that network's gateway router to the Internet. Inside the private network, the host portion of the IP address can be subdivided for use in identifying subnetworks.

Subnetting, as specified in RFC 950, enables the network number of any classful IP address (A, B, or C) to be subdivided into smaller network numbers. A subnetted IP address actually consists of three parts:

- Network address

- Subnetwork address

- Host address

The subnetwork and host addresses are carved from the original IP address's host address portion. Therefore, your ability to subnet depends directly on the type of IP address being subnetted. The more host bits there are in the IP address, the more subnets and hosts you can create. However, these subnets decrease the number of hosts that can be addressed. You are, in effect, taking bits away from the host address to identify subnetwork numbers. Subnets are identified using a pseudo-IP address known as a *subnet mask*.

A subnet mask is a 32-bit binary number that can be expressed in dotted decimal form. The mask is used to tell end systems (including routers and other hosts) in the network how many bits of the IP address are used for network and subnetwork identification. These bits are called the *extended network prefix*. The remaining bits identify the hosts within the subnetwork. The bits of the mask that identify the network number are set to 1s and the host bits are set to 0s.

For example, a mask of 11111111.11111111.11111111.11000000 (255.255.255.192 in dotted-decimal notation) would yield 64 mathematically possible host addresses per subnet. The values of the rightmost 6 bits, the 1s set equal to 0, sum to 64 in the base 10 number system. Therefore, you may uniquely identify 64 devices within this subnet. Only 62 of these addresses, however, are actually usable. The other two host addresses are reserved. The first host number in a subnet is always reserved for identifying the subnet itself. The last host number is also reserved but is used for IP broadcasts within the subnet. Therefore, you must always subtract two from the maximum number of hosts in a subnet to get the maximum number of *usable* host addresses per subnet.

The number of mathematically possible subnets, however, depends on what class of IP address was being subnetted! Each class reserves a different number of the available bits for the network number. Therefore, each class offers a different amount of bits that can be used for subnetting. Table 2-6 demonstrates the tradeoff between the number of subnets and the number of hosts per subnet that can be carved from a Class B IP address. A Class B address uses 16 bits for network number and 16 for host identification. As you peruse Table 2-6, you will notice that the fewest number of bits you can allocate to the network prefix is 2, and the most is 14. The reason for this is simple—a network prefix of 1 bit will only allow you to define 2 subnet numbers: 0 and 1. The rules for subnetting prevent you from using a subnet address that consists of all 0s or all 1s. Such addresses are reserved! Therefore, a network prefix of 1 bit yields no usable subnets addresses.

Similarly, a network prefix of 2 bits yields only two usable subnet addresses. With a 2-bit binary subnet address field, the mathematically possible address combinations are 00, 01, 10, and 11. The first and last combinations aren't valid, leaving only 01 and 10 for use in identifying subnets.

Table 2-6 *Subnetting a Class B Address Space*

Number of Bits in Network Prefix	Subnet Mask	Number of Usable Subnet Addresses	Number of Usable Host Addresses, Per Subnet
2	255.255.192.0	2	16,382
3	255.255.224.0	6	8,190
4	255.255.240.0	14	4,094
5	255.255.248.0	30	2,046
6	255.255.252.0	62	1,022
7	255.255.254.0	126	510
8	255.255.255.0	254	254
9	255.255.255.128	510	126
10	255.255.255.192	1,022	62
11	255.255.255.224	2,046	30
12	255.255.255.240	4,094	14
13	255.255.255.248	8,190	6
14	255.255.255.252	16,382	2

Obviously, the more bits that are allocated to identifying a subnet number, the fewer remain for host identification and vice versa.

Class C addresses can also be subnetted. Because a Class C address allocates 24 bits for network addressing, only 8 bits remain for apportioning between subnet and host addressing. Table 2-7 presents the tradeoffs between subnet and host addressing in a Class C network.

Table 2-7   *Subnetting a Class C Address Space*

Number of Bits in Network Prefix	Subnet Mask	Number of Usable Subnet Addresses	Number of Usable Host Addresses, Per Subnet
2	255.255.192.0	2	62
3	255.255.224.0	6	30
4	255.255.240.0	14	14
5	255.255.248.0	30	6
6	255.255.252.0	62	2

Although Tables 2-6 and 2-7 demonstrate the tradeoffs between the numbers of possible subnets per mask and hosts per subnet, they fall short of actually demonstrating how subnetting works. The best way to demonstrate subnetting is to actually subnet an IP address, which is done in the next section.

A Subnetting Example

Subnetting is perhaps the most difficult aspect of the IP address architecture to comprehend. This is largely because it only really makes sense when viewed in binary numbers, which isn't very intuitive. You need to subnet the Class C address 193.168.125.0, for example. This is your base address; the one that the Internet would calculate routes to. You need to carve this into six subnets. You would need at least three of the eight host bits to create a unique extended network prefix for each of the six subnets. These addresses would be 001, 010, 011, 100, 101, and 110. The last octet is split: three bits are added to the network number to form the extended network prefix, and the remaining five are used to identify hosts. Table 2-8 demonstrates how subnetworks are formed.

In Table 2-8, the extended network prefixes (which consists of the IP network address and the subnetwork address) are in bold. The subnet address is in bold italic. The host addresses are in normal typeface and separated from the extended network prefix with a hyphen. This makes it easier to see how a basic IP network address can be subdivided into subnetworks.

Table 2-8 *Forming Subnets*

Network Number	Binary Address	Decimal Address
Base	**11000000.10101001.01111101.**00000000	193.168.125.0
Subnet 0	**11000000.10101001.01111101.*000*-**00000	193.168.125.0
Subnet 1	**11000000.10101001.01111101.*001*-**00000	193.168.125.32
Subnet 2	**11000000.10101001.01111101.*010*-**00000	193.168.125.64
Subnet 3	**11000000.10101001.01111101.*011*-**00000	193.168.125.96
Subnet 4	**11000000.10101001.01111101.*100*-**00000	193.168.125.128
Subnet 5	**11000000.10101001.01111101.*101*-**00000	193.168.125.160
Subnet 6	**11000000.10101001.01111101.*110*-**00000	193.168.125.192
Subnet 7	**11000000.10101001.01111101.*111*-**00000	193.168.125.224

Each subnetwork number is defined with the first three bits of the last octet. The decimal values of these digits are 128, 64, and 32, respectively. The starting IP address (in decimal) for each subnet is presented in the third column. Not surprisingly, these increment in multiples of 32: the rightmost bit of the subnet number.

NOTE

Subnets 0 and 7, although mathematically possible to define, are not usable. Their subnet addresses are 000 and 111, respectively. As such, they represent reserved addresses and should not be used to address specific subnets. A subnet address of all 0s (regardless of how many 0s) is always

reserved for identifying the subnet itself. A subnet address of all 1s is reserved for broadcasting within the subnet. These subnet addresses are included in Table 2-8 solely to demonstrate the incrementing of the binary
subnet address field from minimum value to maximum value.

Hosts in each subnet would be defined by incrementing the
remaining five bits in the last octet. There are 32 possible combinations of 0s and 1s. The highest and lowest values are
reserved, yielding a usable maximum of 30 hosts per subnet. A
device with an IP address of 193.168.125.193 would be the first
host defined in Subnet 6. Subsequent hosts would be numbered
up to 193.168.125.223, at which point the subnet would be fully
populated. No further hosts could be added.

VLSM

Although subnetting proved a valuable addition to the Internet
addressing architecture, it did suffer from one fundamental limitation: You were limited to a single subnet mask for an entire network. Therefore, after you selected a subnet mask (which dictated
the number of hosts you could support per subnet number) you
couldn't support subnets of a different size. Any requirement for
larger-sized subnets meant you had to change the size of the subnet mask for the entire network. Needless to say, this could be a
complicated and time-consuming affair.

A solution to this problem arose in 1987. The IETF published
RFC 1009, which specified how a subnetted network could use
more than one subnet mask! Ostensibly, each subnet mask would

be a different size. Otherwise, they wouldn't be different masks: Their network prefix would be identical. The new subnetting technique was, therefore, called VLSM.

VLSM enables a more efficient use of an organization's IP address space by enabling the network's administrator(s) to customize the size of a subnet mask to the specific requirements of each subnet. To illustrate this point, assume a base IP address of 172.16.9.0. This is a Class B address, which uses a 16-bit network number. Extending the network prefix by 6 bits results in a 22-bit extended network prefix. Mathematically, there are 62 usable subnet addresses and 1,022 usable host addresses per subnet.

NOTE

The size of an extended network prefixes can be identified using a / followed by the number of bits used for the network and subnetwork addressing. Therefore, 193.168.125.0/27 identifies a specific Class C address, with 27 bits used for the extended network prefix.

This subnetting scheme would make sense if the organization needed more than 30 subnets populated with more than 500 hosts per subnet. If the organization consisted of a few large suborganizations with more than 500 hosts each, however, and many smaller suborganizations with just 40 or 50 host devices each, the majority of possible IP addresses would be wasted. Each organization, regardless of need, would be allocated a subnet with 1,022 host addresses. The smaller organizations would each waste approximately 950 host addresses. Given that a subnetted network could only use a single mask of fixed and predetermined length such address wastage could not be avoided.

As a purely mathematical exercise, subnetting was an ideal solution to a vexing problem: the rapid depletion of the finite IP address space. Enabling private networks to redefine the host field of an IP address into subnetwork and host addresses would greatly reduce the amount of wasted IP addresses. Unfortunately, in a real-world setting, the need for subnets is not homogeneous. It is not realistic to expect an organization, or its networks, to be divided into uniformly sized subcomponents. It is much more likely that there will be organizations (and subnetworks) of all sizes. Therefore, using a fixed-length subnet mask would result in wasted IP host addresses in each subnet defined, as was seen in the preceding example.

The solution to this dilemma was to allow an IP address space to be subnetted flexibly using different sized subnet masks. Using the preceding example, a network administrator could carve a base IP address into different subnet masks. The few large organizations could continue to use the 22-bit extended network prefix, whereas the smaller organizations could be given a 25- or 26-bit extended network prefix. The 25-bit prefix would enable the creation of 126-host subnets, and the 26-bit prefix would permit subnets with up to 62 hosts each. This solution is VLSM.

NOTE

It should be noted that almost all of today's routing protocols support subnetting, if not VLSM. One exception is RIP, which predates the IETF's specification of the various subnetting mechanisms.

CLASSLESS INTERDOMAIN ROUTING

A relatively recent addition to the IP address architecture is CIDR. CIDR was born of the crisis that accompanied the Internet's explosive growth during the early 1990s.

As early as 1992, the IETF became concerned with the Internet's capability to continue to scale upward in response to demand for Internet use. Their specific concerns were as follows:

- Exhaustion of the remaining, unassigned IPv4 network addresses. The Class B space was in particular danger of depletion.

- The rapid, and substantial, increase in the size of the Internet's routing tables as a result of its growth.

All the indications were that the Internet's rapid growth would continue, as more commercial organizations came online. In fact, some members of the IETF even predicted a date of doom. This date, March 1994, was the projected date of the depletion of the Class B address space. Absent any other mechanism for addressing, the Internet's scalability would be seriously compromised. More ominously, the Internet's routing mechanisms might collapse under the weight of their ever-growing routing tables before the Date of Doom.

The Internet was becoming a victim of its own success. The IETF decided that, to avoid the collapse of the Internet, both short- and long-term solutions would be needed. In the long term, the only viable solution was a completely new IP, with greatly expanded address space and address architectures. Ultimately, this solution became known as IPng (Internet Protocol: The Next Generation) or, more formally, as IP Version 6 (IPv6). You can learn more about this emerging protocol in Chapter 15, "The Future of Routing."

The more pressing, short-term needs were to slow down the rate of depletion of the remaining unassigned addresses. The answer was to eliminate the inefficient classes of addresses in favor of a more flexible addressing architecture. The result was CIDR.

In September 1993, the plans for CIDR were released in RFCs 1517, 1518, 1519, and 1520. CIDR had three key features that were invaluable in staving off depletion of the IPv4 address space. These features are the following:

- The elimination of classful addressing

- Enhanced route aggregation

- Supernetting

Classless Addressing

Mathematically, the IPv4 address space still held a substantial number of available addresses. Unfortunately, many of these potential addresses were squandered because they were locked into assigned blocks, or classes, of assigned addresses. Eliminating classes wouldn't necessarily recover the addresses locked into those address spaces that were already assigned, but it would enable the remaining addresses to be used much more efficiently. Ostensibly, this stopgap effort would buy the time needed for IPv6 to be developed and deployed.

Enhanced Route Aggregation

CIDR enables Internet routers (or any CIDR-compliant router) to more efficiently aggregate routing information. In other words, a single entry in a routing table can represent the address spaces of many networks. This can greatly reduce the size of the routing tables that are needed in any given internetwork and directly translates into an increased scalability.

CIDR was implemented in the Internet during 1994 through 1995 and was immediately effective in containing the expansion of the Internet routers' routing tables. It is doubtful that the Internet would have continued to grow had CIDR not been implemented.

Supernetting

Another benefit of CIDR is the capability to supernet. *Supernetting* is nothing more than using contiguous blocks of Class C address spaces to simulate a single, albeit larger address space. If you were to obtain enough contiguous Class C addresses, you could redefine the allocation of bits between network and host identification fields and simulate a Class B address.

Supernetting is designed to alleviate the pressure on the rapidly depleting Class B address space by offering a more flexible alternative. The previous class-based address architecture suffered from a tremendous disparity between its Class B and C networks. Networks that required more than the 254 hosts offered by a Class C had the following two choices, neither of which was highly desirable:

1. Using multiple Class C addresses (which would have necessitated routing between the network domains)
2. Stepping up to a Class B address with its 65,534 usable host addresses

The simpler solution, frequently, was to use the Class B even though it wasted tens of thousands of IP addresses.

How CIDR Works

CIDR was a dramatic break from tradition in that it completely abandoned the rigid classes of addresses. The original IPv4 address architecture used an 8-bit network number for Class A addresses, a 16-bit network number for Class B addresses, and a 24-bit number for Class C addresses. CIDR replaced these categories with a more generalized network prefix. This prefix could be of any length rather than just 8, 16, or 24 bits. This allows CIDR to craft network address spaces according to the size of a network instead of force-fitting networks into presized network address spaces.

Each CIDR-compliant network address is advertised with a specific bit mask. This mask identifies the length of the network prefix. For example, 192.125.61.8/20 identifies a CIDR address with a 20-bit network address. The IP address can be any mathematically valid address regardless of whether that address was originally part of the Class A, B, or C range! CIDR-compliant routers look at the number after the / to determine the network number. Therefore, the former Class C address 192.125.61.8 previously had a network number of 192.125.61 and a host number of 8. As a Class C address, you could provide addresses for a maximum of 254 hosts within the network. Using CIDR, the architectural limitations of the 8-bit boundaries between address components is eliminated. To better understand how this works, it is necessary to translate the decimal number to binary.

In binary, this network portion of this address is 11000000.0111101.00111101. The first 20 bits of this example identify the network number. Figure 2-7 demonstrates the split of this address between network and host numbers.

	Network number	Host number
Binary address	11000000.1111101.0011	1101.00000000

Figure 2-7
A 20-bit CIDR network number.

Notice that the split between the network and host portions of the address falls in the middle of the third octet. The bits that aren't allocated to network number are used to identify hosts. Therefore, an IPv4 address with a 20-bit network prefix has 12 bits left for host identification. Mathematically, this translates to 4,094 usable host addresses. Because none of the leftmost bits are preset (which previously established the address class), virtually the entire range of addresses can be used in a CIDR network. Therefore, a 20-bit network prefix can be assigned a value that was previously reserved for Class A, B, or C networks.

SUMMARY

A solid understanding of IP's address architecture is a prerequisite to appreciating the fundamentals of internetworking with IP. The basics presented in this chapter should help you better appreciate the mechanics of internetworking with the IP. Many of the architectural devices presented in this chapter—including CIDR, subnet masking, and VLSM—are so widely used that not understanding them will compromise your ability to support and design internetworks.

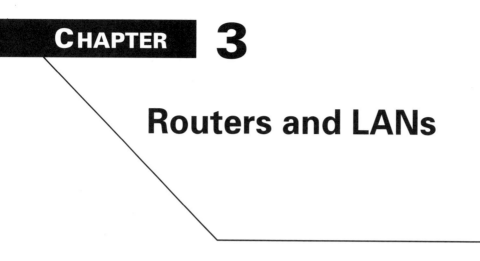

CHAPTER **3**

Routers and LANs

Although routers are often thought of as wide-area network (WAN) devices, they can be equally useful in local-area networks (LANs). Routers, by virtue of their capability to communicate at both the data link layer and the network layer, can provide LAN administrators with a multitude of options for managing LANs and bolstering their performance.

Some of the many things that a router can do in a LAN environment include segment a LAN's media access and MAC broadcast domains, interconnect different LAN architectures, collapse a LAN's backbone into a single device, and provide a gateway to the WAN. This chapter examines all these LAN-level router functions.

LAN DOMAINS

Before delving into the various roles that routers can play in a LAN, it is necessary to first understand some of the functional aspects of a LAN. This will make it easier to understand the effects that routers have when used in a LAN.

A LAN, at its simplest, is a data communications vehicle that operates at the physical and data link layers of the OSI reference model. LANs support two critical functions:

- Media access

- The capability to both address and forward frames of data to other local machines

The key word in the second item is *local*. The definition of *local* may change subtly with context: A LAN has boundaries that constrain its capability to perform these two functions. For example, a LAN has a media access domain and a Media Access Control (MAC) broadcast domain. Each domain forms the boundary around a group of local, LAN-attached devices.

NOTE

Broadcasts can also be performed at the network layer. These broadcasts are bounded by the network layer domain.

The Media Access Domain

A media access domain consists of all the devices connected to a LAN that must share the LAN's bandwidth. The name and nature of this domain depends on the media access methodology employed in a LAN. The two primary methodologies for regulating media access are contention and token passing.

Other media access arbitration techniques exist, but these two account for the vast majority of existing LANs. More importantly, they will adequately demonstrate the differences between a media access domain as well as a MAC broadcast domain.

The Contention Domain

In a LAN that uses contention to arbitrate permission to transmit, such as the various Ethernets, this domain is known as a *contention*, or *collision*, domain. These names reflect the fact that this is a competition-based, chaotic, and less-than-perfectly reliable access-arbitration technique.

In essence, any device in the contention domain may begin transmitting if it detects no other traffic on the transmission media. The lack of traffic is presumed to mean an idle LAN. In fact, because transmissions are not instantaneous, silence of the LAN may just mean that a device is transmitting but that transmission hasn't reached all the peripheral devices yet. Therefore, a device may begin transmitting only to have its transmissions collide with another. In such cases, both transmission streams are compromised and must be retransmitted.

In an Ethernet network, regardless of the media type or transmission speed, a contention domain consists of all the devices that must compete for the right to transmit. IEEE-compliant Ethernet LANs can support up to a maximum of 1,024 station devices in a single contention domain. This means that there can be up to 1,024 total devices competing for the right to transmit in an Ethernet contention domain.

The Token-Passing Domain

In LANs that pass tokens to regulate media access, such as Fiber Distributed Data Interface (FDDI) or Token Ring, the media access domain is called the *token-passing domain*. Media access is arbitrated by passing a token in an orderly, circular fashion between the LAN's peripheral devices. A token is a special pattern of bits that is circulated around the media access domain.

The token can be modified by a LAN-attached device to form the header of a data frame. Without this token, the data frame's header cannot be constructed and there can be no transmission. Recipient peripheral devices copy the data in the frame from the LAN. This device also inverts some of the bits in the frame's header to acknowledge its receipt. The frame is then allowed to continue traversing the ring. When it returns to its originator, that device takes the frame off the network and strips out the data. If that device needs to send more data, it may do so. Otherwise, the header is reconverted back into a token and placed on the transmission media, where it travels to the next device downstream. Although this may seem complicated, token passing is a highly organized and efficient means of arbitrating media access permissions.

In a token-passing LAN, regardless of the media type or transmission speed, a token-passing domain consists of all the devices that pass tokens. Here is where a discontinuity in definitions occurs between Token Ring and FDDI, the two most common token-passing LAN architectures. They enjoy similar media access domain characteristics, but they define *device* differently.

In a Token Ring network, only the LAN's peripheral devices are counted as devices. The hubs are nothing more than repeaters; they are incapable of modifying token bits. Therefore, they cannot be considered devices in the parlance of this LAN architecture.

FDDI, on the other hand, does count hub ports as devices. This has some significant ramifications on the sizes of the media access domains in these two LAN architectures. Token Ring LANs can support up to a maximum of 260 peripheral devices in a single token-passing domain. FDDI can support up to 500 total devices (including hub ports) in its token-passing domain. Therefore, you can connect more peripheral devices to a Token Ring LAN than you can to FDDI.

Additionally, FDDI enables devices to be either single-attached (SA) or dual-attached (DA) to the LAN. These describe the number of connections made to the LAN. DA FDDI, while providing redundancy, effectively doubles the device count in the token-passing domain. Each attached port must be counted as a separate device. Therefore, only 125 DA peripheral devices may be connected to a FDDI LAN.

Expanding Media Access Domains

Many of today's LANs are constructed using repeating hubs. The result is a star-shaped physical topology; peripheral devices are interconnected via a central hub. In other words, their connections to the LAN radiate out from a single point much like the rays of a star. Consequently, the physical topologies of LANs are identical, regardless of their media access methodology.

Figure 3-1 illustrates a media access domain in a star-shaped LAN.

NOTE

Given the previously described discontinuities in the definition of the term *device* that exists between Ethernet, Token Ring, and FDDI, the examples in this section apply only to Ethernet, Token Ring, and SA FDDI.

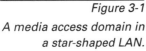

Figure 3-1

A media access domain in a star-shaped LAN.

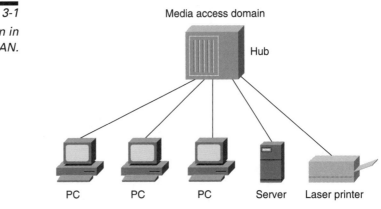

If a given work environment were to install a second Ethernet hub for a second workgroup, it would have two separate Ethernet LANs. That is, each LAN would be completely autonomous and define its own media access and MAC broadcast domains. Figure 3-2 illustrates this.

Figure 3-2

Two separate LANs, each with its own media access domain.

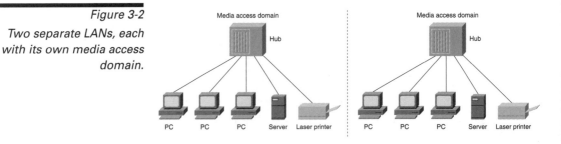

If the two LANs in Figure 3-2 were to be directly interconnected, the result would be a single LAN. This LAN's media access domain would consist of all the devices that populated the original two LANs. The media access domain would also include the two ports used to interconnect the LANs. Therefore, this consolidated LAN would consolidate all LAN-attached devices into a single media access domain. This is depicted in Figure 3-3.

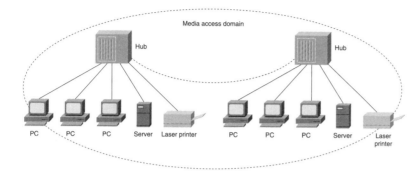

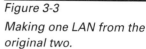

Figure 3-3
Making one LAN from the
original two.

Interconnecting the repeating hubs of LANs, both contention based and token passing, results in a functional consolidation of their media access domains. Depending on the LAN architecture, the expanded media access domain may also have to include the hub ports that were interconnected. This is the only way to expand a media access domain!

Other forms of LAN expansion and LAN-to-LAN interconnection are possible but require additional hardware. This hardware can include LAN switches, bridges, and routers. These devices, however, decrease the size of the media access domain, the MAC broadcast domain, or both. Therefore, they enable the overall size of a LAN to increase without a commensurate increase in the size of its media access or MAC broadcast domains. Such asymmetric expandability is the key to a LAN's scalability. These concepts are examined throughout the remainder of this chapter.

The MAC Broadcast Domain

A MAC broadcast domain consists of all the devices connected to a LAN that receive framed data broadcast by a machine to all other machines on the LAN. The concept of a MAC broadcast is virtually universal throughout all IEEE-compliant LANs, regardless of their media access methodology. Consequently, this chapter examines MAC broadcast domains only in the context of Ethernet LANs.

NOTE

FDDI is considered an IEEE-compliant LAN, even though it was not created by the IEEE. This is because the IEEE standards are passed to the American National Standards Institute (ANSI) for integration with their national standards. FDDI is an ANSI specification that complies with the ANSI equivalents of the IEEE 802.1 and 802.2 standards. Therefore, FDDI is IEEE compliant.

In essence, a MAC broadcast domain is the set of devices that can communicate directly without requiring higher-layer protocols or addressing. To better illustrate the difference between MAC broadcast and media access domains, compare Figures 3-1 and 3-4.

Figure 3-4

An Ethernet MAC broadcast domain with five devices.

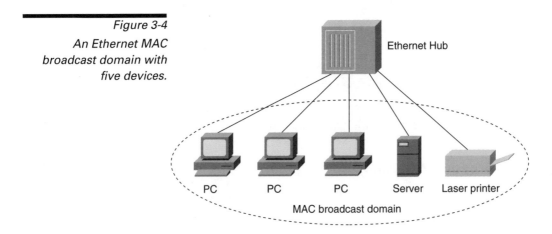

Figure 3-4 uses the same LAN configuration depicted in Figure 3-1, but identifies its MAC broadcast domain rather than the media access domain. The key distinction between MAC broadcast and media access domains will become obvious as the various LAN segmentation mechanisms are examined.

As with the media access domain, adding a second isolated LAN creates a second, fully separate broadcast domain. Figure 3-5 identifies the MAC broadcast domains of the LAN configuration presented in Figure 3-2.

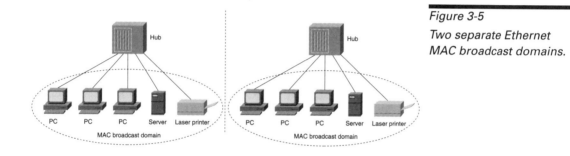

Figure 3-5
Two separate Ethernet
MAC broadcast domains.

Interconnecting these LANs in the manner demonstrated in Figure 3-3 results in a single, but larger, MAC broadcast domain. Figure 3-6 illustrates this new broadcast domain.

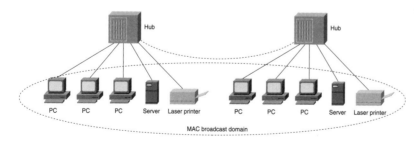

Figure 3-6
Making one Ethernet LAN
and MAC broadcast
domain of the original two.

This LAN's MAC broadcast domain consists of all the devices that populated the original two LANs' broadcast domains. In this scenario, any given broadcast message is now propagated across the network to twice as many devices as before. Therein lies the proverbial double-edged sword of LANs with large MAC broadcast domains: They can become quite large due to the segmentation of their media access domains, but suffer from the flatness, or lack of a hierarchy, to their MAC broadcast domain.

The Trouble with Flat LANs

LANs built with a single MAC broadcast domain are known as *flat LANs*. They are flat because there is no structure or hierarchy to their broadcast domains. The benefit of having a large broadcast domain is that it is extremely easy to reach all the devices that are interconnected on the LAN. The potential danger, also, is that it is extremely easy to reach all the devices on the LAN. The more devices you connect to a flat LAN, the more resources are consumed by each MAC broadcast message. Using the wrong communications protocol (that is, one that makes extensive use of MAC broadcasting) could easily compromise the performance of the network, as well as all the devices that populate it.

NOTE

MAC broadcasts are performed by setting the destination MAC address of a frame of data to its highest possible value: FF:FF:FF:FF:FF:FF. This reserved address value, when placed in a frame's destination address field, is interpreted by all IEEE-compliant LANs as being addressed to all local machines. Therefore, it is accepted by all machines, regardless of what their actual MAC address is.

This paradox shouldn't be misinterpreted as meaning flat LANs are undesirable. On the contrary! The introduction of LAN switching led to a flattening of LANs. The larger a flat LAN is (in terms of its population), however, the more important it is to segment it. Segmentation is a technique that allows the overall size of a LAN to be expanded, by controlling the sizes of its media access and/or MAC broadcast domains.

LAN SEGMENTATION

Although the preceding series of examples seem a bit redundant, it is necessary to develop the context for better appreciating the differences between a LAN's MAC broadcast and/or media access domains. Although these two domains are so closely related as to be virtually synonymous from a user's perspective, they can be intentionally and unambiguously separated. This separation, as demonstrated throughout the preceding section's examples and illustrations, is known as *segmentation*.

Segmentation is the process of splitting a LAN's domain(s) into two or more separate domains. This allows a LAN to grow beyond its inherent limitations without compromising its performance. It is possible to segment LANs' media access domains, MAC broadcast domains, or both. Segmentation is usually done to improve the performance of a LAN, although it could be done proactively to ensure the continued scalability of the LAN.

Some of the devices that could be used to segment a LAN are bridges, switches, and routers. The functional distinctions between these different segmentation devices lie in the layers of the OSI reference model that they operate in. The point is that there are different tools for segmenting different aspects of a LAN.

Selecting the right one for your particular needs absolutely requires understanding the ways that each operates and the effects they have on the LAN's domains.

Segmenting with Bridges

A bridge is a hardware segmentation device that operates at the first two layers of the OSI reference model—the physical and data link layers. Bridges segment a LAN's media access domain. Therefore, installing a bridge between two LAN hubs results in two media access domains that share a common MAC broadcast domain.

In general, all bridges work by building address tables. These tables are built and maintained by a bridge. Each is populated with a two-dimensional array or table. The bridging table maintains an up-to-date listing of every MAC address on the LAN, as well as the physical bridge port connected to the segment containing that address.

In operation, the bridge listens to all LAN traffic. The source and destination MAC addresses of each frame received by the bridge are examined. This allows the bridge to learn which MAC addresses reside on which port and, consequently, which LAN segment.

The destination address is hashed against the bridging table to identify the appropriate port to transmit it from. If the MAC address exists on the same LAN segment that the frame came from, the bridge needs to do nothing with it; it safely assumes that the frame has already been carried to its intended destination.

If the bridging table identifies that MAC address as being on a different segment, however, the bridge then forwards that frame to that segment. It is important to note that the bridge, as far as media access is concerned, must adhere to the media access protocol. In a token-passing network, the bridge must await the token before it can forward the frame. In a contention-based LAN, the bridge must compete for available bandwidth before it can forward the frame.

It is quite possible that the bridge will occasionally receive a frame addressed to a MAC address that the bridge doesn't know about. This can happen when a new device is connected to the network, a bridge's bridging table is "lost," or a new bridge is installed. In such cases, the bridge will propagate that frame to all its attached LAN segments, except for the one the frame came from.

Bridging, in an IEEE 802–compliant LAN, occurs at the MAC layer. For this reason, bridges are frequently referred to as *MAC bridges*. MAC bridging is an unnecessarily broad technical term. It effectively describes the layer at which the device operates but does not describe its functionality. In fact, there are three types of MAC bridges:

- Transparent bridges

- Translating bridges

- Speed-buffering bridges

Transparent Bridges

Transparent bridges link together segments of the same type of LAN. The simplest transparent bridge contains just two ports, but transparent bridges may also contain more ports. Figure 3-7 illustrates how a transparent bridge isolates the traffic of two LAN segments by creating two media access domains.

Figure 3-7

Transparent bridges segment the media access domain of a single LAN architecture.

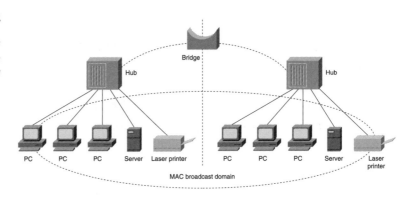

The transparent bridge segments one LAN with one communications channel into two distinct communications channels within a common architecture. This is significant because it means that a bridge can reduce the number of devices in a media access domain by creating two such domains.

It is important to note that transparent bridges do not segment a LAN's MAC broadcast domain. Therefore, in Figure 3-7, MAC broadcasts are still carried throughout the entire LAN. Despite this, the LANs on each side of the bridge function as separate media access domains.

Translating Bridges

A translating bridge, sometimes also referred to as a *translational bridge*, works in exactly the same manner as a transparent bridge, but it has the added capability to provide the conversion processes needed between two or more LAN architectures. It does this by literally translating the frames of one LAN architecture into the frame structure of another. This is useful for interconnecting Token Ring and Ethernet devices.

Figure 3-8 illustrates using a translating bridge to interconnect a Token Ring and Ethernet LANs. The stations on both LANs may communicate with each other through the bridge as easily as they communicate among themselves.

NOTE

In Figure 3-8, the Token Ring LAN is depicted as a ring, and the Ethernet is depicted as a bus. This visually reinforces the differences between these two LAN architectures that would not otherwise be evident if they were illustrated using the more familiar star topology.

The Token Ring and Ethernet LANs in Figure 3-8 retain separate media access domains. Given the radical differences in their media access arbitration techniques, this shouldn't be surprising. What may be surprising, however, is that the bridge unifies their MAC broadcast domains! Therefore, a Token Ring–connected computer can send MAC broadcasts to Ethernet-connected machines.

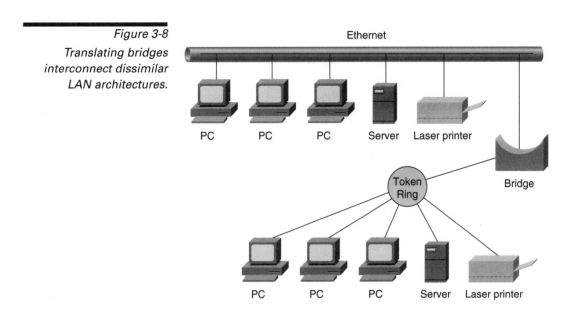

Figure 3-8
Translating bridges
interconnect dissimilar
LAN architectures.

Perhaps a more useful application of translation bridging is using a more robust LAN architecture as a backbone for client/server LANs. It is quite common, for example, to use FDDI to interconnect Ethernet segments. This is illustrated in Figure 3-9.

Figure 3-9
Translating bridges can
also be used to
interconnect client/server
LANs using a
high-performance LAN
architecture.

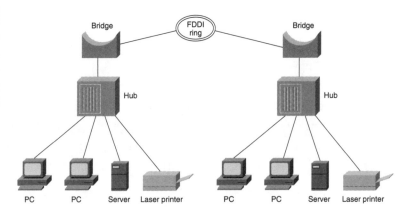

In this scenario, the use of translating bridges creates three separate media access domains: two Ethernet and one FDDI. These bridges, however, do not segment the LANs' MAC broadcast domains. Instead, the bridges unify the three different LANs into a single MAC broadcast domain.

Translation bridging is only possible among LANs that adhere to the IEEE's standards for MAC addressing.

Translating bridges are highly specialized devices. Therefore, unless a bridge is specifically identified as a translating bridge, do not assume that it can bridge dissimilar LAN architectures.

Speed-Buffering Bridges

The last type of bridge is the speed-buffering bridge. Speed-buffering bridges have long been used to interconnect LAN segments with similar architectures but different transmission rates. Examples of this include the following:

- 4 Mbps to 16 Mbps Token Ring

- 1 Mbps to 10 Mbps Ethernet

- 10 Mbps to 100 Mbps Ethernet

NOTE

You could argue that translating bridges are, in effect, also speed-buffering bridges. To the extent that most of the translations occur between LAN architectures with different transmission rates, translation bridges must also perform speed buffering. Their primary function is translation, however; speed buffering is an adjunct task made necessary by the translation.

Figure 3-10 illustrates a speed-buffering bridge interconnecting a 10 Mbps Ethernet LAN with a 100 Mbps Ethernet LAN. In this illustration, the servers are concentrated together on a single high-speed LAN segment, and the clients share a lower-speed segment.

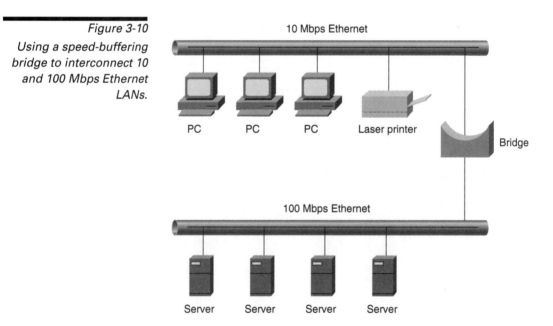

Figure 3-10

Using a speed-buffering bridge to interconnect 10 and 100 Mbps Ethernet LANs.

In Figure 3-10, the clients and the servers enjoy separate media access domains, but now they share a common MAC broadcast domain.

Bridging Today

Generally speaking, bridges are simple and inexpensive devices. They are self-learning, so the administrative overheads are negligible. A bridge is usually a two-port device, but bridges can also have more ports. Such multiport bridges are useful in internetworking more than two LAN environments.

Bridges function transparently from both a user's and an administrator's perspective. The variety of bridges makes them a flexible mechanism for improving the performance of a LAN. Bridging is on the decline. This isn't due to their functions no longer being needed. Quite the contrary: Their functionality is required more today than ever before! Consequently, their functions have been almost completely usurped by other networking devices.

Their functionality has been built in to routers, multitopology LAN hubs, and, most importantly, LAN switches. Many standalone and stackable hubs are also available with higher performance up-link ports. All are either translating, speed-buffering, or transparent bridges in disguise.

Segmenting with Switches

A switch is a multiport, data link layer (Layer 2) device. Much like a bridge, a switch "learns" MAC addresses and stores them in an internal lookup table. Temporary logical paths are constructed between the frame's originator and its intended recipient, and the frames are forwarded along that temporary path. The capability to create and sustain temporary paths with their own dedicated bandwidth is what separates bridges from switches. Bridges use a shared backplane to interconnect LAN segments. Switches use temporary, but dedicated, logical paths to interconnect LAN segments as needed. This architecture results in each port on a switch functioning as a separate media access domain.

Beyond this architectural distinction, switches and bridges are similar enough in their mechanics that switches are frequently described as nothing more than fast bridges. This is a gross over-simplification, of course, that does not adequately describe a switch's many benefits.

Switching can be used to interconnect either hubs or individual devices. These approaches are known as segment switching and port switching, respectively.

Segment Switching

Using a switch to interconnect shared hubs is known as *segment switching*. This name indicates that each port functions as its own segment. In this scenario, each hub connected to a switched port becomes its own media access domain although that domain must include the switched port.

Figure 3-11 illustrates the media access and MAC broadcast domains of a segment-switched LAN.

As is now somewhat predictable with data link layer segmentation mechanisms, segment switching does not segment the MAC broadcast domain. Segment switching does, however, segment media access domains. The net effect is an increase in the available bandwidth on the LAN, a decrease in the number of devices sharing each segment's bandwidth, yet no compromise in the

Layer 2 connectivity (as defined by the MAC broadcast domain).
A MAC broadcast would be propagated throughout all the
switched segments.

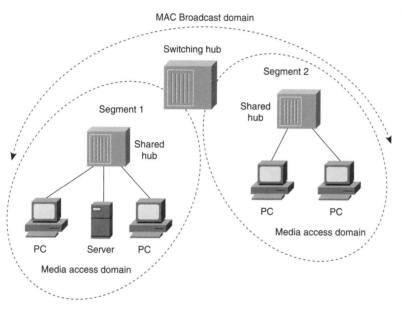

MAC Broadcast domain

Figure 3-11
Media access and MAC
broadcast domains in a
segment-switched LAN.

Port Switching

In a port-switched LAN, each port on the switching hub is connected to a single device. The switching port and the device it connects to become their own self-contained media access domain.
All devices in the network remain part of the same MAC broadcast domain, however. This is illustrated in Figure 3-12.

Port switching is also sometimes referred to as *microsegmenta-
tion* because it chops a LAN's media access domain into the
smallest possible segments. Switching has proven to be so successful at improving LAN performance in both segment and
port-level configurations that it has been broadly implemented.

Today, it is easy to find a switching hub for virtually every LAN architecture, including both contention-based and token-passing LAN architectures.

Figure 3-12

*Media access and MAC
broadcast domains in a
port-switched LAN.*

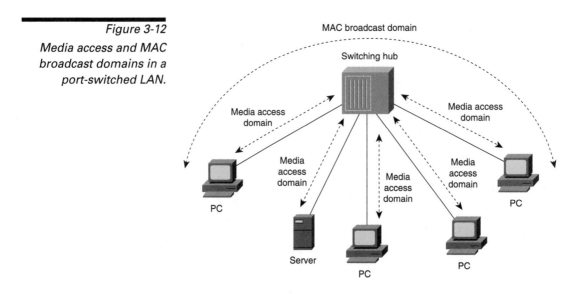

Switching Contention-Based Networks

In a contention-based protocol, port switching effectively reduces the collision domain to just the switch port and the device that it connects to the network. The single greatest performance constraint in contention-based networks, such as Ethernet networks, is competition for bandwidth. Therefore, it shouldn't be a surprise that segmenting media access domains has always been the preferred means of improving performance in such networks.

Switching builds on this success model and takes it to the extreme with port segmentation. Competition for bandwidth, and the chaos that inevitably ensues on busy networks no longer need to be the performance constraints that they once were. In fact, port switches are frequently designed for full-duplex operation. A separate physical wire path exists for both transmit and receive operations. Therefore, even the competition between a switch port and its attached peripheral is eliminated.

Switching Token-Passing Networks

Port switching can improve token-passing LANs in much the same way it can improve contention-based LANs. The number of devices that pass tokens is reduced to an absolute minimum number of two: the switch port and the device connected to it. The only difference is that these devices pass tokens back and forth, rather than compete with each other for available bandwidth.

IP Switching

The last form of switching is called *Layer 3 switching*, or *Internet Protocol (IP) switching*. Layer 3 switches are, essentially, a cross between a LAN switch and a router. Each port on the switch is a separate LAN port, but the forwarding engine actually calculates and stores routes based on IP addresses, not MAC addresses.

Each LAN port functions as a port-switched LAN port. Layer 3 switches available today tend to only support IP or both IP and IPX, to the exclusion of other network layer protocols. Similarly, selection of LAN port technologies is frequently limited to either 10 or 100 Mbps Ethernet.

Segmenting with Routers

It is important to note that, for the most part, segmentation doesn't create two separate LANs. LANs exist only at the first two layers of the OSI reference model: the physical and data link layers. The segmentation devices examined up to this point have been limited to just these first two layers of the OSI reference model. However, there's another way to segment LANs: by using routers.

Routers can be used in two different ways to segment LANs:

- To emulate a bridged connection between LANs

- To route between LANs

Bridge Emulation

Routers are designed to be a universal interconnector in both LANs and WANs. To support their flexibility, they are available with interfaces for virtually every standardized LAN architecture and WAN transmission facility imaginable. Therefore, they can be configured with any or all the interfaces that are required to mimic the functionality of all three types of LAN bridges.

Having already seen that all three types of bridges segment media access domains while unifying MAC broadcast domains, it should be sufficient to say that a router can be programmed to function *exactly* as a bridge. That is to say, a router can isolate the media access domains of two or more LANs while simultaneously bridging their MAC broadcast domains. This is done by configuring the router interfaces for the two LANs. By virtue of connecting to different router interfaces, the media access domains of these LANs are automatically kept isolated from each other. However, the router will forward any MAC broadcasts, or any other MAC-addressed frames, that a bridge would propagate across the segments.

NOTE

In deference to their bridging capabilities, routers were sometimes called *brouters*. This term is a shortened form of *bridge-router*. Because bridging, as a LAN segmentation technique, has matured and declined, the term *brouter* has disappeared. Today, it is rare to encounter anyone who still uses it.

Using routers to emulate bridges has fallen out of favor for several reasons. First, bridged networks were unable to scale to meet growing demand for network connectivity. Second, the emergence of LAN switching provided networks with a very cost-effective and highly scalable means of scaling upward. Therefore, bridges became superfluous. Finally, routers tend to be more sophisticated and expensive than bridges. Simple economics reveal that a router's resources are better applied to more sophisticated uses. Using routers to interconnect LANs was an invaluable step, however, in the evolution from flat networks to switched networks.

Routing Between Segments

Routers, unlike bridges or switches, have the capability to operate at the first *three* layers of the OSI reference model—the physical, data link, and network layers. Consequently, they aren't as limited in their segmentation capabilities as bridges and switches are. They can interconnect two or more LANs without consolidating their MAC broadcast domains! In fact, using a router to segment a LAN creates fully separate LANs, each with its own media access and MAC broadcast domains. Figure 3-13 illustrates a router being used to segment a LAN.

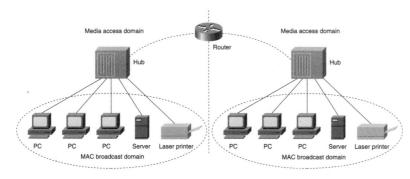

Figure 3-13

Routers can segment both media access and MAC broadcast domains.

In Figure 3-13, two Ethernet LANs are interconnected via a router. Each LAN's media access domain now includes the hub port and router port that provide the interconnection. The two LANs' MAC broadcast domains, however, remain fully separate.

Commonality between these LANs is established at the network layer. In other words, a Layer 3 addressing architecture and protocol suite, such as IP, is required for communications between any two devices that reside on different LANs. Given this, a third domain must be considered whenever segmenting a LAN: the network domain. A network domain consists of all the networked devices that can communicate directly using IP (or other Layer 3 protocols) for addressing across a LAN. Implicit in this definition is that IP packets are not *routed* to other networks, even though they use a routable address format. Routers are unique in their capability to segment network domains.

The Differences Between Bridges, Switches, and Routers

Routers can do several things that data link layer segmentation devices, such as bridges and switches, can't:

- Routers can look inside the payload of data frames and identify the packets that are enveloped by the frame.

- Routers strip away the framing and reconstruct the packets contained in the frame's data field.

- Routers can forward packets (as opposed to just frames).

Another key difference between bridges and routers is that routers do not just identify which port they need to forward the packet or frame to. They were designed for operation in a potentially more complex, and even circuitous, environment: the WAN. In a WAN, there may be multiple paths through the network to get from any point to any point. The router can identify all the potential paths through the network to any given destination address. More significantly, the router can discriminate between the alternatives and select the best path.

LAN BACKBONES

A LAN backbone is any mechanism or facility that interconnects all the LAN's hubs. There are many different ways to construct a LAN backbone. Some of these are clever and highly functional. Others are simplistic and shortsighted. Some are easy to scale, and some are not. Regardless of its components or topology, a LAN backbone unifies the disparate mini-LANs that would exist if the hubs were not interconnected.

The simplest of all LAN backbones is a hub that interconnects other hubs. As discussed earlier in the chapter, this creates large, flat LANs with singular media access and MAC broadcast domains. Although this may be, in fact, the most economical backbone for small LAN environments, it does not scale very well. Adding new users may require the addition of hubs. It doesn't take a great imagination to see that all the ports available on the backbone hub can quickly be consumed by connections to other hubs. When this happens, the solution, typically, is to just keep adding hubs to the backbone. This is known as a *serial*, or *daisy-chained*, backbone. Daisy-chained hubs can quickly become an administrative nightmare; it is difficult to maintain accurate records of the LAN's topology and wiring schemes over time.

Routers can be used to form a highly scalable LAN backbone in one of two main ways:

- Collapsed backbones
- Parallel backbones

Collapsed Backbones

A collapsed backbone topology features a single, centralized router that interconnects all the LAN segments in a building. The router effectively creates multiple media access and broadcast domains, and thereby increases the performance of each of the LAN segments.

The simplest, and most typical, collapsed backbone topology segments a building according to its physical wire distribution. That is, all the computing and/or communications devices whose wiring is physically terminated in a single telephone closet become a segment. A single physical connection to this telephone closet (and its hubs and their computers, printers, and so on) runs back to a single port on a router. Therefore, they form a self-contained LAN segment, complete with their own media access domain, MAC broadcast domain, and IP addressing. A LAN segmented with a router using a collapsed backbone topology is illustrated in Figure 3-14.

An important consideration in collapsed backbone topologies is that user communities are seldom conveniently distributed throughout a building. Instead, the users are scattered far and wide, which means that there is a good chance that they will be found on different LANs interconnected via a collapsed backbone router. Subsequently, simple network tasks among the members of a workgroup are likely to traverse the router. As fast as routers may be, they are still software driven. Therefore, in comparison to purely hardware devices, such as hubs and switches, routers are slow. Consequently, collapsed backbones might actually introduce a performance penalty not present with Layer 2-only LAN backbone solutions.

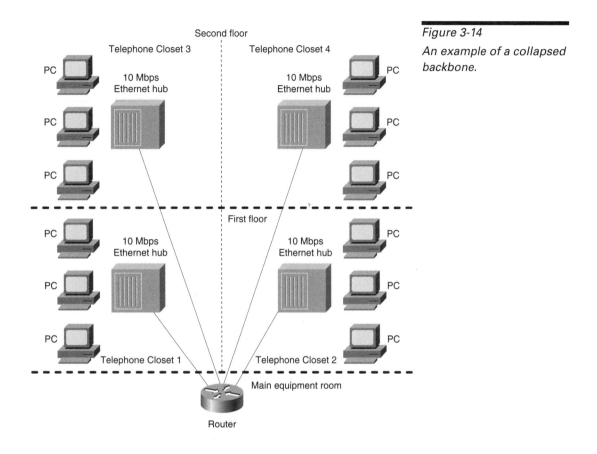

Figure 3-14
An example of a collapsed backbone.

Today, Layer 3 LAN switches are available that duplicate the functionality of the router in a collapsed backbone without duplicating its slow performance. In other words, the IP switch performs inter-LAN routing at wire speeds!

CAUTION

Care should be taken when designing collapsed backbone LANs to absolutely minimize the amount of traffic that must cross the router. Use it as a traffic aggregator for LAN-level resources, like WAN facilities, and not indiscriminately, like a bridge.

Collapsed backbones, like the one shown in Figure 3-14, have another flaw: They introduce a single point of failure in the LAN. This is not necessarily a fatal flaw. In fact, many of the other LAN backbone topologies also introduce a single point of failure into the LAN. Nevertheless, that weakness must be considered when planning a network topology.

Parallel Backbones

In some of the cases where collapsed backbones are untenable, a modified version may prove ideal. This modification is known as the *parallel backbone*. The reasons for installing a parallel backbone are many. User communities may be widely dispersed throughout a building; some groups and/or applications may have stringent network security requirements; or high network availability may be required. Regardless of the reason, running parallel connections from a building's collapsed backbone router to the same telephone closet enables supporting multiple segments to be run from each closet, as shown in Figure 3-15.

The parallel backbone topology is a modification of the collapsed backbone. Much like the collapsed backbone, this backbone topology can create multiple media access and MAC broadcast domains. The key distinction is that this topology can achieve a finer degree of segmentation than a collapsed backbone can provide.

This approach marginally increases the cost of the network, but can increase the performance of each segment and satisfy additional network criteria, such as security and fault tolerance.

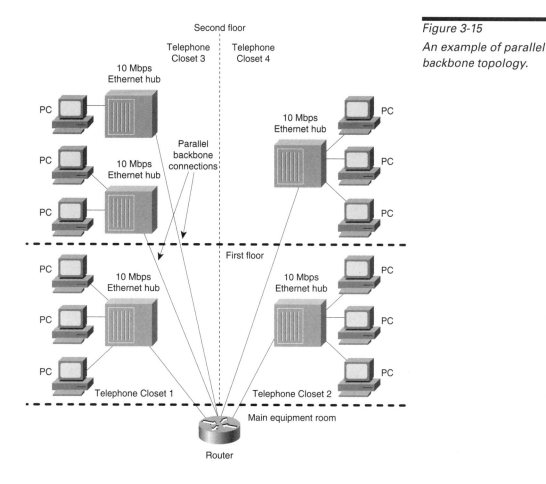

Figure 3-15

An example of parallel backbone topology.

WAN Gateway

Perhaps the most familiar, and important, of a router's LAN-level functions is its use as a gateway to the WAN. This is the function that LAN-based routers were originally designed for. In this original context, a LAN's router was its gateway to the internetwork that lay beyond its border. The router can function in this capacity because it supports operation at Layer 3, the network layer, of the OSI reference model.

The network layer encompasses all the protocols, address architectures, and other mechanisms needed to pass data beyond the domain boundaries of LANs. To utilize network layer protocols requires the use of a networking protocol, such as IP. Networking protocols, known more specifically as either *routed* or *routable* protocols, each have their own addressing schemes. These addresses must be used by any/all devices that need to communicate beyond the LAN's boundaries. Communications within a LAN's boundaries can be affected through data link layer addressing.

Implementing IP addresses, as well as other internetworking protocols, creates a new domain: a Layer 3 domain. In the case of the IP protocol, this new domain is the IP network domain.

IP Network Domains

Much like a MAC broadcast domain defines the boundaries of a LAN, IP also defines its borders. All devices within a given IP network domain must have the same IP network address. They have unique host numbers that, when appended to the network address, yield a unique address that can be used across network domains. For example, an IP network address might be 192.168.9.0. The 192.168.9 portion of this address is the network's numeric address. The last digit (0) identifies a specific host within that network number. Zero is a reserved value, which cannot be assigned to a host. It always identifies a network's number. Hosts addresses can range from 1 to 255, for a total of 254 usable addresses in this particular type of IP address. It is important to remember that the IP boundaries described in this section are applicable regardless of which type of IP addressing is used. Subnets, VLSM, classful addresses, and even IPv6 addressed networks all conform to this description of the IP boundaries.

NOTE

For a more detailed examination of the two IP protocols, refer to Chapter 5, "Internet Protocols Versions."

Figure 3-16 illustrates a typical LAN that is using a router as a gateway to an IP WAN. In this example, every device in the LAN has its own IP address, and they are all part of the 192.168.9.0 network.

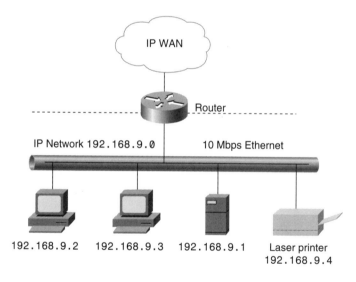

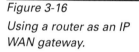

Figure 3-16

Using a router as an IP WAN gateway.

As indicated in Figure 3-16, the LAN's IP network domain extends up to, and includes, the router interface port. The domain does not include the entire router or all its ports. Each port can be programmed to function as the interface for a different IP network domain. This is one of the attributes that make a router so uniquely capable of internetworking. It can function as a point of intersection for two or more different networks. More importantly, it can support the physical intersection of networks (either LANs or connections to other routers) with a series of services that facilitate forwarding of data between different networks.

Using the Gateway

As explained in Chapter 1, "An Introduction to Internetworking," LAN-attached devices transmit framed data. The payloads of these frames, more likely than not, contain network layer packets. Therefore, users of LAN-attached devices access the WAN gateway via transmitted frames.

The gateway router enables devices to communicate and share data with devices that lie beyond their LAN's boundaries. This requires only the use of a routed protocol suite, such as Transmission Control Protocol/Internet Protocol (TCP/IP) or Internetwork Packet Exchange/Sequenced Packet Exchange (IPX/SPX), and proper use of that protocol suite's addressing mechanisms. Transmitting devices (better described as *originating devices*) must specify the full network (for example, IP) address, including the network and host numbers as the destination. This destination address is recorded in the header of each IP packet transmitted, along with other pieces of information. IP packets are placed in the framing required by the LAN that the device is connected to and transmitted over the LAN.

NOTE

Devices that initiate, or originate, a communications session are properly identified as *originating*, or *source*, devices rather than transmitting devices. The reason for the distinction is simple: After the communications session is established, data may flow in both directions. Therefore, differentiating between a transmitting and a receiving device becomes a per-packet endeavor. However, the source and destination of any given communications session remain constant for the duration of that session.

LAN frames, too, contain header information such as source and destination addressing. These addresses are the data link layer's MAC addresses. In the case of the LAN's gateway router, the MAC address corresponds to the router interface port's MAC address. This port accepts the transmitted frames, strips off the framing, and examines the network address of any embedded packet(s). This network address determines where the router forwards the packet. This forwarding process is examined in more detail in Chapter 7, "The Mechanics of Routing Protocols."

SUMMARY

Routers are extremely intelligent, capable, and versatile devices. They can provide all the functions of any bridge, and they can even segment adjacent LANs by IP domains instead of either of the Layer 2 domains. This makes them the most powerful of all LAN segmentation mechanisms.

As useful as they may be in a LAN environment, routers were originally designed to internetwork using network layer addresses and protocols. Their capabilities in this capacity are what make routers absolutely indispensable in today's networks. For more information on how routers operate in internetworks, read Chapter 4, "Routers and WANs."

CHAPTER 4

Routers and WANs

Routers are designed to interconnect multiple networks. This interconnection enables machines on different networks to communicate with each other. Interconnected networks can be colocated (as shown in Chapter 3, "Routers and LANs") or geographically dispersed. Networks that are geographically dispersed are usually interconnected via a wide-area network (WAN). WANs are constructed of numerous different technologies including routers, transmission facilities, and line drivers. It is the router's capability to interconnect networks in a WAN that has made it indispensable.

This chapter begins with an overview of the physical components and logical functions of a router as well as the various specialized roles a router may have within a WAN. This chapter concludes with a look at some of the ways to measure the effectiveness of your WAN.

A CLOSER LOOK AT ROUTERS

A router is an intelligent network device that operates predominantly at the first three layers of the OSI reference model. Routers, like any host, are actually capable of operating at all seven layers of the OSI reference model. Depending on your particular configuration, you may or may not use all seven layers of functionality. However, the need for the first three layers is virtually universal. Communications across the first two layers allows routers to communicate directly with LANs (data link layer constructs). More importantly, routers can identify routes through networks based on Layer 3 addresses. This enables routers to internetwork multiple networks, regardless of how near or far they may be, by using network layer addressing.

Understanding routers and routing requires examining a router from two different perspectives: physical and logical. From a physical perspective, routers contain myriad parts that each have a specific function. From a logical perspective, routers perform many functions including finding other routers in the network, learning about potential destination networks and hosts, discovering and tracking potential routes, as well as forwarding datagrams toward their specified destination. Together, these physical components and logical functions enable you to build and use internetworks, including WANs.

Physical Components

A router is a remarkably complex device. Its complexity lies in its routing engine—logic that enables the physical device to perform the various routing functions. The complexity of routing logic is hidden by the relative simplicity of the router's physical form. The most common type of router is actually a highly specialized type of computer; it contains the same basic components as any other computer. These include the following:

- A central processing unit (CPU)

- Random access memory (RAM)

- A basic input/output system (BIOS)

- An operating system (OS)

- A motherboard

- Physical input/output (I/O) ports

- A power supply, chassis, and sheet-metal skin

The vast majority of a router's components will remain forever shielded from the eyes of network administrators by the chassis' sheet-metal skin. These components are extremely reliable and under normal operating conditions shouldn't see the light of day. The obvious exceptions to this general statement are borne of expansion. Any time you need to add more resources to the router, you will have to take its cover off. Such resources usually include either memory or I/O ports.

The components that a network administrator will encounter most often are the operating system and the I/O ports. A router's operating system (in Cisco System's case the *Internetwork Operating System*—IOS) is the software that controls the various hardware components and makes them usable. Network administrators use a command-line interface to develop a logical configuration. The configuration is a profile of the system: the numbers, locations, types of each I/O port, and even details such as addressing and bandwidth information. A router's configuration can also include security information such as which users are permitted access to specific I/O ports and their transmission facilities.

The I/O ports are the one physical router component that network administrators see on a routine basis. These are the tangible proofs of the router's unique capability to interconnect seemingly endless combinations of LAN and WAN transmission technologies. Each one of these, whether LAN or WAN, must have its own I/O port on the router. These ports function like a network interface card (NIC) in a LAN-attached computer; they define the medium and framing mechanisms expected and provide the appropriate physical interfaces. Many of these physical interfaces appear quite similar to each other. This physical similarity belies the differences between the higher-layer functions of those technologies. Therefore, it is more useful to examine transmission technologies than examine specific physical interfaces. Chapter 6, "Transmission Technologies," provides this coverage.

Router Functions

Equally important as providing physical interconnectivity for multiple networks are the logical functions a router performs. These functions make the physical interconnections usable. For example, internetworked communications requires that at least one physical path interconnect the source and destination machines. However, having and using a physical path are two very different things. Specifically, the source and destination machines must speak a common language (a *routed protocol*). It also helps if the routers that lie in between them also speak a common language (a *routing protocol*) and agree on which specific physical path is the best one to use.

Therefore, some of the more salient functions that a router provides are

- Physical interconnectivity

- Logical interconnectivity

- Route calculation and maintenance

- Security

Physical Interconnectivity

A router has a minimum of two, and frequently many more, physical I/O ports. I/O ports, or *interfaces* as they are better known, are used to physically connect network transmission facilities to a router. Each port is connected to a circuit board that is attached to the router's motherboard. Thus, it is the motherboard that actually provides the interconnectivity among multiple networks.

The network administrator must configure each interface via the router's console. Configuration includes defining the interface's port number in the router, the specific transmission technology and bandwidth available on the network connected to that interface, and the types of protocols that will be used through that interface. The actual parameters that must be defined vary based on the type of network interface.

Logical Interconnectivity

As soon as a router interface is configured, it can be activated. The interface's configuration identifies the type of transmission facility it connects to, the interface's IP address, and the address of the network that it connects to. Upon activation of a port, the router immediately begins monitoring all the packets that are being transmitted on the network attached to the newly activated port. This allows it to "learn" about network and host IP addresses that reside on the networks that can be reached via that port. These addresses are stored in tables called *routing tables*. Routing tables correlate the port number of each interface in the router with the network layer addresses that can be reached (either directly or indirectly) via that port.

A router can also be configured with a *default route*. A default route associates a specific router interface with all unknown destination addresses. This allows a router to forward a datagram to destinations that it has not yet learned of. Default routes can be useful in other ways, too. Default routes can be used to minimize the growth of routing tables, for example, or be used to reduce the amount of traffic generated between routers as they exchange routing information.

Route Calculation and Maintenance

Routers communicate with each other using a predetermined protocol, a *routing protocol*. Routing protocols enable routers to do the following:

- Identify potential routes to specific destination networks and/or hosts

- Perform a mathematical comparison, known as a calculation, to determine the best path to each destination

- Continuously monitor the network to detect any topology changes that may render known routes to be invalid

Many different types of routing protocols exist. Some, such as Routing Information Protocol (RIP), are quite simple. Others, such as Open Shortest Path First (OSPF), are remarkably powerful and feature-rich but complicated. In general, routing protocols can use two approaches to make routing decisions: distance vectors and link states. A distance-vector protocol makes its decisions based on some measurement of the distance between source and destination machines. A link-state protocol bases its decisions on various states of the links, or transmission facilities, that interconnect the source and destination machines. Neither one is right or wrong: They are just different ways of making the same decisions. They will, however, result in different levels of performance, including convergence times. The implications of convergence times will become more apparent as you read about specific routing protocols in Part III, "Routing Protocols."

You can evaluate routing protocols using numerous, more specific criteria than just which approaches they use. Some of the more meaningful criteria include the following:

- *Optimality*—Optimality describes a routing protocol's capability to select the best available route. Unfortunately, the word *best* is ambiguous. There are many different ways to evaluate different routes to any given destination. Each way could result in the selection of a different "best" route depending on the criteria used. The criteria used by routing protocols to calculate and evaluate routes are known as *routing metrics*. There is a wide variety of metrics, and they vary widely by routing protocol. A simple metric is *hop count*—the number of hops, or routers, that lie between the source and destination machines.

• *Efficiency*—Another criterion to consider when evaluating routing protocols is their operational efficiency. Operational efficiency can be measured by examining the physical resources, including router RAM and CPU time, and network bandwidth required by a given routing protocol. You may need to consult your router manufacturer or vendor to determine the relative efficiencies of any protocols you are considering.

• *Robustness*—A routing protocol should perform reliably at all times, not just when the network is stable. Error conditions, including hardware or transmission-facility failures, router configuration errors, and even heavy traffic loads, adversely affect a network. Therefore, it is critical that a routing protocol function properly during periods of network failure and/or instability.

• *Convergence*—Because they are intelligent devices, routers can automatically detect changes in the internetwork. When a change is detected, all the routers involved must converge on a new agreement of the network's shape and recalculate their routes to known destinations accordingly. This process of mutual agreement is called *convergence*.

Each routing protocol uses different mechanisms for detecting and communicating network changes. Therefore, each one converges at a different rate. In general, the slower a routing protocol converges, the greater the potential for disrupting service across the internetwork.

- *Scalability*—A network's scalability is its capability to grow. Although growth isn't a requirement in every organization, the routing protocol you select should be capable of scaling upward to meet your network's projected growth.

Numerous protocols are specifically designed to calculate routes. Many of the more popular of these are explored in Part III, "Routing Protocols."

Security

Providing security is among a router's many logical functions. Securing a network that uses an intentionally open protocol, such as IP, is not a trivial undertaking. The type of security that a router can provide is based on access permissions. You can explicitly define permissions, per port, on your routers. The list of permissions is known as an *access control list* (ACL).

ACLs are a remarkably simple mechanism. A router's administrator configures access permissions per port. These permissions are stored in the ACL. Each datagram received from any given port is buffered temporarily while the router determines what to do with it. Part of this requires looking up the destination address and matching that address with a table of known addresses per port. The other part of this process is checking to see whether that datagram actually has the permissions required to be forwarded to its destination. If there are no restrictions that preclude it from being forwarded, it is forwarded. Otherwise, the router drops the data-gram and, if appropriate, sends an error message to its source machine.

Figure 4-1 shows a typical, small networked environment. One of the router's interface ports, Serial Port 0 (S0), is connected to the Internet. The user community is connected via two Ethernet segments. Each segment has its own interface port to the same router. They are numbered E0 and E1 in this illustration.

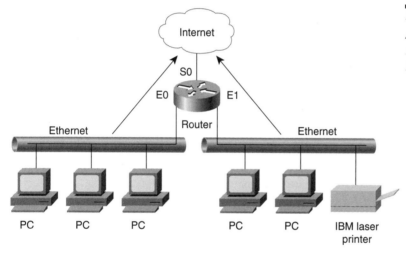

Figure 4-1
An access control list can reduce the risks of internetworking.

The users in this network require access to the Internet's content for marketing purposes. This requires that TCP/IP sessions be permitted to flow in both directions through the connection to the Internet. The users are concerned, however, about exposing their internal hosts to attack from the Internet. Therefore, access control lists can be used to exclude UDP access to ports E0 and E1 from S0 either universally or per application type. In this example, anyone attempting to access these ports from the S0 port using the UDP protocol will be denied access. No such restrictions are placed on ports E0 and E1. The cumulative access control lists (one per port) would resemble the contents of Table 4-1.

Table 4-1 *Access Control Lists for the Network in Figure 4-1*

Port Number	Allowed Access To	Denied Access To
E0	E1	N/A
	S0	N/A
E1	E0	N/A
	S1	N/A
S0	N/A	E0 using UDP
		E1 using UDP

The access control list example presented in Figure 4-1 and Table 4-1 is based on port-level and application-level permissions. It is possible to program access based on IP addresses, too. You can explicitly allow or deny access based on an individual IP address or an entire range of addresses.

As useful as ACLs may be, they are not a panacea: You must view them in the perspective of the entire networked computing environment. Therefore, it is important to remember two factors about securing an IP network. First, ACLs must be kept current. Daily administrative activities might include such things as moves, changes, deletions, and additions of both interfaces and address ranges. Lists that are not kept up to date to reflect such changes in the network become less and less effective. Second, ACLs are best regarded as just one layer in an overall network security scheme. Other valid, and valuable security mechanisms include host-level authentication, encryption of transmitted data, use of firewalls at network borders, as well as many others. You must assess the risks inherent in your own operating environment and identify specific controls to minimize your exposure to those risks. Access control lists may be quite useful, but they provide only one type of protection for one part of your internetwork. Therefore, it is highly unlikely that you can adequately protect your networked computing assets without supplementary security mechanisms.

Roles of the Router in WANs

More often than not, internetworks are quite extensive in terms of the number of routers, transmission facilities, and attached end systems. In an extensive internetwork, such as the Internet or even large private networks, it would be virtually impossible for any given machine to know about every other machine. Therefore, some semblance of hierarchy is needed. Hierarchical organization of internetworked machines creates the need for specialized routing functions.

Routers can specialize in learning about and distributing routing information about end systems within their domain. These routers are called *interior gateways*. Alternatively, routers can specialize in collecting routing information about machines that lie beyond their domain. These routers are known as *exterior gateways*.

Networking is often used as a generic, or universal, term. However, networked machines communicate in tremendously different ways. Routers can function in different capacities in an internetwork, for example, as interior, exterior, or border routers.

NOTE

It is not uncommon to find interior routers, exterior routers, and border routers described as *interior gateways*, *exterior gateways*, and *border gateways*, respectively. The term *gateway* is as old as routing itself. Over time, this term has lost some of its descriptive value. Consequently, both sets of terms are technically correct, except in the presence of technological purists. Then you will have to determine which terminology they consider correct!

These functional specializations are more than merely academic. In fact, many routing protocols were specifically designed for use in one of these three capacities. Part III, "Routing Protocols," describes some of the most common of the specialized routing protocols. Understanding the differences among them requires examining them in the context of a WAN. Therefore, a logical starting point is an examination of the context! The terms *WAN*, *network*, *internetwork*, and *autonomous system* are all used interchangeably, yet each has a slightly different meaning:

- *WAN*—A WAN is a collection of related LANs linked together via routers and serial transmission facilities such as leased lines or Frame-Relay circuits. Implicit in this definition is that the LANs in the WAN may be geographically dispersed, but they still fall under the auspices of a single organization such as a company, school, and so on.

- *Network*—Network is a more nebulous term that defies specificity. Everything from LANs to WANs can be classified as a network. Consequently, for the purposes of this book, a network identifies a generic collection of related networking mechanisms. Therefore, a network may be a LAN or a WAN, but it must belong to a single organization and feature a consistent addressing architecture.

- *Internetwork*—Internetwork is only slightly more concrete than *network*. An internetwork is a collection of loosely related networks that are interconnected. The interconnected networks can belong to different organizations. For example, two companies can use the Internet to interconnect their private WANs. The resulting internetwork consists of one public network and two private networks linked together.

- *Autonomous system*—An autonomous system (AS) is a network (either LAN or WAN) that is relatively self contained. It is administered by a single person (or group of persons), features a single routed protocol, address architecture, and usually just one routing protocol. An autonomous system may support connections to other autonomous systems owned and operated by the same organization. Alternatively, an AS may have connections to other networks, such as the Internet, yet it retains autonomy of operation. This term is usually used in conjunction with specific routing protocols, such as OSPF, that enable a network to be carved into numbered subsections.

Given these definitions, it is possible to better define the functional classes of routers. An *interior router* is one that can be used by end systems in a network to access other end systems within the same network. The interior router supports no connections to any other network.

Figure 4-2 illustrates a small network and identifies those devices that function as interior routers.

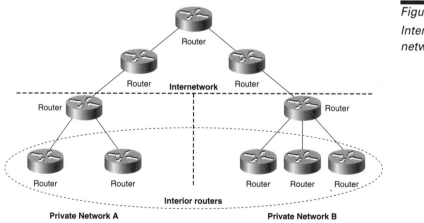

Figure 4-2
Interior routers in a network.

An exterior router is one that lies beyond the boundaries of any given network. In Figure 4-1, the Internet is depicted as a feature-less cloud. In reality, this cloud has a specific topology. Figure 4-3, although not pretending to depict the Internet's actual topology, presents a highly simplified Internet topology that is solely intended to demonstrate what an exterior router is.

Figure 4-3

Exterior routers from the perspective of the private networks.

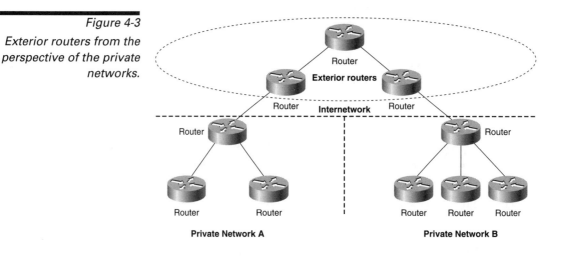

The last functional class of router is the border router. As the name implies, border routers interconnect a network with other networks. It is important to note that a single entity may own and operate multiple autonomous systems. Therefore, a border router may denote the boundary between two autonomous systems rather than the border between a private network and some other network.

Figure 4-4 identifies the border routers in the sample network that has been used in the preceding two figures.

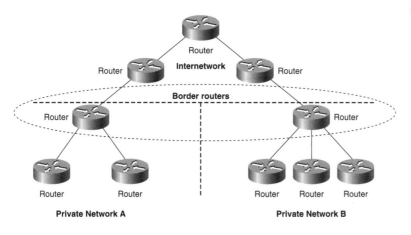

Figure 4-4

The border routers from the perspective of the private networks.

Internetworking Scenarios

Having examined the concepts underlying routing and internetworking, as well as some of the terminology indigenous to these topics, you can see how they are used by examining three internetworking scenarios. Each scenario demonstrates some of the issues that need to be addressed in any network or internetwork:

- Routing within a network

- Routing between adjacent networks

- Routing between nonadjacent networks

These three generic aspects encompass virtually every form of internetworking that you are likely to encounter. Each one holds different implications for the network administrator, including such routing aspects as route calculation and distribution, convergence, and security. The following sections provide an overview of each internetworking scenario and highlight the areas of concern for a network administrator. The various potential resolutions to these routing concerns are presented throughout this book.

Routing Within a Network

The simplest form of routing is routing within the confines of a single network. Such a network consists of just interior routers. In theory, this form of network would use just one routed protocol, one address architecture, and a minimum number of destinations. This would greatly reduce the workload of each router and maximize potential network performance. Therefore, the routing issues in intranetwork routing are more closely related to the network's size and topology rather than its address architectures and routing protocols. Topology, which is examined in more detail in Chapter 13, "Building Internetworks," must be carefully selected to match the requirements of the user community.

If the network were small enough, it might be feasible for the administrator to preprogram all the possible routes statically rather than introduce the complexity of a dynamic routing protocol. Statically programmed routes, however, can become an onerous burden in a growing or constantly changing network.

Routing Between Adjacent Networks

A small step up in complexity from intranetwork routing is internetwork routing between adjacent networks. Physical adjacency means that the two networks are directly connected to each other. Such an adjacency may have been designed to promote rapid convergence, improve security, or satisfy any number of other performance criteria.

The logical separation of the multiple networks implies that the border routers between them must summarize and redistribute routing information between them. In this fashion, the end systems of one network can directly address the end systems in another network. Figure 4-5 illustrates this type of routing.

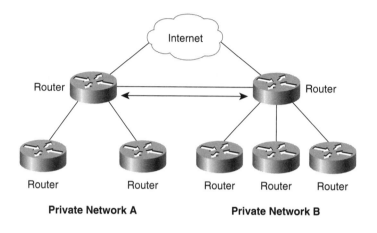

Figure 4-5

Routing between adjacent networks.

The routing issues that need to be addressed in this type of internetwork arise from the differences between the two networks. Some of the potential differences that must be identified include the following:

- Do the networks belong to the same organization? If not, the border routers need to secure their network's perimeter.

- Do the networks use the same routing protocol? If not, some mutually acceptable metric must be found.

- Do the networks use the same routed protocol? If not, you may have to support a second routed protocol in your network to facilitate internetworking. More specific details about internetworking with dissimilar protocols, both routed and routing, are in Chapter 14, "Internetworking with Dissimilar Protocols."

Additionally, topology can affect routing between adjacent networks. Using a single point of interconnection between the two networks, for example, makes it easy to control the calculation and redistribution of routing information between the networks.

This convenience introduces a single point of failure, however, it might not be acceptable to your users. Introducing a second (or even more) interconnection point solves the single point of failure problem but can create the opportunity for infinite routing loops to occur. Resolving such a dilemma requires an understanding of your users' tolerance for downtime and risk. Armed with this understanding, you can evaluate specific routing protocols for their capabilities to converge quickly and compensate for potential routing problems. Part III, "Routing Protocols," provides a survey of the most commonly used routing protocols, and should provide you with enough information to make intelligent protocol choices.

Internetworking Nonadjacent Networks

Routing between nonadjacent networks is, simultaneously, the most complicated and useful type of routing. Two networks can use a third network as an intermediary. It is highly likely that the three different networks will use different routing protocols, routed protocols, and address architectures. Therefore, the boundary router's job is to overcome these obstacles to communication while also guarding the border of its network.

Figure 4-6 illustrates routing between nonadjacent small networks.

Figure 4-6

Routing between nonadjacent networks.

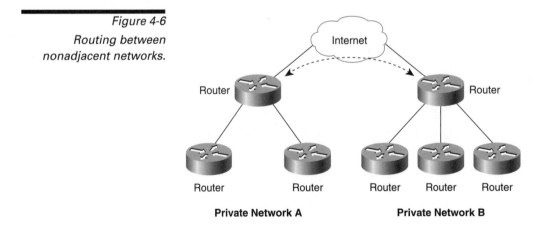

The border router of each private network in this illustration needs to protect the border of its network from unwanted intrusion. Given that the two networks that need to communicate aren't adjacent and the intermediary network is beyond their control, the risks of unwanted intrusion are much higher than if they were directly internetworked. Therefore, the network administrators must develop a set of criteria for allowing specific external users into their network, while disallowing access to everyone else. The border router would implement these criteria in an ACL.

Another responsibility of the border router would be to summarize the internal routes and redistribute this information to the networks beyond. This enables users outside the bounds of the private network to access its end systems. If this routing information weren't distributed, no one outside that private network would be able to access its end systems.

Finally, it is highly likely that the border routers will have to be configured to use multiple routing protocols. An interior gateway protocol will likely be selected for intranetwork routing purposes. Calculating routes across the internetwork, however, might require a different protocol—one that features stronger support for route summarization.

WAN Performance Criteria

Having reviewed some of the various ways to construct networks using routers, it is also important to establish some criteria for measuring the efficacy of your network. Many different criteria, or metrics, can be applied. Some of these are fairly objective and can be automatically extracted from the network monitoring protocols native to virtually every network device. Others are subjective and can be next to impossible to determine in advance. Some of the more common metrics include the following:

- Component uptime

- Traffic volumes

- Delay

- Resource utilization rates

Each of these metrics is discussed in more detail in the following sections.

Component Uptime

Each physical component of the WAN can be monitored and measured for its availability using uptime. *Uptime* is the opposite of downtime: It is the amount of time that the device is functional and in service relative to the users' requirements for its availability. It is quite common for uptime to be statistically overstated by measuring it on a 7×24 basis, even though the users' requirements may only be for 5×12. Remember to tailor this and every other metric as closely as possible to your users' stated requirements for network performance.

Electronic devices, although highly reliable, eventually fail. Most manufacturers provide a *mean time between failures* (MTBF) rating for their equipment as a reassurance of how reliable their products really are. Typically, MTBF ratings are in the tens of thousands of hours. This could, conceivably, translate into years of trouble-free service. Unfortunately, these ratings are statistically derived. The actual time between failures of any given device depends greatly on a number of factors. These factors include the following:

- Ambient temperature ranges of the operating environment

- Cleanliness of the commercial electric power

- How well devices are handled before and during operation

In other words, your mileage *will* vary! Monitoring and tracking uptime of individual components will enable you to demonstrate to your user community how well you are satisfying their requirements for the network's availability.

Component uptime data can also be trended over time to identify potentially problematic components in your network infrastructure. Such trends can provide information about the general reliability of a given type or brand of hardware, which then can be used to identify individual components that may be at risk of failure.

Availability Versus Uptime

The term *availability* is sometimes used to generically describe aggregate network uptime. Unfortunately, it is not a good metric. In theory, network availability provides a quantified synopsis of the network's readiness. In practice, availability is so nebulous as to be virtually meaningless.

To illustrate this point, if a router at a premise location fails, the entire network is unavailable to the users at that location. The network, however, is available to users at every other location. They will not be able to access hosts at the impacted location, but they will also not be impeded from accessing every other host in the network. The extent to which the network is available varies greatly by location and by usage requirements. Therefore, quantifying network availability can be more onerous than it is valuable.

Traffic Volumes

One of the more important metrics for any WAN is the volume of traffic that it is expected to support. Volume is almost always volatile; it varies with time, business cycles, seasons, and so on. In other words, you can count on traffic volumes being anything but constant. Given this volatility, it is important to measure volumes in two different ways, maximum volumes and average volumes:

- The *maximum volume* that you expect the network to support is known as the peak volume. As its name implies, this is the greatest amount of traffic that you expect the network to have to support.

- *Average volumes* are the traffic loads that you can reasonably expect during the course of a business day from any given work location.

Establishing these two traffic volumes is critical to the sizing of the WAN's transmission facilities, as well as its routers. If you expect any given location to generate a traffic load of 100 kbps during the course of a business day, for example, it is clear that a 56 kbps transmission facility will be inadequate.

Delay

Delay is one of the more common metrics that can be used to measure network performance. Delay is the time that elapses between two events. In data communications, these two events are typically the transmission and reception of data. Therefore, delay is the total amount of time that is required by the network to transport a packet from its point of origin to its destination. Given this definition, delay is an aggregate phenomenon with many potential causes. Three of the more common causes are

- *Propagation delays*—Propagation delays are the cumulative amount of time required to transmit, or propagate, the data across each transmission facility in the network path that it must take. The size and quantity of each transmission facility in the network path directly contribute to the aggregate forwarding delay of any given transmission. An additional contributor to propagation delay is traffic volumes. The more traffic flowing across a given facility, the less bandwidth is available for new transmissions. Propagation delays are indigenous to terrestrial circuits, regardless of whether they traverse glass or copper media or are transmitted through the air using microwave radio frequencies.

- *Satellite uplink/downlink delays*—Some transmission facilities are satellite based. These require the signal to be transmitted up to the satellite and transmitted back down from the satellite. Due to the potentially great distances between the terrestrial transmission facilities and the satellite, these delays can be quite noticeable.

- *Forwarding delays*—Forwarding delays in a network are the cumulative amount of time that each physical device needs to receive, buffer, process, and forward data. The actual forwarding delay of any given device may vary over time. Individual devices operating at or near capacity will likely experience a greater forwarding delay than comparable devices that are lightly utilized. Additionally, forwarding delays can be exacerbated by heavy traffic or error conditions in the network. Forwarding delays are *latency* in individual components.

Resource Utilization Rates

The degree to which the various physical resources of the WAN are being utilized is also a good indicator of how well, or how poorly, the WAN is performing relative to the performance requirements. There are two main categories of resource utilization rates that should be monitored carefully:

- Router CPU and memory utilization rates

- Transmission facility utilization rates

Router Physical Resources' Rates

Routers are one of the most vital components of any WAN. And, unlike the transmission facilities, they are outside the purview of the telecommunications carrier. Therefore, they are distinctly the responsibility of the customer. Fortunately, routers are intelligent devices that contain their own CPU and memory. These physical resources are indispensable in the calculation of WAN routes and the forwarding of packets. They can also be used to monitor the performance of the router.

If either CPU or memory utilization rates approach 100%, performance will suffer. Numerous conditions can result in either utilization rate temporarily spiking upward with consequential performance degradation. One example would be a sudden increase in transmissions from the LAN to the WAN. LANs can operate at speeds up to 1 Gbps, but they usually operate only at either 10, 16, or 100 Mbps. Any of these speeds are a gross mismatch against the typical WAN transmission facility, which offers a paltry 1.544 Mbps of bandwidth. This mismatch in bandwidth must be buffered by the router's memory. It wouldn't take long for a router to become resource constricted given a sustained period of heavy LAN transmissions.

If such situations are rarely experienced, they should be considered aberrations. Aberrations should be monitored, but they shouldn't drive physical upgrades. If these resource constrictions recur or constitute a trend, however, something needs to be done. Usually, this requires an upgrade, either to the next larger router or via an expansion of memory. If a router is chronically at or near 100% of capacity with its memory, it is time to purchase additional memory.

Responding to chronically high CPU utilization rates might not be as simple as a memory upgrade. There are really only three options for improving high CPU utilization rates:

- If possible, add another CPU to the router.

- Upgrade to a more powerful router.

- Investigate the WAN's traffic patterns to see whether the load on the problematic router can be reduced.

Manipulating traffic patterns is really only a viable option in larger WANs with complex topologies that afford route redundancy. Even so, if the router in question is a premise-edge vehicle (as opposed to a backbone router), your only option will likely be the forklift upgrade.

Transmission Facility Rates

Transmission facilities can also be monitored for utilization. Typically, this utilization rate is expressed in terms of the percentage of consumed bandwidth. If you are using a T1, for example, a given sample might indicate that 30% of its 1.544 Mbps of available bandwidth is currently being utilized.

These rates can be tricky to analyze, and may even be misleading. It is not uncommon, for example, for network-management software packages to capture utilization data in time intervals. These can be one hour, five minutes, or just about any other interval. The sampling frequency, if set too coarsely, can miss short-duration fluctuations in bandwidth consumption. If the sampling is too frequent, you could find yourself mired in a meaningless morass of data points. The trick is finding the right frequency that provides meaningful data about how the network is performing relative to the users' expectations.

Beyond merely selecting the sampling rate is the issue of sampling window. The sampling window should be determined by the users' requirements for WAN availability. If the utilization samples are spread over a 24-hour day and 7-day week, whereas the users work only 10 hours per day, 5 days per week, the statistical data is not indicative of how well the users' requirements are being met.

Utilization rates are a wonderful statistical tool for monitoring and measuring the status of transmission facilities. They are not, however, the only metric for assessing a network's performance. The network is successful only if it satisfies the users' requirements. Therefore, a combination of performance metrics that provides a multifaceted, composite perspective is likely to provide a better assessment of the network's success.

Costs of the WAN

Tempering the various performance criteria is cost. The costs of owning and operating a WAN include the initial startup costs as well as the monthly recurring expenses. Not surprisingly, the larger and more powerful network components are much more expensive than smaller, less robust components. Therefore, designing a WAN becomes an economic exercise in which a careful balance of performance and cost is achieved.

Achieving this balance can be painful. No one wants to design a WAN that will disappoint the users with its performance, but no one wants to design a WAN that blows the budget, either! Fortunately, the following truisms can help guide the design of a WAN that satisfies existing requirements, provides flexibility for future growth, and doesn't exceed the budget:

- The capital investments in routers and other network hardware become a fixed part of the network. After they are placed in operation, the logistics of replacing hardware become quite complicated. And, depending on your depreciation schedule for capital equipment, you might find yourself obligated to use it for five or more years! It might behoove you to purchase a larger but relatively unpopulated router. You can add hardware (memory, CPUs, and interfaces) in the future as the need for them arises. This allows future expansion at modest incremental costs and little (if any) operational downtime.

- The transmission facilities are relatively easy to replace with other transmission facilities. They are an expense item, not a capital investment, so there is no depreciation expense to retire. They can be replaced with other facilities as often as your lease agreement with the carrier permits. Therefore, you might want to explore your options for meeting performance requirements with the various available transmission facilities and technologies.

Applying the wisdom behind these truisms can help you meet your users' present and future expected requirements all within the constraints of your budget.

SUMMARY

WANs are complex structures that don't necessarily adhere to any published or open standard. Designing, building, and operating one that consistently satisfies your users' requirements can be a Herculean task. Success lies in understanding the capabilities, limitations, and costs of each WAN component technology. This understanding forms the context for their integration. Each component technology will be well matched with the performance capabilities of each other component and balanced against any budgetary constraints.

PART II

The Inner Workings of Routers

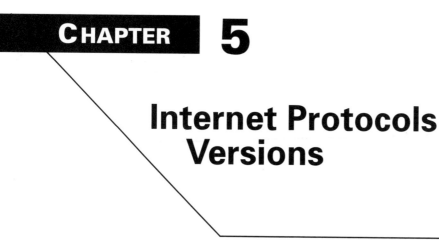

Internet Protocols Versions

A necessary prerequisite to examining the inner workings of a router is to first examine the data structures that they forward. These data structures, better known as *packets* or *datagrams*, are indigenous to routed protocols. Routed protocols encapsulate data and instructions for transport through a network. Routers forward these packets of data toward their specified destinations. Each packet of a routed protocol must contain all the necessary information to enable routers to move them from their source to their destination.

NOTE

Although it is not uncommon to find *packet* and *datagram* used interchangeably, there is a subtle distinction between them. This distinction is addressed later in this chapter. For now, the more familiar term, *packet,* will be used solely to facilitate clear communication.

133

The bad news is that routed protocols are remarkably complex. The good news is that it isn't necessary to master the intricacies of a routed protocol before you can appreciate the mechanics of routing. This chapter focuses on the world's leading routed protocol: the Internet Protocol (IP). There are two versions of IP:

- IP version 4 (IPv4)

- IP version 6 (IPv6)

This chapter provides a quick survey of the these two versions of IP, their header structure, and some of their basic functionality. This will form the context for a more meaningful examination of the router's internal components, both hardware and software, in subsequent chapters.

THE NETWORK LAYER

As demonstrated in Chapter 3, "Routers and LANs," the network layer (Layer 3) of the OSI Reference Model enables devices to communicate, regardless of their proximity. The network layer defines the functions and services necessary for such communications to occur.

There are actually two types of networking protocols that operate at Layer 3: routed protocols and routing protocols. *Routing protocols* are used in communications between routers. Routers need to communicate with each other about routes, their status, and availability. Routing protocols are further examined in Part III, "Routing Protocols."

Routed protocols are those that encapsulate user information and data into packets, and transport packets of data to their destinations. These protocols provide addressing that can be accessed and interpreted by routers. The routers then forward that data across unspecified distances, beyond the domain of the sender's LAN, to wherever the destination may be. Nonrouted protocols also exist; they perform a similar function to routed protocols. Unlike routed protocols, routers aren't designed to access and interpret their header information. For that matter, nonrouted protocols aren't designed to be forwarded across wide-area networks.

THE TRANSPORT LAYER

Although Layer 3 protocols provide routers with the various mechanisms required for forwarding packets, there are limits to their capabilities. Layer 3 only provides the mechanisms for internetwork data transfers. Layer 4, the transport layer, can provide the Layer 3 network protocols with end-to-end reliability and integrity.

The transport layer may be required to guarantee error-free delivery of packets and sequencing of delivered packets, as well as provide quality-of-service guarantees. The functions of these two layers are highly interrelated. Consequently, they are usually bundled into protocol stacks.

An example of a Layer 4 protocol is the Transmission Control Protocol (TCP). TCP is almost always referenced in combination with its Layer 3 counterpart, the Internet Protocol (IP), as *TCP/IP*. TCP cannot be used without its complementary Layer 3 protocol, IP. Similarly, Sequenced Packet Exchange (SPX) can only be used with its Layer 3 Protocol, Internetwork Packet Exchange (IPX).

The Differences Between Reference Models

Although this discussion thus far has described network and transport protocols in terms of the OSI Reference Model, very few protocols are actually implemented in such strict accord with that model. From this perspective, the OSI model can be viewed as a dismal failure.

Its success, however, has been in its usefulness as an academic vehicle. Its rigid adherence to a hierarchical structure of functions is marvelous for explaining the mechanics of data communications. Consequently, most people tend to think of the various layered functions in terms of the OSI model's layer names and numbers.

Despite this academic success, the dominant paradigm has been for each new stack of networking protocols to be implemented within its own reference model framework. Usually, these new models collapse the OSI's seven layers into five, or fewer, layers. These models, and their protocols, still contain all the necessary functionality to support communications; they just don't separate them to the degree that the OSI model does.

This can be a source of confusion, because there can be quite a difference between layer numbers and names that contain any given function. To minimize any confusion, each of the Internet protocols described in this chapter is compared, side-by-side, to a block diagram of the OSI Reference Model. This will help you see exactly what the correlation is between the two models.

This chapter provides an overview of just IPv4 and IPv6, the two implementations of the Internet Protocol.

INTERNET PROTOCOL, VERSION 4 (IPv4)

IP was developed approximately 20 years ago for the U.S. Department of Defense (DoD). The DoD needed a way to interconnect the various brands of proprietary computers and their equally proprietary support networks across a common internetwork. This was achieved by way of a layered protocol that insulated applications from networking hardware. This protocol uses a model that is slightly different from the OSI Reference Model. It is known as the TCP/IP Reference Model.

Unlike the OSI Reference Model, the TCP/IP model focuses more on delivering interconnectivity than on rigidly adhering to functional layers. It does this by acknowledging the importance of a hierarchical arrangement of functions, but still leaving protocol designers ample flexibility for implementation. Consequently, the OSI Reference Model is significantly better at explaining the mechanics of intercomputer communications, but TCP/IP has become the internetworking protocol of choice in the marketplace. Its success was largely due to its openness. Other protocol suites enjoyed limited success but tended to tie you needlessly to a single vendor. This limited your options for implementing third-party software and, ultimately, doomed the proprietary protocols.

The flexibility of the TCP/IP Reference Model is shown in Figure 5-1 in comparison with the OSI Reference Model.

OSI Reference Model Layer Description	OSI Layer Number	TCP/IP Equivalent Layer Description
Application	7	Process/ Application
Presentation	6	
Session	5	Host-to-Host
Transport	4	
Network	3	Internet
Data link	2	Network Access
Physical	1	

Figure 5-1

A comparison of OSI and TCP/IP reference models.

The TCP/IP Reference Model was developed long after the protocol it explains. This model offers significantly more flexibility than its OSI counterpart because it emphasizes the hierarchical arrangement of functions rather than strict functional layering.

Dissecting TCP/IP

The TCP/IP protocol stack includes four functional layers: network access, internet, host-to-host, and process/application. These four loosely correlate to the seven layers of the OSI Reference Model without compromising functionality.

The Process/Application Layer

The application layer provides protocols for remote access and resource sharing. Familiar applications such as Telnet, FTP, SMTP, and HTTP all reside and operate in this layer and depend on the functionality of the underlying layers.

The Host-to-Host Layer

The IP host-to-host layer correlates loosely to the OSI Reference Model's session and transport layers. It consists of two protocol entities: Transmission Control Protocol (TCP) and User Datagram Protocol (UDP). A third entity is being defined to accommodate the increasingly transaction-oriented nature of the Internet. This protocol entity is tentatively called Transaction Transmission Control Protocol (T/TCP). T/TCP is currently languishing because it lacks the impetus afforded by market support. Unless support coalesces for this third entity, it will be relegated to little more than a footnote in the annals of the Internet.

Transmission Control Protocol

TCP provides a connection-oriented data transmission between two hosts, can support multiple data streams, and provides for flow and error control and even the reordering of packets that may have been received out of order.

Figure 5-2 illustrates the structure of the TCP protocol's header, as well as the sizes of its fields.

16-bit TCP source port	16-bit TCP destination port	32-bit sequence number	32-bit acknowledgment number	4-bit data offset field	6-bit reserved field	6-bit flags field	16-bit window size field	16-bit checksum	Padding

Figure 5-2

TCP header structure.

The TCP protocol header is a minimum of 20 octets and contains the following fields:

- *TCP Source Port*—The 16-bit source port field contains the number of the port that initiates the communications session. The source port and source IP address function as the packet's return address.

- *TCP Destination Port*—The 16-bit destination port field is the address of the port for which the transmission is destined. This port contains the interface address of the application on the recipient's computer that the packet's data will be passed to.

- *TCP Sequence Number*—The 32-bit sequence number is used by the receiving computer to reconstruct the application's data back to its original form. In a dynamically routed network, it is quite possible for some of the packets to take different routes and, consequently, arrive out of order. This sequencing field compensates for this inconsistency of delivery.

- *TCP Acknowledgment Number*—TCP uses a 32-bit ac-knowledgment (ACK) of the first octet of data contained in the next expected segment. The number used to identify each ACK is the sequence number of the packet being acknowledged.

- *Data Offset Field*—This 4-bit field contains the size of the TCP header, measured in a 32-bit data structure known as a "word."

- *Reserved Field*—This 6-bit field is always set to 0. It is reserved for an as-yet-unspecified future use.

- *Flags Field*—The 6-bit flag field contains six 1-bit flags that allow the control functions of urgent field, acknowl-edgment of significant field, push, reset connection, syn-chronize sequence numbers, and finish sending data.

- *Window Size Field*—This 16-bit field is used by the desti-nation machine to tell the source host how much data it is willing to accept.

- *Checksum*—The TCP header also contains a 16-bit error-checking field known as a checksum. The source host calculates a mathematical value, based on the segment's contents. The destination host performs the same calculation. If the content remains intact, the result of the two calculations is identical, and thereby prove the validity of the data.

- *Padding*—Extra zeros are added to this field to ensure that the TCP header is always a multiple of 32 bits.

User Datagram Protocol

UDP is IP's other host-to-host layer protocol (corresponding to the transport layer of the OSI Reference Model). UDP provides a basic, low-overhead data transmission. In essence, UDP provides a connectionless session between two end systems and does not provide for the acknowledgment of received datagrams. UDP's simplicity makes it inappropriate for some applications but perfect for more sophisticated applications that can provide their own connection-oriented functionality. Alternatively, there are applications whose data has an extremely high time value. One example would be a videoconference session. Such applications would prefer to use UDP because data delivered late or out of sequence is just discarded.

NOTE

UDP raises an interesting and potentially contentious issue: What is the difference between a datagram and a packet? Both are Layer 3 data-bearing constructs, and both are supported by the IP networking protocol. The critical distinction is that datagrams do not require acknowledgment of receipt by the recipient.

This implies that all Layer 3 data-bearing constructs are inherently datagrams because Layer 3 internetworking is connectionless, best-effort service. Reliability is provided by Layer 4 transport protocols, such as TCP or SPX. Therefore, the term *packet* really only describes Layer 3 data-bearing constructs that also contain the segments of a reliable Layer 4 protocol. Otherwise, they are just datagrams.

Alternatively, UDP can be used for exchanges of such data as broadcasted NetBIOS names, system messages, and so forth, because these exchanges do not require flow control, acknowledgments, reordering, or any of the functionality that TCP provides.

Figure 5-3 illustrates the structure of the UDP header, as well as the sizes of its fields.

16-bit UDP source port	16-bit UDP destination port	16-bit length field	16-bit checksum

The UDP protocol header has the following fields:

- *UDP Source Port Number*—The 16-bit source port is the logical port number on the source computer. The source port and source IP address function as the packet's return address.

- *UDP Destination Port Number*—The 16-bit destination port is the connection number on the destination computer. The UDP destination port is used to forward the packet to the correct application after the packet arrives at the intended destination machine.

- *UDP Message Length*—The 16-bit UDP Message Length field informs the destination computer of the size of the message. This provides another mechanism for the destination computer to use in determining the message's validity.

- *UDP Checksum*—UDP Checksum is a 16-bit error-checking field that is calculated based on the contents of the datagram. The destination computer performs the same mathematical function as the originating host. A discrepancy in the two calculated values indicates that an error has occurred during the transmission of the packet.

The major functional difference between TCP and UDP is reliability. TCP is highly reliable, and UDP is a fast, but simple "best-effort" delivery mechanism. This fundamental difference results in vastly different uses of the two host-to-host layer protocols. The primary functional similarity between TCP and UDP is that they both contain information that can only be used by the destination machine. Routers generally do not use any TCP or UDP information when calculating their routes or making forwarding decisions. Instead, routers rely extensively on the header information contained in Layer 3 data structures, such as the IP header.

The Internet Layer

The Internet layer of IPv4 consists of all the protocols and procedures necessary to allow data communications between hosts to traverse multiple networks. This means that the data-bearing packets must be routable. IP makes data packets routable.

Figure 5-4 illustrates the structure of the IP header, as well as the sizes of its fields.

4-bit IP version number	4-bit header length	8-bit type of service flags	16-bit total length field	16-bit packet identifier	Three 1-bit flag	13-bit fragment offset field	8-bit time-to-live field	8-bit protocol identifier field	16-bit checksum	32-bit source IP address	32-bit destination IP address	Padding

Figure 5-4

The structure of an IP header.

The IP header has the following size and fields:

- *IP Version Number*—The first 4 bits of the IP header identify the operating version of IP (for example, version 4 or version 6).

- *Internet Header Length*—The next 4 bits of the header contain the length of the header, expressed in multiples of 32.

- *Type of Service Flags*—The next 8 bits contain 1-bit flags that can be used to specify precedence, delay, throughput, and reliability parameters for that packet of data.

- *Total Length Field*—This 16-bit field contains the total length of the IP packet measured in octets. Valid values can range up to 65,535 octets.

- *Packet Identifier*—Each IP packet is given a unique 16-bit identifier that is used to identify the fragments of a datagram.

- *Flags*—The next field contains three 1-bit flags that indicate whether fragmentation of the packet is permitted, and if it is used.

- *Fragment Offset Field*—This 13-bit field measures the offset of the fragmented contents relative to the beginning of the entire packet. This value is measured in 64-bit increments.

- *Time-to-Live (TTL) Field*—The IP packet cannot be permitted to roam the WAN in perpetuity. It must be limited to a finite TTL. The 8-bit TTL field is set by the sender to any value up to 255. This value is decremented by at least one for each hop the packet makes. After decrementing to 1, the packet is assumed to be undeliverable. An ICMP message is generated and sent back to the source machine, and the undeliverable packet is destroyed.

- *Protocol Identifier Field*—This 8-bit field identifies the protocol that follows the IP header, such as VINES, TCP, UDP, and so forth.

- *Checksum*—The Checksum field is a 16-bit error-checking field. The destination computer, and every gateway node

in the network, will recompute the mathematical calculation on the packet's header as the source computer did. If
the data survived the trip intact, the results of these two
calculations are identical. This field also informs the destination host of the amount of incoming data.

- *Source IP Address*—The source address is the IP address
  of the source computer.

- *Destination IP Address*—The destination address is the IP
  address of the destination computer.

- *Padding*—Extra zeros are added to this field to ensure that
  the IP header is always a multiple of 32 bits.

These header fields reveal that IPv4's Internet layer is inherently
connectionless: The packet-forwarding devices in the network are
free to determine the ideal path for each packet to take through the
network. It also doesn't provide any of the acknowledgments, flow
control, or sequencing functions of higher-level protocols such as
TCP. It leaves such functions to those higher-level protocols.

The Internet layer must also support other route-management
functions beyond just IP's packet formatting. It must provide
mechanisms for resolving Layer 2 addresses into Layer 3
addresses and vice versa. These route-management functions are
provided by peer protocols to IP, which are described in Chapter
1, "An Introduction to Internetworking." These protocols include
Interior Gateway Protocol (IGP), Exterior Gateway Protocol
(EGP), Address Resolution Protocol (ARP), Reverse Address Resolution Protocol (RARP), and Internet Control Message Protocol
(ICMP).

Typical IPv4 Operation

The application layer places a header onto the data packet, identifying the destination host and port. The host-to-host layer

protocol (either TCP or UDP, depending on the application) breaks that block of data into smaller, more manageable pieces. Each piece has a TCP or UDP header prepended to it. This structure is known as a TCP *segment*.

The segment's header fields are populated appropriately, and the segment is passed to the Internet layer. The Internet layer adds the addressing, protocol type (TCP or UDP), and checksum information. If the segment was fragmented, the Internet layer populates that field as well.

The destination machine performs the reverse of the operation just described. It receives the packets and passes them to its host-to-host layer protocol. If necessary, the packets are reordered into data segments that are passed up to the appropriate application.

IPv4 Addressing Scheme

IPv4 uses a 32-bit binary addressing scheme to identify networks, network devices, and network-connected machines. These addresses, known as IP addresses, are strictly regulated by the *Internet Assigned Numbers Authority* (IANA) to ensure their uniqueness in the Internet. This function is currently being transitioned out of the hands of the U.S. government in favor of a private organization. This reflects both the desire of the U.S. government to control its expenses, and the undeniably global nature of the Internet.

RFC 1597 and RFC 1918

If your WAN will not be directly interconnected with the Internet or to any other network, internetwork addresses could be arbitrarily selected. Generally speaking, arbitrarily selecting internetwork addresses is short-sighted and a gross dereliction of duties. That being said, Request for Comment (RFC) 1597 was released in May 1993, and posited a plan to the contrary.

RFC 1597 was obsoleted by RFC 1918 in February, 1996. This new RFC made only extremely minor changes to the original specification, however. The most substantial of these changes was the abandonment of alphabetic classes, such as A, B, and C. Instead, RFC 1918 posited the use of the new CIDR-compliant addressing. Under CIDR, address classes are no longer used. Instead, the number of bits reserved for the network number are identified with a slash (/) followed by the number of bits. Thus, a Class A address of 10 is identified as 10/8 because only 8 bits are used to designate network numbers. Classless network numbering is covered in more detail in Chapter 2, "Understanding Internetwork Addresses."

Three ranges of addresses that could be used for internal networking purposes only were identified and reserved. These ranges include one each of IPv4's Class A, B, and C addresses. They are

- `10.0.0.0—10.255.255.255`

- `172.16.0.0—172.31.255.255`

- `192.168.0.0—192.168.255.255`

These ranges were reserved by IANA for use in private networks. One stipulation of RFC 1597 was that these addresses couldn't be used when directly accessing the Internet. Companies that used these addresses and subsequently found the need to access the Internet faced a tough decision. They could renumber all their devices to comply with IANA, or they could use a proxy server or a network address translator (NAT) as an intermediary between their intranet and the Internet. Using such devices would enable the company to keep their spurious addressing, without compromising access to and from the Internet.

If you choose to implement RFC 1597 or 1918's reserved addresses for your intranet, you must consider the long-term implications of that decision. Over time, you may need to interconnect with other company networks through an extranet, or to the Internet itself. In either event, you may not be able to guarantee the uniqueness of any given made-up address.

Finally, if you implement one of the address ranges reserved for private networks in RFC 1597 or 1918, you must still guarantee the uniqueness of each device's address within your private network domain. The addresses won't be unique globally, but they must be unique locally.

Ipv4 provided for five classes of IP addresses, each identified by a single alphabetic character: A, B, C, D, and E. Each address consists of two parts, a network and host address. The five classes represent different compromises between the number of support-able networks and hosts. Although these addresses are binary, they are normally identified with a dotted-decimal–style format (for example, 192.168.121.6) to facilitate human usage. The dots are used to separate the address's four octets.

> **NOTE**
>
> Dotted-decimal notation refers to the conversion of the binary address to the decimal (base 10) number system. A dot (.) is used to separate the node and network numbers. For example, 192.168.251.99 refers to device 99 on network 192.168.251.

The classes of addresses that were supported by IPv4 include

- *Class A IP address*—The first bit of a Class A address is always a 0. The next 7 bits identify the network number. The last 24 bits (that is, three dotted-decimal numbers) of a Class A address represent possible host addresses. The range of possible Class A addresses is from 1.0.0.0 to 126.0.0.0. Each Class A address can support 16,774,214 unique host addresses.

- *Class B IP address*—The first 2 bits of a Class B address are 10. The next 16 bits identify the network number, and the last 16 bits identify potential host addresses. The range of possible Class B addresses is from 128.1.0.0 to 191.254.0.0. Each Class B address can support 65,534 unique host addresses, which are addressed using the last 14 bits of this address space.

- *Class C IP address*—The first 3 bits of a Class C address are 110. The next 21 bits identify the network's number. The last octet is used for host addressing. The range of possible Class C network addresses is from 192.0.1.0 to 223.255.254.0. Each Class C address can support 254 unique host addresses.

- *Class D IP address*—The first 4 bits of a Class D address are 1110. These addresses are used for multicasting, but have seen only limited usage. A multicast address is a unique network address that directs packets with that destination address to predefined groups of IP addresses. Class D network addresses are from 224.0.0.0 to 239.255.255.254.

- *Class E IP address*—A Class E address has been defined, but is reserved by the IETF for its own research. This range is, by the faculty of deduction, 240.0.0.0 to 255.255.255.0. No Class E addresses have been released for use in the Internet.

The large gaps between these address classes have wasted a considerable number of potential addresses. Consider, for example, a medium-sized company that requires 300 IP addresses. A Class C address (254 addresses) is inadequate. Using two Class C addresses provides more than enough addresses, but results in two separate domains within the company. Alternatively, stepping up to a Class B address provides all the needed addresses within a single domain, but wastes 65,234 addresses.

Fortunately, this is no longer the case. A new interdomain routing protocol known as classless interdomain routing (CIDR) has been developed to enable multiple smaller address classes to function as a single routing domain.

IP addressing requires each machine to have its own unique address. Subnet masks can compensate for the tremendous gaps between address classes by customizing the length of the host and/or network addresses. These two numbers are used to route any given IP datagram to its destination.

As TCP/IP is capable of supporting multiple sessions from a single host, it must then provide a way of addressing specific communications programs that may operate on each host. TCP/IP does so with port numbers. The IETF has assigned some of the more common applications their own *well-known port numbers*. These numbers are reliably constant, per application, from host to host. Other applications are just assigned an available port number.

IPv4 Conclusion

IPv4 is almost 20 years old. It has endured substantial changes, including technological advances and a radical change in the demographics of its user base.

Perhaps the most significant of these changes has been the commercialization of the Internet. This has brought with it an unprecedented growth in the Internet's user population and a shift in its demographics. This, in turn, has created the tandem need for more addresses and Internet layer support for new types of service. IPv4's limitations have been driving the development of a completely new version of the protocol. This new version is called IP Version 6 (IPv6), but is also commonly referred to as Internet Protocol: Next Generation (IPng).

INTERNET PROTOCOL, VERSION 6 (IPv6)

IPv6 is designed to be a simple, forward-compatible upgrade to the existing version of IP. This upgrade is also intended to resolve all the weaknesses that IPv4 is currently manifesting including: the shortage of available IP addresses, the inability to accommodate time-sensitive traffic, and its lack of network layer security.

NOTE

IPv6 is sometimes referred to as IPng, or IP: Next Generation. IPng was the name of the original initiative to develop a next generation IP. As the protocol's specifications were being developed, the protocol was named IP version 6 (which was then abbreviated to IPv6).

Although IPng and IPv6 really refer to different things (that is, a development initiative versus a protocol), the two terms are used interchangeably to identify the new protocol. Aside from a few references to acknowledge the unintentional "synonymity," this book will adhere to the proper term for this new routed protocol: IPv6.

In addition to these issues, routing is also driving the development and deployment of the new IP protocol. IPv4 is hampered by its 32-bit address architecture, its two-level addressing hierarchy, and its address classes. This two-level addressing hierarchy (host and domain name) just does not allow construction of efficient address hierarchies that can be aggregated by routers on the scale that today's global Internet requires.

IPv6 resolves all these issues. It will offer a vastly expanded addressing scheme to support the continued expansion of the Internet, and an improved capability to aggregate routes on a large scale.

IPv6 will also support numerous other features such as real-time audio and/or video transmissions, host mobility, end-to-end security through Internet layer encryption and authentication, as well as autoconfiguration and autoreconfiguration. It is expected that these services will provide ample incentive for migration as soon as IPv6-capable products become available. Many of these features still require additional standardization. Therefore, it would be premature to expound on them at any great length.

The one aspect of IPv6 that can, and should, be expounded on is its addressing. IPv4's 32-bit address length gave the protocol a theoretical capability to address 2^{32}, or about four billion devices. Inefficient subnet masking techniques, among other wasteful practices, has squandered this resource.

IPv6 uses a 128-bit address and is theoretically capable of 2^{96} times the size of the IPv4 address space. This is 340,282,366,920,938,463,463,374,607,431,768,211,456 mathematically possible addresses. Only about 15% of this potential address space is currently allocated. The remainder is reserved for unspecified future use, and appears as a string of hexadecimal zeros in the address field.

In reality, the assignment and routing of addresses requires the creation of hierarchies. Hierarchies can reduce the number of potential addresses, but increase the efficiency of IPv6-capable routing protocols. A four-fold increase in the size of the address space means that the new addressing format will be very user-hostile. Exacerbating this situation is the fact that the IPv6 address is annotated in a coloned (:) hexadecimal format rather than the now-familiar dotted decimal. The practical implication of this is that users will rely increasingly on user-friendly mnemonic names.

Therefore, Domain Name Service (DNS) becomes an absolute necessity, and not the optional service that it had been in the IPv4 network environment.

NOTE

Domain Name Service is the network utility responsible for translating mnemonic host names into numeric IP addresses.

As significant as the increased potential address space is, even greater flexibility is afforded with IPv6's new address structures. IPv6 dispenses with the previous class-based addressing. Instead, it recognizes three kinds of unicast address, replaces the former Class D address with a new multicast address format, and introduces a new address type. You *must* understand these new addressing structures prior to undertaking an IPv6 migration.

IPv6 Unicast Address Structures

Unicast addressing provides connectivity from one endpoint to one endpoint. IPv6 supports several forms of unicast addresses. They are described in the following sections.

Internet Service Provider Unicast Address

Whereas IPv4 preassumed clusters of users requiring connectivity, IPv6 provides a unicast address format designed specifically for use by Internet service providers (ISPs) to connect *individual* users to the Internet. These provider-based unicast addresses offer unique addresses for individuals or small groups who access the Internet through a provider. The architecture of the address provides for efficient aggregation of routes in an environment characterized by individual users, as opposed to large concentrations of users.

The ISP unicast address format is as follows:

- A 3-bit ISP unicast address flag that is always set to 010

- A Registry ID field that is n bits in length

- A Provider ID field that is m bits in length

- A Subscriber ID field that is o bits in length

- A Subnet ID field that is p bits in length

- An Interface ID field that is 125 (n+m+o+p) bits in length

The alphabetic characters n, m, o, and p denote variable-length fields. The length of the Interface ID is 125 bits (maximum length of an IPv6 address is 128 bits, minus the 3-bit flag) minus the sum of these variable fields.

An example of this type of address would be 010:0:0:0:0:x, where x can be any number. Given that much of the new address space has yet to be allocated, these addresses will contain lots of zeros. Therefore, groups of zeros may be shortened with a double ::. This shorthand notation is 010::x.

The other unicast address types are designed for local use. Local use addresses can be assigned to networked devices within a stand-alone intranet or to devices on an intranet that need to have access to the Internet.

Link-Local Use

The link-local is for use on a single link for purposes such as auto-address configuration, neighbor discovery, or when no routers are present. Link-local addresses have the following format:

- A 10-bit local use flag that is always set to 1111111011

- A reserved, unnamed field that is n bits in length but defaulted to a value of 0

- An Interface ID field that is 118 n bits in length

The interface ID can be the Media Access Control (MAC) address of an Ethernet network interface card (NIC). MAC addresses, being theoretically unique addresses, can be concatenated with standard IP address prefixes to form unique addresses for mobile or transitory users. An example of a link-local address with a MAC address is 1111111011:0:mac_address.

Site-Local-Use Unicast Address

Site-local addresses are designed for use in a single site. They may be used for sites or organizations that are not connected to the global Internet. They do not need to request or "steal" an address prefix from the global Internet address space. IPv6 site-local addresses can be used instead. When the organization connects to the global Internet, it can then form unique global addresses by replacing the site-local prefix with a subscriber prefix that contains a registry, provider, and subscriber identification.

Site-local addresses have the following format:

- A 10-bit local use flag that is always set to 1111111011

- A reserved, unnamed field that is n bits in length but defaulted to a value of 0

- A Subnet ID field that is m bits in length

- An Interface ID field that is 118 (n+m) bits in length

An example of a site-local address is 1111111011:0:subnet:interface.

IPv6 Transitional Unicast Address Structures

Two special IPv6 unicast addresses have been defined as transition mechanisms to allow hosts and routers to dynamically route IPv6 packets over IPv4 network infrastructure and vice versa.

IPv4-Compatible IPv6 Unicast Address

The first unicast address type is called an IPv4-compatible IPv6 address. This transitional unicast address can be assigned to IPv6 nodes and can contain an IPv4 address in the last 32 bits. Figure 5-5 illustrates the format of these addresses.

Figure 5-5

The structure of an IPv4-compatible IPv6 unicast address.

80-bit reserved field set to 0	16-bit reserved field set to 0	32-bit IPv4 address

IPv4-Mapped IPv6 Unicast Address

A second, similar type of IPv6 address that also contains an IPv4 address in its last 32 bits is known as an IPv4-mapped IPv6 address. This address is constructed by a dual protocol router and permits IPv4-only nodes to tunnel through IPv6 network infrastructure. The only difference between IPv4-mapped IPv6 addresses and IPv4-compatible IPv6 addresses is that IPv4-mapped addresses are constructs only. They are built automatically by dual protocol routers, and cannot be assigned to any nodes. Figure 5-6 illustrates the format of these addresses.

Figure 5-6

The structure of an IPv4-mapped IPv6 unicast address.

80-bit reserved field set to zeros	16-bit reserved field set to Fs	32-bit IPv4 address

Both the IPv4-mapped and the IPv4-compatible unicast addresses are essential to tunneling. *Tunneling* enables the transport of packets through an otherwise incompatible network region by wrapping those packets in an externally acceptable framework.

IPv6 Anycast Address Structures

The *anycast* address, introduced in IPv6, is a single value assigned to more than one interface. Typically, these interfaces belong to different devices. A packet sent to an anycast address is routed to only one device. It is sent to the "nearest" interface having that address as defined by the routing protocol's measure of distance. For example, a World Wide Web (WWW) site may be mirrored on several servers. By assigning an anycast address to these servers, requests for connectivity to that WWW site are automatically routed to only one server: the server nearest the user.

NOTE

In a routed environment, the "nearest" interface might not be the one that is physically closest. Routers can use a surprising array of metrics to calculate routes. Identifying the nearest one depends on the actual routing protocol used, as well as that protocol's metrics. This topic is addressed in detail in Part III, "Routing Protocols."

Anycast addresses are formed from the unicast address space and may take the form of any unicast address type. Anycast addresses are formed by just assigning the same unicast address to more than one interface.

IPv6 Multicast Address Structures

Multicasting was supported in IPv4, but required the use of obscure Class D addressing. IPv6 eliminates Class D addresses in favor of a new address format that permits trillions of possible multicast group codes. Each group code identifies two or more packet recipients. The scope of a particular multicast address is flexible. Each address can be confined to a single system, restricted within a specific site, associated with a particular network link, or distributed globally.

It should be noted that IP broadcasts have also been eliminated in favor of the new multicasting address format.

Despite the potential benefits of IPv6, the migration from IPv4 is not risk free. The extension of the address length from 32 to 128 bits automatically limits interoperability between IPv4 and IPv6. *IPv4-only nodes cannot interoperate with IPv6-only nodes because the address architectures are not forward-compatible*. This business risk, in combination with the ongoing evolution of IPv4, will likely continue to forestall the acceptance of IPv6 in the marketplace.

SUMMARY

The two versions of routed protocols described throughout this chapter, IPv4 and IPv6, are remarkably dissimilar in many respects. Together, they represent the past, present, and future of routing. Understanding these routed protocols, particularly their addressing and subnetting schemes, will help you understand how routers actually forward data from source to destination machines.

As you examine the other aspects of internetworking, it will become increasingly apparent why some of the header fields are necessary, as well as how they are used.

CHAPTER 6

Transmission Technologies

One of the router's most important capabilities is the interconnection of virtually any combination of different LAN and WAN technologies. As demonstrated in Part I, "Internetworking Fundamentals," LANs and WANs differ significantly from one another. Although a detailed examination of the myriad LAN and WAN technologies is beyond the scope of this book, a review of their "speeds and feeds" is pertinent to understanding exactly what a router can do. Therefore, this chapter provides an overview of the physical transmission media, data rates, and distance limitations (if any) of the more commonly encountered LAN and WAN technologies. Additionally, the industry and national standards that support long-distance carrier systems are also examined.

LAN TECHNOLOGIES

As explained in Chapter 2, "Understanding Internetwork Addresses," routers are an indispensable part of the LAN. Therefore, it is not surprising that most router vendors offer I/O ports for virtually all the most common physical implementations of today's LANs. Some of the more commonly encountered LAN architectures include Ethernet, Token Ring, FDDI, and ATM.

Of course, numerous other LAN architectures abound, including such esoteric networks as Token Bus, ARCnet, and even ARCnet Plus. It is highly unlikely that you will ever encounter them, however; they have long since passed into obsolescence. It is important to note that even the LAN architectures examined in this chapter may have some physical layer specifications that are either not supported or not universally supported by router manufacturers.

Ethernet

Ethernet was born of internal research conducted at Xerox's famed Palo Alto Research Center in the early 1970s. Rather than being some bold and innovative new technology that researchers strove to bring to market, Ethernet's origins are quite pedestrian. The researchers needed a way to share their expensive laser printer between their desktop workstations. The answer: a crude and somewhat chaotic data link layer protocol that relied on higher-layer protocols to behave properly. Somewhat tongue in cheek, these researchers named their new pet Ethernet, a subtle play on words. From this humble beginning spawned a tremendous family of related products, protocols, and technologies.

Today, many different varieties of Ethernet exist. This family includes at least five different frame structures, three different media access arbitration techniques, and an ever-growing collection of medium-dependent interfaces (MDIs). The MDI is the most visible aspect of the 802.3 physical layer; it defines and describes the expected type of transmission medium, as well as its transmission and impedance characteristics. For the LAN to operate properly, the correct transmission media must be connected to the corresponding network interface card (NIC), which contains the MDI's logic.

There are multiple IEEE-supported Ethernet MDIs, each one describing the mechanisms needed to support transmission via a different transmission medium. The following sections identify each specific MDI and categorize them by their transmission speed.

10 Mbps Ethernet MDIs

As defined by the IEEE, 10 Mbps baseband Ethernet has five distinct MDIs. These MDIs are bundled into modules that define every aspect of the physical layer for the different transmission media. Of these five MDIs, two are based on coaxial cable, two are based on fiber-optic cable, and one is for twisted copper pairs of wire.

The 10 Mbps Ethernet MDIs include the following:

- 10Base2—Also known as thinnet, 10Base2 gets its name from the following convention: the signaling speed (in Mbps), the transmission method (baseband, in this case), and the maximum number of meters that the cable can be (rounded to the nearest 100, and then divided by 100). This specification describes a 10 Mbps baseband network protocol. It uses a 50 ohm coaxial cable that can be a maximum length of 185 meters. Rounding 185 yields 200. Dividing 200 by 100 yields 2, the last digit of the MDI's name. 10Base2 networks can be extended beyond 185 meters by using repeaters, bridges, or routers. Each 10Base2 LAN can support a maximum of 30 taps. A *tap* is a device that physically splices two pieces of coaxial cable without splitting them. This allows user devices to be interconnected to a LAN's backbone.

- 10Base5—As its name implies, the maximum length for 10Base5 coaxial cable is 500 meters. This MDI uses a much thicker coaxial cable than 10Base2; therefore, it is often referred to as *thicknet*. Transmission efficacy, in copper media, is a function of the conductor's thickness. The greater the conductor's diameter, the more bandwidth can be achieved. Consequently, 10Base5 can be tapped up to 100 times.

NOTE

It is highly unlikely that you will encounter a router that can be configured with an I/O port for a coaxially cabled Ethernet. These cables, besides taking up a lot of space, are functionally obsolete. If you must support a coaxially cabled Ethernet, however, routers may be configured with an AUI port. A transceiver can be attached to this port, which can be connected to your coaxial Ethernet.

- 10BaseT—If 10BaseT had adhered to the naming conventions applied to the coaxial specifications, its name would have been 10Base1, because it is limited to a 100-meter segment length. For whatever reason, the IEEE broke from convention and designated this MDI with a *T* to symbolize its physical media: twisted pair. 10BaseT can operate over a minimum of Category 3 unshielded twisted-pair.

Twisted-Pair Wiring

Twisted-pair wiring is a commodity: Regardless of the manufacturer, one can reasonably expect consistent performance. This is due to the degree of standardization that has occurred in the telecommunications industry. If this sounds a bit vague, that's intentional. No single standards body is responsible for the care and maintenance of standards that define twisted pair. Instead, a loose collaboration of ANSI, the FCC, the EIA/TIA, and many other organizations provides the standards for cabling, and even cable components such as terminators.

This confederation has not developed specifications that define either shielded twisted-pair (STP) or unshielded twisted-pair (UTP) cabling! Although some standards do establish guidelines for cabling and/or cable components, twisted pair is defined via *categories of performance*. They are functional standards, not physical standards. In other words, all a given manufacturer has to do to prove compliance is to demonstrate performance, regardless of how the wire was made, how thick it is, what it is made from, or anything else.

Originally, five series of tests established benchmark performance categories for twisted-pair wiring. These were numbered 1 through 5, and compliant wire was identified as being Category *x*, or Cat-*x*, with *x* being the numeric test series that was achieved. Over time, the market has coalesced into just two viable performance levels: Category 3 and Category 5. Categories 1 and 2 were officially made obsolete in 1995 because of inadequate performance vis-à-vis requirements. Category 4 offers a median level of performance, relative to 3 and 5, but is seldom (if ever) used.

Category 3 UTP offers 16 MHz of bandwidth, which translates into signaling speeds up to 10 Mbps at 100 meters. Category 4 can support 20 MHz (which equates to a theoretical maximum bandwidth of 20 Mbps). Category 5 can support up to 100 MHz.

This range demonstrates why Category 4 has failed to gain support in the market. It does not provide enough of a performance differential to be worth the bother. If someone needs more bandwidth than Category 3 can provide, he can just install Category 5. He must adhere to the distance limitations of whichever LAN architecture is chosen. Category 5 can provide 100 Mbps, 155 Mbps, and even 256 Mbps.

- 10BaseFL—The 10BaseFL specification provides for the baseband transmission of 10 Mbps Ethernet over multimode 62.5/125 micron fiber-optic cable. The maximum distance for a cable run is 2,000 meters. 10BaseFL can be used to interconnect repeaters, or even to connect servers to a repeater. Such connections tend to be slightly more expensive than a comparable 10BaseT connection, but 10BaseFL can be extended over much greater distances.

- 10BaseFOIRL—A relatively recent addition to the 802.3 series is 10BaseFOIRL—quite a mouthful for a mnemonic intended to facilitate the remembrance of 10 Mbps baseband transmission over Fiber-Optic Inter-Repeater Links! Implicit in this definition is that this technology is strictly limited to the interconnection of repeaters. In other words, it is for hub-to-hub connectivity over fiber-optic cabling. No other devices can be attached. This includes routers. Therefore, you will not find a router I/O port configured for this MDI.

  10BaseFOIRL uses a 8.3 micron diameter fiber-optic cable that must be driven by an injection laser diode (ILD). This hardware/media combination provides effective transmission of 10 Mbps baseband signals for up to 5,000 meters.

NOTE

The fiber-optic cable's 8.3-micron diameter width is almost always referred to in a rounded form: 9-micron diameter. Inexplicably, the width of multimode 62.5-micron diameter fiber-optic cable is always referred to as 62.5-micron diameter.

---

100 Mbps Ethernet MDIs

The Fast Ethernet MDIs include the following:

- 100BaseTX—100BaseTX defines the original 100BaseX specification for Category 5 unshielded twisted-pair (UTP) and for Type 1 shielded twisted-pair (STP). Both are limited to 100-meter transmission distances.

- 100BaseFX—This specification defines 100 Mbps Ethernet over fiber-optic cabling. 100BaseFX can support the 100 Mbps data rate up to 400 meters over two strands of 62.5/125-micron fiber-optic cable.

- 100BaseT4—100BaseT4 is designed to allow transmission of 100 Mbps over four pairs of voice-grade wiring for distances up to 100 meters. Voice-grade wiring is defined to be a minimum of Category 3 UTP. It can also transmit using Categories 4 and 5 UTP.

Gigabit Ethernet MDIs

Additionally, the IEEE has developed new MDIs for its Gigabit Ethernet specification:

- 1000BaseSX—100BaseSX is the IEEE 802.3z proposed specification for multimode transmission using short-wavelength lasers rather than the lower-bandwidth, light emitting diodes (LEDs). Short wavelength is defined to be those lasers that produce light in the 850-nanometer range. This proposal actually recognizes two different media: 50-micron and 62.5-micron diameter fiber-optic cabling. The 50-micron variant can support the full gigabit signaling rate for a maximum of 550 meters. The 62.5-micron diameter variant is limited to a maximum of 260 meters per cable segment.

- 1000BaseLX—1000BaseLX is the proposed specification for long-wavelength laser transmissions. Long wavelengths are those laser transmissions that are 1,300 nanometers in length. This proposal includes 62.5-micron multimode fiber-optic cabling, 50-micron multimode fiber-optic cabling, and 8.3-micron single-mode fiber-optic cabling. In its current form, the 62.5-micron multimode fiber can extend to a maximum of 440 meters. The 50-micron multimode can be up to 550 meters. The 8.3-micron single-mode fiber specification, ostensibly the most expensive to manufacture and install, can support gigabit signaling for up to 3 kilometers.

- 1000BaseCX—1000BaseCX defines the 802.3 proposed specification for transmission over either high-quality shielded twisted-pair or coaxial cabling. The maximum distance for transmission over either media is limited to just 25 meters. The very short transmission distance limits this physical interface significantly. One of the proposed uses is to interconnect colocated Gigabit switches by using a low-cost copper alternative to fiber optics.

- 1000BaseT—A separate IEEE task force is still working on the standard for 1000BaseT. This team, and its would-be standard, is called 802.3ab. Its goal is to match the performance of Fast Ethernet over four pairs of Category 5 UTP, albeit at a data rate of 1024 Mbps.

Token Ring

IBM originally conceived Token Ring as a data-center technology for networking mainframe computers. It was first proposed to the IEEE for standardization in 1969 for this purpose. After personal computers (PCs) were developed, it became apparent that Token Ring could serve to interconnect them as well. This was the impetus behind its inclusion in the IEEE's Project 802. IBM was a major proponent of the IEEE standardization efforts. Today, both technologies are known as Token Ring.

Standardization under the 802 umbrella necessitated making some changes to Token Ring's data link layer so that it would support the 802 style of hardware-level addressing. This would make the IEEE's Token Ring bridgeable with other 802 LAN architectures.

The IEEE designated Token Ring as its 802.5 specification. This specification is almost identical to IBM's Token Ring. In addition to the aforementioned hardware-level changes, the IEEE also standardized the message format and Layer 2 protocols. Perhaps the most significant change was that the 802.5 specification did not specify either a topology or a physical transmission media! This was a major departure from the IBM version, which specified the use of a star topology and unshielded twisted-pair wiring. This meant that repeaterless peer-to-peer Token Ring LANs could be built, instead of using a star topology with a repeating hub to form the star's center.

Token Ring Transmission Media

Both of the early Token Ring networks specified a 4 Mbps LAN that used what is now known as Category 3 UTP. Over time, the data rate was increased to 16 Mbps in response to increases in the number and speed of devices that were being interconnected. This new specification required a minimum of Category 4 UTP, although it is more frequently encountered running over Category 5 UTP.

FDDI

FDDI is an acronym for Fiber Distributed Data Interface, but nobody uses that mouthful of a name. In fact, most people don't even spell out F-D-D-I; they slur the letters together and pronounce it "fiddy." FDDI is a robust and reliable LAN technology that dates back to the mid-1980s. FDDI features a 100 Mbps data rate and dual counter-rotating rings. These rings can span up to 200 kilometers, using fiber-optic cables. This maximum distance means that FDDI can be used effectively as both a local and a metropolitan-area network (MAN).

Access to FDDI's transmission media is regulated through a token-passing scheme that is similar to Token Ring. Only the device that holds the token may transmit. Also, similarly to Token Ring, the token can pass in only one direction on a ring.

FDDI Transmission Media

FDDI has three different physical-layer specifications, which are called physical layer medium, or PMD. (That's not a typo; it really is abbreviated as PMD). Originally, FDDI was limited to a single PMD: 62.5/125-micron diameter multimode fiber-optic cabling. It remained a glass-only technology until the 1990s. Then, the high cost of fiber-optic cable started cutting into its market share. The answer seemed obvious: develop a copper-based PMD that could support the FDDI protocols.

In June of 1990, ANSI formed a working committee to build the specification for a twisted-pair PMD (TP-PMD). Originally, the TP-PMD was a proprietary product that grafted the FDDI Layer 2 on to a Category 5 UTP physical layer. The end result was marketed as CDDI, for Copper Distributed Data Interface. This specification became an ANSI standard in 1994. Today, CDDI is obsolete. Its biggest benefit was a 100 Mbps data rate over copper wires. With the arrival of Fast Ethernet, the market had a 100 Mbps LAN with copper wires *and* a familiar data-link protocol that easily integrated with their existing networks. Consequently, support for CDDI has been dropped by Cisco Systems, the original owner of the technology.

A single-mode fiber-optic version (SMF-PMD) has also been developed. Based on 8.3-micron diameter fiber-optic cabling, and driven by a laser rather than an LED, this PMD is more expensive than its multimode counterpart. It also consumes more energy and dissipates more heat than FDDI's other two PMDs. In its favor, the SMF-PMD can maintain the integrity of transmitted signals for much greater drive distances: up to 60 kilometers versus the paltry 2 kilometers of the multimode fiber, or 100 meters of twisted pair.

NOTE

It is important to note that a drive distance is the distance between two devices. It is not the maximum diameter of the network.

FDDI Connection Types

FDDI actually has a much more complex physical layer than most other LANs. Given that FDDI is frequently used to interconnect LANs and premise edge routers, it is imperative to examine this complexity in detail. FDDI supports two types of connections:

- Single-attached stations (SAS)
- Dual-attached stations (DAS)

This means that FDDI network interface cards can have two sets of physical media interfaces. They are known as ports A and B. Port A is the primary interface, and port B is the secondary interface.

DASs feature two sets of media interfaces. This enables a DAS device to have a physical connection to each of FDDI's two rings. Figure 6-1 illustrates the way that a dual-attached station connects to the LAN. Each DAS device has two sets of media interface ports, each containing both A and B ports. Each port contains physical connections for two physical media: one for transmitting and the other for receiving data. Thus, a DAS device on a fiber-optic FDDI network actually has four fibers connected to it.

Figure 6-1

Dual-attached stations in a FDDI ring.

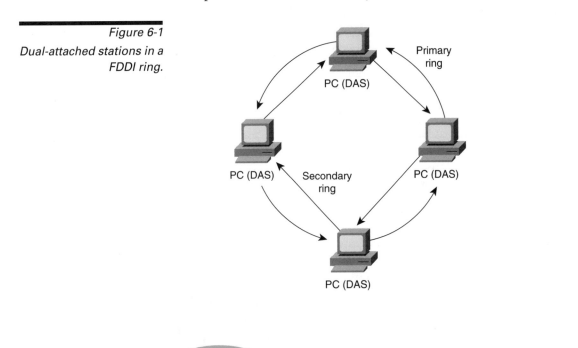

NOTE

A concentrator is a device that aggregates multiple LAN connections on to a common electrical backplane. The most common type of LAN concentrator is known as a hub. Concentrators can also be dual attached. Consequently, it would be correct to refer to both concentrators and stations with the phrase *dual attached* (DA) without specifically identifying the devices.

As shown in Figure 6-1, the physical device actually becomes an integral part of the two rings because the NIC provides physical continuity for the two rings in the interval between the A and B ports. Each of the illustrated physical rings actually consists of two strands of fiber-optic cabling: one for transmit and one for receive.

DAS connections can form a repeaterless, peer-to-peer LAN. This is accomplished by connecting the A port of one device's interface to the B port of another device, and vice versa. The drawback to this is that each DAS device must be powered on and functioning for the rings to be complete. FDDI can wrap around a break in the ring, but this directly impacts the performance of the entire ring. More significantly, multiple stations are simultaneously powered down or otherwise out of service; the net result might be two or more smaller ring pairs.

SASs eliminate the potential performance problems inherent in DAS by eliminating the wraparound feature. Each SAS device has just a single communications interface, S, with two media ports. The separate fibers are used to transmit and receive. Both fibers terminate at the concentrator, which provides the connectivity to both rings. Figure 6-2 illustrates a single-attached station with its concentrator.

As is the case in Figure 6-1, the physical connections indicated in Figure 6-2 actually consist of two strands of fiber-optic cabling.

Wraparounds

FDDI supports a self-healing capability in its dual-attached configuration by using the two rings to *wraparound* a failure. When this capability is used, the actual direction of the token's flow through the rings will vary from the norm. Given that wraparound is indicative of an error state, this shouldn't be surprising. To better understand FDDI's self-healing capability, consider the example presented in Figure 6-3. This figure builds on the topology presented in Figure 6-1, and demonstrates what would happen in the event of a cable failure. The network components detect a break in the ring, and automatically seek to restore the integrity of the ring by wrapping around the failed component. In this manner, service is restored to as much of the original network as possible.

Figure 6-2
Single-attached stations in
a tree topology.

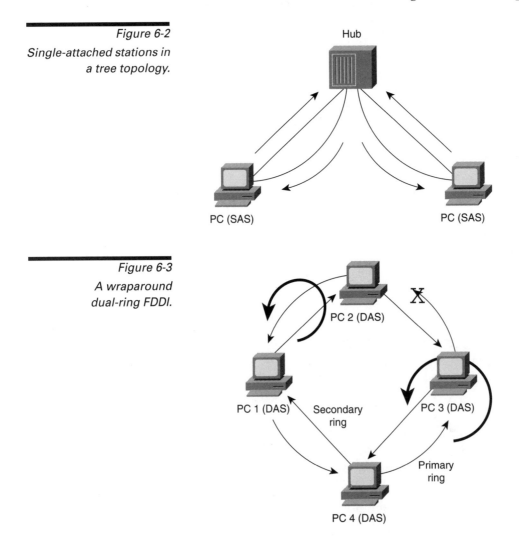

Figure 6-3
A wraparound
dual-ring FDDI.

It is important to note that FDDI is equally capable of recovering from failures of physical devices on the network, as well as just cable breaks.

ATM

Adapting Asynchronous Transfer Mode (ATM) to the LAN environment created the need for supporting copper-based transmission media that would be consistent with its existing optically based specifications. Additionally, it was strongly believed that a rate less than the 51.84 Mbps would have to be developed for ATM. Two competing proposals were developed: 25.6 and 25.9 Mbps. The 25.9 Mbps proposal was more logical, because it could be evenly scaled upward into the OC architecture. Unfortunately, politics prevailed and the ATM Forum embraced the 25.6 Mbps proposal.

The 25.6 Mbps specification was cobbled together from IBM's Token Ring chip set. It was believed that such a basis would make 25.6 Mbps ATM more reliable than any proposal that lacked a similar, well-engineered heritage. Its heritage, however, resulted in an odd (but relatively functional) data rate. This specification could provide connectivity over Category 3 UTP for up to 100 meters.

The copper-based variant of OC-1 was designed to provide 51.84 Mbps over a maximum of 100 meters of Category 5 UTP. Unfortunately, this specification was based on a new modulation technology known as carrierless amplitude phase modulation (CAP or CAP-M). Although proven to be successful in laboratory environments, this technology proved virtually impossible to manufacture on a large scale at that time.

ATM's full rate of 155.52 Mbps was also treated to a pair of new physical media interfaces for the LAN environment. The first was Category 5 UTP, which could be up to 100 meters long. The other was 62.5-micron, multimode fiber-optic cabling. This media could stretch for up to 2 kilometers.

In a LAN environment that has actually embraced ATM, you will likely find the 155.52 Mbps version used as a LAN's backbone, connections to servers and routers, and maybe even connections to high-end workstations. The 25.6 Mbps version is distinctly a station-connect technology, and it is doubtful that it will see much service even in that capacity.

WAN TECHNOLOGIES

Transmission facilities used to construct the WAN present the richest array of options for the network planner. These facilities come in optic cabling and can support numerous framing formats.

Transmission facilities also vary greatly in the manner in which they provide connections. There are four primary types of facilities:

- Dedicated, or leased, lines

- Circuit switched

- Packet switched

- Cell switched

These four types encompass all versions of facilities although technological innovation may be blurring their boundaries somewhat. The following sections briefly describe these technologies.

Leased Lines

The leased line is the most robust and flexible of the circuit-switched transmission facilities. These circuits are called leased lines because they are leased from telecommunications carriers for a monthly fee.

In North America, the dominant system for providing digital +-line service is known as the T-carrier system. The T-carrier allows 1.544 Mbps of bandwidth to be channelized into 24 separate transmission facilities over two pairs of wire. Each channel is 64 kbps wide and can be further channelized into even smaller facilities, such as 9.6 kbps. The 1.544 Mbps facility is known as the T-1. A higher capacity facility also exists within the T-carrier system. This is the 44.736 Mbps T-3 facility.

For more information on carrier systems, including SONET and T-carrier, refer to the section titled "Carrier System Standards" near the end of the chapter.

NOTE

Leased lines are frequently called *dedicated* or *private* lines because their bandwidth is reserved only for the company that is leasing them. Leased lines are the vehicle that virtually every form of business-grade telecommunications service is delivered over.

Circuit-Switched Facilities

Circuit switching is a communications method that creates a switched, dedicated path between two end stations. A good example of a circuit-switched network is the telephone system. A telephone is hard-wired to a central office telecommunications switch that is owned and operated by an exchange carrier. Although many exchange carriers exist, including local exchange carriers (LECs) and intermediary exchange carriers (IXCs), and many more telecommunications switches in the world, any telephone can establish a connection to any other telephone through a series of switches. That connection is a physical circuit and is dedicated to that session for the duration of the communications session. When the telephones terminate their sessions, the physical circuit through the switched telecommunications infrastructure is torn down. The resources are then freed up for the next call.

The creation of a dedicated, physical circuit through switches is the essence of circuit switching. Every unit of transmission, regardless of whether it is a cell, frame, or anything else that may be constructed, takes the same physical path through the network infrastructure. This concept may be applied in several different formats. Three examples of circuit-switched transmission facilities include ISDN and Switched 56, both of which are discussed in the sections that follow.

Integrated Services Digital Network

Integrated Services Digital Network (ISDN) is a digital circuit-switched technology that can transport voice and data simultaneously over the same physical connection. Connections are made on-demand by dialing another ISDN circuit's telephone number. This type of service is known as *dial-on-demand*. ISDN can be ordered in either Basic Rate Interface (BRI) or Primary Rate Interface (PRI).

The BRI offers 144 kbps in a format known as *2B+D*. The 2B refers to two 64 kbps B (for *bearer*) channels that can be linked together, or bonded, to form one logical connection at 128 kbps.

The D channel is a 16 kbps control channel used for call setup, take-down, and other control functions. Originally the ISDN BRI was distinctly a remote access technology, as opposed to a true, multiuser, WAN transmission facility. Today, this transmission technology is finding increasing acceptance as a low-cost backup facility for dedicated-line networks. As a backup facility, ISDN may be pressed into service whenever a dedicated line either fails or becomes severely congested.

Typically the PRI is delivered over a T-1 facility at a gross transmission rate of 1.544 Mbps. This is usually channelized into 23 64 kbps B channels and one 64 kbps D channel. Higher-rate H channels of either 384, 1536, and 1920 kbps can be used rather than, or in combination with, the B and D channels. Although ISDN is often described as a circuit-switched facility, it can support circuit-switched, packet-switched, and even semipermanent connections. The reason why ISDN is capable of such flexibility is relatively simple: The B channels are circuit switched, whereas the D channel is packet switched.

Switched 56

Another dial-on-demand circuit-switched variant is Switched 56. Switched 56 offers 56 kbps of bandwidth between any two points that subscribe to this service. As with any dial-on-demand service, no circuit exists until a call is placed. Then, the circuit is constructed between the origination and requested destination points. The actual path taken through the switched communications infrastructure is invisible, and immaterial, to the end users. This circuit is torn down when the session terminates.

The nondedicated nature of Switched 56 makes it an affordable alternative to leased lines. You pay based on usage rather than for the luxury of having bandwidth reserved for you, regardless of whether it is being used. Balanced against affordability is performance. Switched 56 circuits must set up calls to requested destinations. This takes time. Therefore, establishing a communications session over a 56 kbps leased line is much faster than over a Switched 56. After the call is established, performance should be comparable.

NOTE

56 kbps modems, unlike a Switched 56 link, rely on compression to achieve their advertised throughput. The extent to which data can be compressed depends on the data itself, and not on the modem encrypting it. Consequently, it is quite likely that some application types will find the 56 kbps of bandwidth available via a Switched 56 circuit to be superior to a compression-based 56 kbps modem!

Switched 56 is a mature and declining technology. It once offered a combination of lower cost than leased lines and much higher performance than modems and basic telephone lines. Today, advances in signaling techniques have enabled modems to close the performance gap. Switched 56 still offers a slight improvement over the so-called 56 kbps modems (despite what the name says, it cannot sustain that transmission rate) but not much. Today, Switched 56 is probably best suited as an emergency contingency (or backup) to leased lines.

Packet-Switched Facilities

Packet-switching facilities feature an internal packet format that is used to encapsulate data to be transported. Unlike circuit-switched facilities, packet-switched facilities do not provide a dedicated connection between two locations. Instead, the premise access facility interconnects with the telecommunications carrier's switched infrastructure. Customer data packets are forwarded through this commercial packet-switched network (PSN). Two examples of packet-switched networks are the old, but familiar, X.25 and its more up-to-date cousin, Frame Relay, both discussed in the following sections.

X.25

X.25 is a very old WAN communications protocol developed by the CCITT (now known as the International Telecommunications Union, or ITU). Telecommunications carriers first offered it as a commercial service in the early 1970s.

NOTE

The ITU's specifications are sometimes identified with the prefix ITU-T. The *T* suffix identifies the specification as part of the ITU's telecommunications standards.

X.25 supports the use of both switched and permanent virtual circuits. *Switched virtual circuits* (SVCs) are established as needed, and are dismantled after the communications session ends. *Permanent virtual circuits* (PVCs) are predefined, logical connections through a switched network between two points. The advantage of SVCs is that they are flexible and can be used to connect any two points within the X.25 network on demand. Their limitation lies in the call setup time that must be endured prior to exchanging information with another device on the network.

PVCs aren't flexible and must be defined in advance. Their primary benefit lies in the elimination of a call setup period. Therefore, PVCs are typically used to support communications between devices that need to communicate on a routine and ongoing basis. SVCs are used for ad hoc communications.

X.25 contains a robust suite of error detection and correction mechanisms that enables it to be a highly reliable protocol having to traverse a noisy electromechanical switching equipment infrastructure. In essence, X.25 sacrificed throughput for reliability. Today, in the era of digital and optical communications, the error detection/correction mechanisms of X.25 are unnecessary overhead. These functions are now more appropriate at the communicating devices rather than embedded in every network device. Applications that still require the use of the X.25 protocol may find better performance in emulating that protocol over a different transmission facility.

Despite the availability of technically superior transmission technologies, X.25 hasn't been completely supplanted. X.25 is used extensively in Europe, and even in the United States! Many organizations either cannot afford to migrate to newer technologies, or are locked into older infrastructures for a variety of reasons. Therefore, it is still widely deployed around the world.

Frame Relay

Frame Relay is often described as a faster version of X.25. This claim has some merit, because Frame Relay is quite similar to X.25. It is a packet-switching technology, but features smaller packet sizes and fewer error-checking mechanisms. Frame Relay currently supports transfer of packets only through permanent virtual circuits (PVCs) between the network's end point routers.

Eventually, SVCs will be supported in this protocol, although no timelines for its deployment have been suggested by any of the commercial service providers.

NOTE

Frame Relay is classified as a packet-switched technology even though, as its name implies, it is a data link layer protocol that uses frames!

The PVCs' end points are defined by data link connection identifiers (DLCIs) and are given a committed information rate (CIR) through the Frame Relay network. DLCI pairs are also given a minimum available quantity of bandwidth with the option to temporarily burst beyond that limit under certain circumstances. Figure 6-4 illustrates the use of DLCIs in Frame Relay networks. Each dashed line between two locations represents a DLCI pair. Also, note that Location D does not use a router to connect to the Frame Relay network. Frame Relay, as with any data link layer protocol, contains native mechanisms for addressing. Such mechanisms are primitive in comparison to comparable network layer mechanisms, but may suffice for interconnecting stub networks. In Figure 6-4, Location D only connects to one other location, and thus can dispense with the cost and complexity of a routed connection. Instead, it uses a Frame Relay access device (FRAD) to connect the LAN to the WAN.

Frame Relay WANs are built by provisioning a point-to-point private line from the work location to the nearest central office that provides this service. At the central office, this private line terminates in a Frame Relay switch that is either fully or partially meshed with the other Frame Relay switches that comprise that carrier's Frame Relay commercial infrastructure. Much like the central office voice switches that comprise the Public Switched Telephone Network (PSTN), the Frame Relay switches remain invisible to the user community and its applications. Frame Relay's primary benefit is that it can reduce the cost of networking locations that are geographically dispersed by minimizing the length of transmission facilities. These circuits are commercially available at 1.544 Mbps, with CIRs used to create logical subrate connections to multiple locations.

Figure 6-4

Frame Relay requires the establishment of logical pairs of data link connections.

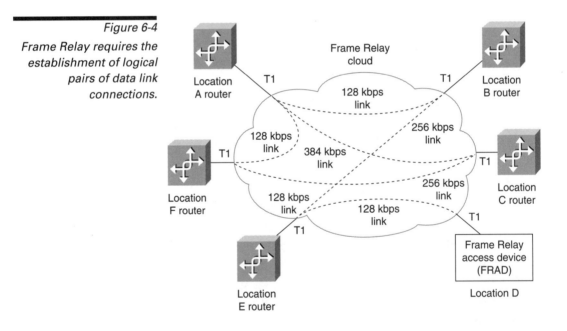

Balanced against this minimization of access facilities cost is a reduction in performance relative to point-to-point leased lines. Frame Relay introduces a significant amount of overhead in terms of framing and protocol, which is added to the overheads of the point-to-point leased line. The rule of thumb that guides engineering the DLCI and CIRs on a Frame Relay connection is to subscribe a maximum of 1.024 Mbps of the 1.544 Mbps of available bandwidth. This guarantees that each DLCI receives its committed information rate, and that there is a margin of extra bandwidth for temporarily *bursting* beyond this preset rate. Frame Relay supports bursting beyond the CIR, up to the amount of unused bandwidth currently on the transmission facility.

It is possible to define a series of DLCIs with a cumulative CIR that is greater than the bandwidth available on the transmission facility. Continuing the example of T-1–based Frame Relay, one could configure 2.048 Mbps of CIRs over the 1.544 Mbps facility. This is known as *oversubscription*. Oversubscription is, from the consumer's perspective, an undesirable practice. It assumes that not all the DLCIs will be active and, therefore, will not be consuming their entire CIR at any given time. This is not an unreasonable assumption, but will most likely result in the sporadic degradation of service during peak usage periods.

Cell-Switched Facilities

A close relative to packet switching is cell switching. The difference between a packet and a cell is the length of the structure. A packet is a variable-length data structure, whereas a cell is a fixed-length data structure. The most familiar cell-switched technology is ATM. Although, technically speaking, ATM is currently a circuit-switched technology, it is best categorized independently.

ATM

ATM was originally designed as an asynchronous transport mechanism for broadband ISDN. It was speculated that its low latency and high bit rate would make it equally ideal for use in LANs. The subsequent market hype has almost completely cemented its reputation as a LAN technology, to the exclusion of its capabilities as a WAN technology.

ATM can operate at many different transmission rates. These rates were, originally, to be based on the Optical Carrier (OC) line specifications. This was consistent with its original mission. Therefore, the basic rate of ATM transmission was set to the OC-3 standard of 155.52 Mbps. Provisions were made to support the OC-1 rate of 51.84 Mbps, as well as for scaling upward to the 2.488 Gbps of the OC-48 specification. This ensured that ATM would scale well within the well-accepted architecture of the public switched networks. For more information on the OC standards, refer to the section titled "The OC System" later in this chapter.

NOTE

There is even work in progress, under the auspices of the ATM Forum, to scale ATM up to a 10 Gbps rate.

As a cell-switched WAN technology, ATM is commercially available at either 1.544 Mbps (DS-1) or 44.736 Mbps (DS-3) over copper transmission facilities, although this availability varies geographically. In some locations, carriers are offering ATM service over fiber-optic transmission facilities. These services range from 622 Mbps (OC-12) to 2 Gbps (OC-48) and even up to approximately 10 Gbps (OC-192).

Initially, wide area ATM was only made available using permanent virtual circuits, much like the DLCIs of Frame Relay. Ultimately, however, wide area ATM will be a switched technology capable of forwarding individual cells without requiring the overheads of establishing a permanent virtual circuit or reserving bandwidth.

CARRIER SYSTEM STANDARDS

Like any other standard networking technology, WAN transmission facilities feature standardized transmission schemes. Such schemes define transmission rates and media types, as well as framing formats and multiplexing methodologies. There are many such schemes and they vary by both geography and technology. Some of the more commonly encountered standards include the following:

- ANSI's Digital Signal Hierarchy

- ITU's Digital Signal Hierarchy

- SONET's Optical Carrier System

- SONET's Synchronous Transport Signal System

These standards are implemented in carrier systems. The remainder of this chapter provides an overview of some of the more useful signaling standards, as well as the carrier systems that are their physical embodiment.

ANSI's Digital Signal Hierarchy

The American National Standards Institute (ANSI) set the standards for digital signal transmission during the early 1980s. This family of standards became known as the Digital Signal Hierarchy (DSH). This hierarchy consists of six specifications, numbered DS-0 through DS-4. Table 6-1 presents these specifications, their corresponding bandwidths, and the number of supported voice channels.

Table 6-1   *ANSI's Digital Signal Standards*

Digital Signal Standard	Bandwidth	Number of Voice Channels
DS-0	64 kbps	1
DS-1	1.544 Mbps	24
DS-1C	3.152 Mbps	48
DS-2	6.312 Mbps	96
DS-3	44.736 Mbps	672
DS-4	274.176 Mbps	4,032

NOTE

DS-0 defines the minimum amount of bandwidth required to transport digitized voice. Given that voice communication typically occurs using an 8 KHz circuit, and digitizing it requires an eight-fold increase in bandwidth, the DS-0 band was defined at 64 kbps. It is not, however, the basic building block of leased lines. That honor goes to the DS-1 specification. DS-0 describes the voice channels that are carved from the other digital signaling specifications.

ANSI's DS standards have been implemented in the telephony carrier system called the *T-carrier system*. There is a direct, one-to-one correlation between T-carrier circuits and their DS namesakes. For example, the DS-1 standard is embodied in the T-1 transmission facility. T-3 is the physical implementation of the DS-3. For more information on the T-carrier system, refer to the section titled "The T-Carrier System" later in this chapter.

After even a cursory glance through Table 6-1, you can probably recognize at least one of the standards. In North America and Japan, the T-1 has become so prevalent in networking that almost every network-aware technical person recognizes the 1.544 Mbps bandwidth and associates it with that transmission facility. Some people might even recognize the 44.736 Mbps of the T-3. The other standards might not be as readily recognized.

The DS-1C, from a functional perspective, is two DS-1s integrated into a common transmission facility. The DS-2 and DS-4 standards have never achieved widespread utilization. This is primarily due to their cost-versus-performance ratios. DS-3 service is also expensive, but offers a better combination of price and bandwidth than its alternatives.

Today, virtually every situation that requires bandwidth in excess of the DS-3 is satisfied with SONET technology (covered in a following section). Therefore, the T-carrier system is used only for T-1, fractional T-1, and T-3 services. The remaining T-n specifications have fallen into disuse.

ITU's Digital Signal Hierarchy

It is important to note that the DSH presented in Table 6-1 was standardized by ANSI. ANSI, an American standards body, doesn't necessarily receive worldwide acceptance of its standards work. In Europe, for example, the ITU (formerly CCITT) created its own family of standards for digital signaling. These standards were named after the committee that recommended them to the ITU: the Conference of European Posts and Telecommunications Administration (CEPT). Table 6-2 lists these CEPT standards.

Table 6-2   *ITU's CEPT Digital Signal Standards*

Digital Signal Standard	Bandwidth	Number of Voice Channels
CEPT-1	2.048 Mbps	30
CEPT-2	8.448 Mbps	120
CEPT-3	34.368 Mbps	480
CEPT-4	139.264 Mbps	1,920
CEPT-5	565.148 Mbps	7,680

Although the ITU standards use the same basic channel as the 64 kbps DS-0, their aggregations are very different. Therefore, the European version of a T-1 is known as the E-1, and it supports 2.048 Mbps compared to the T-1's 1.544 Mbps. Internetworking between Europe and North America presents the challenge of mismatched standards and usually results in unusable channels.

NOTE

If you perform the mathematics, you can see that the CEPT-1 standard (implemented in the European E-1 transmission facility) actually contains enough bandwidth for 32 channels of 64 kbps each. The CEPT-1, and consequently the E-1 circuit, can support a maximum of 30 usable channels. The remaining two channels are reserved for synchronization and signaling. This differs from ANSI's approach in its DS specifications. ANSI imposes framing and timing within each channel, and thereby reduces available bandwidth from the stated transmission rate.

SONET's Carrier Systems

SONET, which stands for Synchronous Optical Network, is basically a series of optically based transmission systems. It is a highly specialized technology set that was designed expressly for use by telecommunications carriers. It was intended to provide interoperability among switching systems made by different manufacturers, as well as to buffer the disparities in capacity and transmission rates of those myriad systems.

To fulfill this role, physical interfaces, framing conventions, and two families of signaling standards were developed. These two families range from 51.84 Mbps to 2.48 Gbps.

NOTE

SONET is an ANSI standard that has been embraced, but not wholly adopted, by the ITU. The ITU's version varies subtly, but in significant ways, and is known as the Synchronous Digital Hierarchy (SDH). The basic rate of transmission in SDH is 155.52 Mbps, unlike the 51.84 Mbps basic rate of SONET.

Another fairly minor difference is that SDH's copper-based transmission standards are known as synchronous transport modules (STMs) rather than synchronous transport signals (STSs).

SONET supports two transmission systems, both discussed in the following sections:

- The OC system

- The Synchronous Transport Signal (STS) system

The OC System

One last series of standards that warrants examination is the Optical Carrier (OC) system. Table 6-3 presents the OC standards, their bandwidth, and the number of DS-0 and DS-1 channels that each supports.

Table 6-3   *Optical Carrier Bandwidths*

Optical Carrier Line	Bandwidth	DS0 Channels	DS1 Channels
OC-1	51.84 Mbps	672	28
OC-3	155.52 Mbps	2,016	84
OC-9	466.56 Mbps	6,048	252
OC-12	622.08 Mbps	8,064	336
OC-18	933.12 Mbps	12,096	504
OC-24	1.244 Gbps	16,128	672
OC-36	1.866 Gbps	24,192	1,008
OC-48	2.488 Gbps	32,256	1,344

In theory, this table can be expanded almost indefinitely by continuing to multiply the basic OC-1. Service is available at OC-192 rates, for example, even though OC-192 has not yet been standardized. Of these specified standards, only OC-1, OC-3, OC-12, and OC-48 are commonly used. The other standards have fallen into disuse. They are defined, but not used.

As optical signaling technology continues to improve, it is reasonable to expect greater multiples of the OC-1 rate to become standardized. In fact, the technology exists to transmit at an OC-192 rate! It is also likely that these larger multiples will be retrofitted into the SONET and/or SDH standards.

The STS System

SONET's OC rates can also be implemented over an electrical signaling system using copper wiring. These electrical rates are indicated with an STS designation rather than the OC designation. Aside from this physical difference, there is a one-to-one correlation between the two standards. In other words, STS-1 is directly equivalent to OC-1; STS-3 equals the OC-3 rate of 155.52 Mbps; and so forth.

It is important to note that the STS-n standards span up to STS-48, which yields 2.488 Gbps of bandwidth. Providing this bandwidth to electrical signals over copper presents some significant technical challenges. For that matter, driving a copper wire at rates in excess of 155.52 Mbps becomes problematic over distances longer than 100 meters. Consequently, only STS-1 and STS-3 are actually defined and usable. The remainder are little more than theoretical constructs.

The T-Carrier System

The digital signaling standards listed in Table 6-1 are implemented through a physical carrier system. The most prevalent carrier system in North America is the T-carrier system. The leased lines delivered by this carrier system are prefaced with the letter *T*. A leased line delivered by T-carrier that conforms to the DS-1 standard is known as a T-1, for example. This important distinction is frequently lost on even the most technical people! Consequently, the terms DS-n and T-n (where n identifies a specific number) are often incorrectly used interchangeably. They are *not* interchangeable. DS-n identifies a standard, whereas T-n identifies a standards-compliant circuit.

The T-carrier system was originally designed to provide multiplexed voice communications over a single transmission facility. These facilities were used to transport calls between the various switching centers. A single T-1 circuit could carry 24 calls. Because the calls were in digital form, they could be amplified and regenerated en route to their destination. Therefore, digitized voice signals were inherently clearer than analog voice communications, which couldn't be regenerated.

Digitization of voice signals, however, presented some technical challenges. The T-carrier system implemented several improvements over the earlier carrier systems. These improvements were specifically designed to improve the quality of digitized voice transmission. In effect, these improvements made the T-carrier system a better transport mechanism for digitized transmissions, without bias toward voice or data. Specific improvements were made in line encoding techniques and framing formats.

T-Carrier Services

As described earlier in the section titled "ANSI's Digital Signal Hierarchy," only two of the DS standards are available as commercial services: T-3 and T-1. A third service is also available: fractional T-1. However, fractional T-1 is a T-1 with a fraction of the 24 available channels actually in use.

The T-3 transmission facility provides 44.736 Mbps of bandwidth. This bandwidth can be channelized into 672 separate channels of 64 kbps each or 28 T-1–equivalent channels. T-3s tend to be very expensive, especially as geographic distances increase. For any networking application that requires more bandwidth than a couple of T-1s can provide, a T-3 may actually prove to be the more economical solution.

The T-1 transmission facility is the foundation of the T-carrier system. This basic service provides customers with 1.544 Mbps of gross bandwidth. This can be channelized into as many as 24 channels of 64 kbps each, or left whole for high-bandwidth networking applications.

Networks that either can't afford the cost of a full T-1 or don't need its bandwidth may find the fractional T-1 service more attractive. Fractional T-1 is actually constructed from a T-1 circuit. Bandwidth on that circuit is fractionalized using a device known as a *channel bank*. The subcircuit is usually a 56 kbps circuit, but can be as small as 9.6 kbps. These subrate channels can then be delivered to different customers.

NOTE

Frames, in the context of the Digital Signaling specification, differ substantially from the highly developed and feature-rich frames used in LANs. DS frames are minimalist structures. Their functionality is limited to the synchronization of the transmission, and in some instances, error detection and network monitoring. As such, a digital signal frame is usually nothing more than a single bit inserted at fixed intervals in a bit stream. The extended superframe (ESF) format of the T-carrier system features one timing bit after 192 data bits, for example. This is its frame, and its sole function is synchronization.

SUMMARY

Routers are uniquely capable of interconnecting LAN and WAN facilities. This is the function for which they were originally designed. Supporting this capability necessitates supporting a very wide variety of both LAN and WAN transmission facilities. This chapter provides a mere overview of some of the more common of these facilities, as well as an introduction to some of the industry and national standards that define these facilities.

CHAPTER 7

The Mechanics of Routing Protocols

The previous chapters examined what routers do, how they can be used, and their various physical mechanisms. This chapter gives you a closer look at how they operate and describes the two primary types of routing: static and dynamic. Of these two, only dynamic uses routing protocols. As a result, dynamic routing is much more powerful and complicated.

Dynamic routing protocols are the technology that enables routers to perform some of their more vital functions. This includes discovering and maintaining routes, converging on an agreement of a network's topology, as well as some of the differences in the ways to calculate routes. Examining the mechanics of these basic functions will provide the context for a more in-depth examination of each of the more commonly encountered dynamic routing protocols, which is provided in Part III, "Routing Protocols."

ROUTING

Routers can route in a two basic ways. They can use preprogrammed *static* routes, or they can dynamically calculate routes using any one of a number of dynamic routing protocols. Dynamic routing protocols are used by routers to perform discover routes. Routers then mechanically forward packets (or datagrams) over those routes.

Statically programmed routers cannot discover routes; they lack any mechanism to communicate routing information with other routers. Statically programmed routers can only forward packets using routes defined by a network administrator.

In addition to static programming of routes, there are three broad categories of dynamic routing protocols:

- Distance-vector

- Link-state

- Hybrids

The primary differences between these types of dynamic routing protocols lie in the way that they discover and calculate new routes to destinations.

Two Functional Classes of Dynamic Routing Protocols

Routing protocols can be classified in many ways, including by many of their operational characteristics such as their field of use, the number of redundant routes to each supported destination, and so on. This book classifies them by the way that they discover and calculate routes. However, it is still useful to reference routing protocols by their field of use. In other words, categorize them by the role that they perform in an internetwork. There are two functional classes of dynamic routing protocols, for example: Interior Gateway Protocols (IGPs) and Exterior Gateway Protocols (EGPs).

Perhaps the easiest way to explain this is that IGPs are used *within* autonomous systems, such as intranets, whereas EGPs are used *between* autonomous systems. Consequently, the Border Gateway Protocol (BGP—an EGP) is the protocol used to calculate routes across the Internet. The Internet, from a routing perspective, is nothing more than a backbone transport for a global collection of privately owned and operated autonomous systems.

The specific protocols covered in Part III are identified as either IGPs or EGPs.

Static Routing

The simplest form of routing is preprogrammed and, consequently, static routes. The tasks of discovering routes and propagating them throughout a network are left to the internetwork's administrator(s).

A router programmed for static routing forwards packets out of predetermined ports. After the relationship between a destination address and a router port is configured, there is no longer any need for routers to attempt route discovery or even communicate information about routes.

There are many benefits to using static routes. For instance, statically programmed routes can make for a more secure network. There can be only a single path into, and out of, a network connected with a statically defined route. That is, of course, unless multiple static routes are defined.

Another benefit is that static routing is much more resource efficient. Static routing uses far less bandwidth across the transmission facilities, doesn't waste any router CPU cycles trying to calculate routes, and requires far less memory. In some networks, you might even be able to use smaller, less expensive routers by using static routes. Despite these benefits, you must be aware of some inherent limitations to static routing.

Drawbacks to Static Routing

In the event of a network failure, or other source of topology change, the onus is on the network administrator to manually accommodate the change. Figure 7-1 illustrates this point.

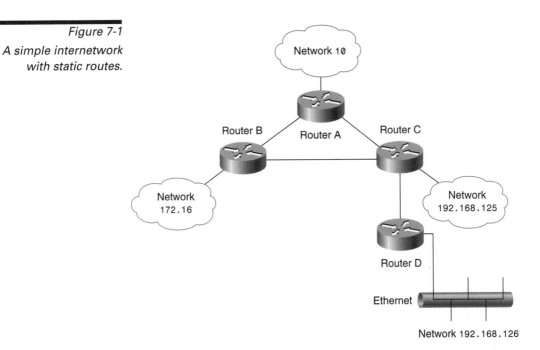

Figure 7-1

A simple internetwork
with static routes.

In this simple example, the networks' administrators have collaborated on a route redistribution scheme that they believe will minimize their workload as well as network traffic loads. The internetwork is relatively small, consisting of three different networks, one of which supports a stub network. Each network uses its own address space and a different dynamic routing protocol. Given the innate incompatibility of the three different routing protocols, the administrators chose not to redistribute routing information among their networks. Rather, they aggregated the routes into network numbers, and statically defined paths for them. Table 7-1 summarizes the routing tables of the three gateway routers. Router D connects a small, stub network to the other networks. As such, this router uses its serial port as a default gateway for all packets addressed to any IP address that does not belong to 192.168.126.

NOTE

For more information on redistributing routing information among dissimilar routing protocols, refer to Chapter 14, "Internetworking with Dissimilar Protocols."

Table 7-1   *Statically Defined Routes*

Router	Destination	Next Hop
A	172.16.0.0	B
A	192.168.0.0	C
B	10.0.0.0	A
B	192.168.0.0	C
C	10.0.0.0	A
C	172.16.0.0	B
C	192.168.126.0	D

In this scenario, Router A forwards all packets addressed to any hosts within the 172.16 network address space to Router B. Router A also forwards all packets addressed to hosts within network 192.168 to Router C. Router B forwards all packets addressed to any hosts within the 192.168 address space to Router C. Router B forwards packets addressed to hosts within Network 10 to Router A. Router C forwards all packets destined for Network 10 to Router A, those packets destined for 172.16 to Router B. Additionally, Router C forwards packets addressed to 192.168.126 to Router D, its stub network. This network is a stub because it is literally a dead end in the network. There is only one way in—and one way out. This small network depends completely on its link to Router C, and Router C itself, for connectivity to all the internetworked hosts.

In this example, a failure will result in unreachable destinations despite the fact that an alternative path is available for use. In Figure 7-2, the transmission facility between Gateway Routers A and C has failed.

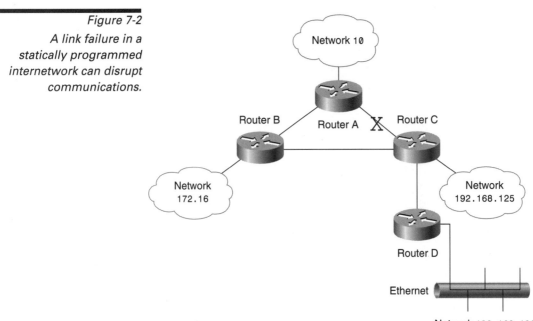

The effect of this failure is that end systems in networks 10 and 192.168 cannot communicate with each other, even though a valid route exists through Router B! Table 7-2 summarizes the effects of this type of failure on the routing tables.

Table 7-2 *Static Routes with a Failed Link*

Router	Destination	Next Hop
A	172.16.0.0	B
A	192.168.0.0	C - Unreachable
B	10.0.0.0	A

Table 7-2 *Static Routes with a Failed Link, continued*

Router	Destination	Next Hop
B	192.168.0.0	C
C	10.0.0.0	A - Unreachable
C	172.16.0.0	B

The lack of any dynamic mechanism prevents Routers A and C from recognizing the link failure. They are not using a routing protocol that would otherwise discover and test the qualities of the links to known destinations. Consequently, they cannot discover the alternative path through Router B. Although this is a valid and usable route, their programming prevents them from discovering it or using it. This situation will remain constant until the network administrator takes corrective action manually.

What's Static Routing Good For?

At this point, you might be wondering what possible benefit there might be in statically defined routes. Static routing is good only for very small networks that only have a single path to any given destination. In such cases, static routing can be the most efficient routing mechanism because it doesn't consume bandwidth trying to discover routes or communicate with other routers.

As networks grow larger, and add redundant paths to destinations, static routing becomes a labor-intensive liability. Any changes in the availability of routers or transmission facilities in the WAN must be manually discovered and programmed in. WANs that feature more complex topologies that offer multiple potential paths absolutely require dynamic routing. Attempts to use static routing in complex, multipath WANs will defeat the purpose of having that route redundancy.

At times, statically defined routes are desirable, even in large or complex networks. Static routes can be configured to enhance security. Your company's connection to the Internet could have a statically defined route to a security server. No ingress would be possible without having first passed whatever authentication mechanisms the security server provides.

Alternatively, statically defined routes might be extremely useful in building extranet connections using IP to other companies that your employer does a lot of business with. Finally, static routes might be the best way to connect small locations with stub networks to your WAN. The point is that static routes can be quite useful. You just need to understand what they can and can't do.

Distance-Vector Routing

In routing based on distance-vector algorithms, also sometimes called Bellman-Ford algorithms, the algorithms periodically pass copies of their routing tables to their immediate network neighbors. Each recipient adds a distance vector—that is, its own distance "value"—to the table and forwards it on to its immediate neighbors. This process occurs in an omnidirectional manner among immediately neighboring routers. This step-by-step process results in each router learning about other routers and developing a cumulative perspective of network "distances."

NOTE

Network distances and costs are somewhat euphemistic in this context. They do not relate directly to either physical distances or monetary costs.

The cumulative table is then used to update each router's routing tables. When completed, each router has learned vague information about the "distances" to networked resources. It does not learn anything specific about other routers, or the network's actual topology.

Drawbacks to Distance-Vector Routing

Under certain circumstances, distance-vector routing can actually create routing problems for distance-vector protocols. A failure or other change in the network, for example, requires some time for the routers to *converge* on a new understanding of the network's topology. During the convergence process, the network may be vulnerable to inconsistent routing, and even infinite loops. Safeguards can contain many of these risks, but the fact remains that the network's performance is at risk during the convergence process. Therefore, older distance-vector protocols that are slow to converge may not be appropriate for large, complex WANs.

Even in smaller networks, distance-vector routing protocols may be problematic at worst, or suboptimal at best. This is because the simplicity that is this genre's strength can also be a source of weakness. Figure 7-3 presents an internetwork with specific geographic locations.

In this example, Network 1 is in New York, Network 2 is in Seattle, Network 3 is in Philadelphia, and Network 4 is in Minneapolis. The distance-vector routing protocol uses a statically assigned cost of 1 for each hop, regardless of the distance of the link or even its bandwidth. Table 7-3 summarizes the number of hops to each of the destination network numbers. Notice that the routers do not have to create separate entries in their routing tables for every known end system. They can do so, but instead usually *summarize* routes. Route summarization is the truncation of the host portion of an IP address; only the network address is stored. In theory, the same path can be used to get to all the hosts or end systems on any given network. Therefore, nothing is gained by creating separate entries for each host address.

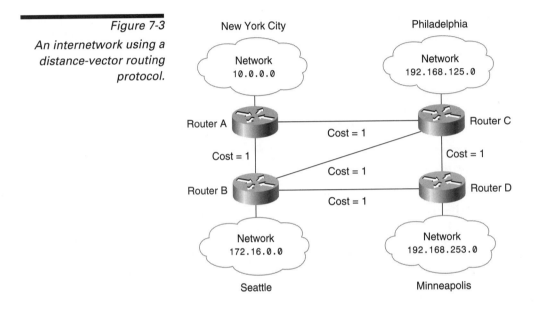

Figure 7-3

An internetwork using a distance-vector routing protocol.

Table 7-3   *The Number of Hops with the Distance-Vector Protocol*

Router	Destination	Next Hop	Number of Hops to Destination
A	172.16.0.0	B	1
A	192.168.125.0	C	1
A	192.168.253.0	B or C	2
B	10.0.0.0	A	1
B	192.168.125.0	C	1
B	192.168.253.0	D	1
C	10.0.0.0	A	1
C	172.16.0.0	B	1
C	192.168.253.0	D	1

Table 7-3 *The Number of Hops with the Distance-Vector Protocol, continued*

Router	Destination	Next Hop	Number of Hops to Destination
D	10.0.0.0	B or C	2
D	172.16.0.0	B	1
D	192.168.125.0	C	1

In any internetwork with redundant routes, it is better to use a distance-vector protocol than to use static routes. This is because distance-vector routing protocols can automatically detect and correct failures in the network. Unfortunately, they aren't perfect. Consider the routing table entries for Gateway Router A, for example. This is the New York gateway. From its perspective, the Minneapolis gateway is two hops away, regardless of whether it goes through Philadelphia or Seattle. In other words, this router would be indifferent to accessing Minneapolis through either Philadelphia or Seattle.

If all the variables in the network were held constant (including such things as traffic levels, the bandwidth of each link, and even transmission technology), the geographically shortest path would incur the least amount of propagation delay. Therefore, logic dictates taking the shorter route, through Philadelphia. In reality, such logic is beyond the capabilities of simple distance-vector protocols. Distance-vector protocols aren't exactly limited by this because propagation delay is often the least significant of the factors driving the performance of a route. Bandwidth and traffic levels can both have much more noticeable effects on the performance of a network.

What's Distance-Vector Routing Good For?

Generally speaking, distance-vector protocols are very simple protocols that are easy to configure, maintain, and use. Consequently, they prove quite useful in very small networks that have few, if any, redundant paths and no stringent network performance requirements. The epitome of the distance-vector routing protocol is *Routing Information Protocol* (RIP). RIP uses a single distance metric (cost) to determine the best next path to take for any given packet. RIP has been widely used for decades, and has only recently warranted updating. For more information on RIP, refer to Chapter 8, "Routing Information Protocol," and Chapter 9, "Routing Information Protocol Version 2."

Link-State Routing

Link-state routing algorithms, known cumulatively as *shortest path first* (SPF) protocols, maintain a complex database of the network's topology. Unlike distance-vector protocols, link-state protocols develop and maintain a full knowledge of the network's routers as well as how they interconnect. This is achieved via the exchange of *link-state advertisements* (LSAs) with other routers in a network.

Each router that has exchanged LSAs constructs a topological database using all received LSAs. An SPF algorithm is then used to compute reachability to networked destinations. This information is used to update the routing table. This process can discover changes in the network topology caused by component failure or network growth.

In fact, the LSA exchange is triggered by an event in the network, instead of running periodically. This can greatly expedite the convergence process because there is no need to wait for a series of arbitrary timers to expire before the networked routers can begin to converge!

If the internetwork depicted in Figure 7-3 were to use a link-state routing protocol, the concerns about connectivity between New York and Minneapolis would be rendered moot. Depending on the actual protocol employed, and the metrics selected, it is highly likely that the routing protocol could discriminate between the two paths and try to use the best one. Table 7-4 summarizes the contents of the gateways' routing tables.

Table 7-4 *Hop Counts in a Link-State Network*

Router	Destination	Next Hop	Number of Hops to Destination
A	172.16.0.0	B	1
A	192.168.125.0	C	1
A	192.168.253.0	B	2
A	192.168.253.0	C	2
B	10.0.0.0	A	1
B	192.168.125.0	C	1
B	192.168.253.0	D	1
C	10.0.0.0	A	1
C	172.16.0.0	B	1
C	192.168.253.0	D	1
D	10.0.0.0	B	2
D	10.0.0.0	C	2
D	172.16.0.0	B	1
D	192.168.125.0	C	1

As is evident in this table's routing entries for the New York-to-Minneapolis routes, a link-state protocol would remember both routes. Some link-state protocols may even provide a means to assess the performance capabilities of these two routes, and bias toward the better-performing one. If the better-performing path, for example the route through Philadelphia, were to experience operational difficulties of any kind (including congestion or component failure), the link-state routing protocol would detect this change and begin forwarding packets through Seattle.

Drawbacks to Link-State Routing

Despite all its features and flexibility, link-state routing raises two potential concerns:

- During the initial discovery process, link-state routing protocols can flood the network's transmission facilities, and thereby significantly decrease the network's capability to transport data. This performance degradation is temporary but can be very noticeable. Whether this flooding process will impede a network's performance noticeably depends on two things: the amount of available bandwidth and the number of routers that must exchange routing information. Flooding in large networks with relatively small links (such as low-bandwidth DLCIs on a Frame Relay network) will be much more noticeable than a similar exercise on a small network with large-sized links (such as T3s).

- Link-state routing is both memory and processor intensive. Consequently, more fully configured routers are required to support link-state routing than distance-vector routing. This increases the cost of the routers that are configured for link-state routing.

These are hardly fatal flaws in the link-state approach to routing. The potential performance impacts of both can be addressed, and resolved, through foresight, planning, and engineering.

What's Link-State Routing Good For?

The link-state approach to dynamic routing can be quite useful in networks of any size. In a well-designed network, a link-state routing protocol will enable your network to gracefully weather the effects of unexpected topological change. Using events, such as changes, to drive updates (rather than fixed-interval timers) enables convergence to begin that much more quickly after a topological change.

The overheads of the frequent, time-driven updates of a distance-vector routing protocol are also avoided. This allows more bandwidth to be used for routing traffic rather than for network maintenance, provided you design your network properly.

A side benefit of the bandwidth efficiency of link-state routing protocols is that they facilitate network scalability better than either static routes or distance-vector protocols. When juxtaposed with their limitations, it is easy to see that link-state routing is best in larger, more complicated networks or in networks that must be highly scalable. It may be challenging to initially configure a link-state protocol in a large network, but is well worth the effort in the long run. For more information on link-state routing, refer to Chapter 12, "Open Shortest Path First."

Hybridized Routing

The last form of routing discipline is hybridization. The balanced hybrid routing protocols use distance-vector metrics but emphasize more accurate metrics than conventional distance-vector protocols. They also converge more rapidly than distance-vector protocols but avoid the overheads of link-state updates. Balanced hybrids are event driven rather than periodic and thereby conserve bandwidth for real applications.

Although "open" balanced hybrid protocols exist, this form is almost exclusively associated with the proprietary creation of a single company, Cisco Systems, Inc. Its protocol, Enhanced Interior Gateway Routing Protocol (EIGRP), was designed to combine the best aspects of distance-vector and link-state routing protocols without incurring any of their performance limitations or penalties. Given that this class of dynamic routing protocol is dominated by EIGRP, its benefits and limitations are examined in more detail in Chapter 11, "Enhanced Interior Gateway Routing Protocol," rather than examined generically in this chapter.

Performance Characteristics of Hybridized Routing

One of the most difficult, yet critical, tasks that must be surmounted when building an internetwork is the selection of a routing protocol. As the preceding sections indicate, a rich palette of options await the prospective internetwork architect. Although the preceding overviews should help you to differentiate among the various classes of dynamic routing protocols, this is just the beginning. You still need to select a specific routing protocol, or protocols, from the variety that may be available in each class.

One of the best ways to start narrowing down the list of potential protocols is by evaluating each protocol's performance characteristics relative to projected requirements. Unlike hardware, you can't just compare routing protocols' packets-per-second or bandwidth ratings. They don't exist! Instead, you should look at how effectively each protocol performs the various tasks that support internetworking.

Two of the most important of these tasks are convergence and route calculation. The remaining sections of this chapter examine each of these concepts in more detail and should adequately prepare you for the more detailed examinations of individual protocols in the following chapters.

NOTE

Of course, many other performance attributes must be considered, including maximum network diameter and how well a given protocol accommodates heavy traffic loads. Such characteristics, however, tend to be more applicable to specific protocols than to the three classes of dynamic routing protocols identified earlier in this chapter. As such, these performance characteristics are examined individually in Part III.

CONVERGENCE

One of the most fascinating aspects of routing is a concept known as *convergence*. Quite simply, whenever a change occurs in a network's topology, or shape, all the routers in that network must develop a new understanding of what the network's topology is. This process is both collaborative and independent; the routers share information with each other, but must independently calculate the impacts of the topology change on their own routes. Because they must mutually develop an agreement of the new topology independently from different perspectives, they are said to *converge* on this consensus.

Convergence is necessary because routers are intelligent devices that can make their own routing decisions. This is simultaneously a source of strength and vulnerability. Under normal operating conditions, this independent and distributed intelligence is a source of tremendous advantage. During changes in the network's topology, the process of converging on a new consensus of the network's shape may actually introduce instability and routing problems.

Accommodating Topological Changes

Unfortunately, the independent nature of routers can also be a source of vulnerability whenever a change occurs in the network's topology. Such changes, by their very nature, change a network's topology. Figure 7-4 illustrates how a change in the network is, in fact, a change in its topology.

Figure 7-4
A four-gateway internetwork.

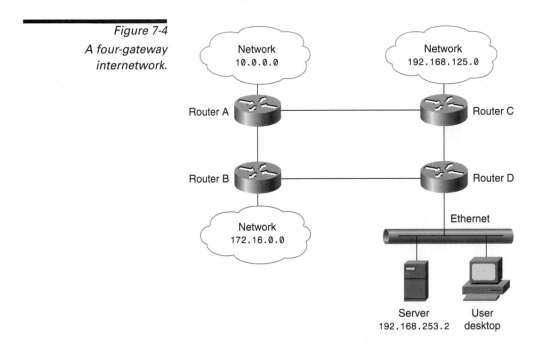

Figure 7-4 features another fairly simple, four-node internetwork with some route redundancy. Table 7-5 summarizes the routing tables of the four routers. For the sake of this example, consider this table to be preconvergence routing table information.

Table 7-5   *Preconvergence Routing Table Contents*

Router	Destination	Next Hop	Number of Hops to Destination
A	172.16.0.0	B	1
A	192.168.125.0	C	1
A	192.168.253.0	B or C	2
B	10.0.0.0	A	1
B	192.168.125.0	A or D	2
B	192.168.253.0	D	1
C	10.0.0.0	A	1
C	172.16.0.0	A or D	2
C	192.168.253.0	D	1
D	10.0.0.0	B or C	2
D	172.16.0.0	B	1
D	192.168.125.0	C	1

If packets sent by Router C to Server 192.168.253.2 suddenly become undeliverable, it is likely that an error occurred somewhere in the network. This could have been caused by a seemingly infinite number of different, specific failures. Some of the more common suspects include the following:

- The server has failed completely (due to either a hardware, software, or electrical failure).

- The LAN connection to the server has failed.

- Router D has experienced a total failure.

- Router D's serial interface port to router C has failed.

- The transmission facility between Gateway Routers C and D has failed.

- Router C's serial interface port to Router D has failed.

Obviously, the new network topology can't be determined until the exact location of the failure has been identified. Similarly, the routers cannot attempt to route around the problem until the failure location has been isolated. If either of the first two scenarios occurred, server 192.168.253.2 would be completely unavailable to all the users of the internetwork, regardless of any route redundancy that may have been built into the network.

Similarly, if router D had failed completely, all the LAN-attached resources at that location would be isolated from the rest of the network. If the failure was either a partial failure of that router, or elsewhere in the network, however, there might still be a way to reach Server 192.168.253.2. Finding a new route to 192.168.253.2 requires the network's routers to recognize and agree on which piece of the network failed. In effect, subtracting this component from the network changes the network's topology.

To continue with the example, assume that Router D's serial interface port to router C has failed. This renders the link between C and D unusable. Figure 7-5 illustrates the new network topology.

Routers using a dynamic routing protocol would quickly determine that Server 192.168.253.2 was unreachable through their current, preferred route. Individually, none of the routers could determine where the actual failure occurred, nor could they determine whether any viable alternative routes still existed. By sharing information with each other, however, a new composite picture of the network can be developed.

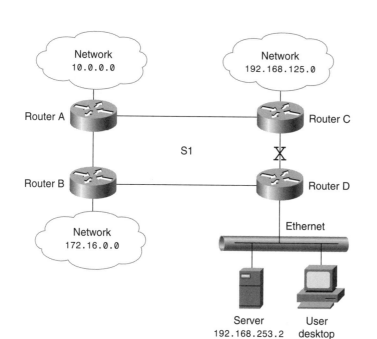

Figure 7-5
The link between Routers C and D is unusable.

NOTE

For the purposes of this chapter, this example uses an intentionally generic method of convergence. More specific details about each routing protocol's convergence characteristics are presented in Part III.

The routing protocol used in this internetwork is relatively simple. It limits each router to exchanging routing information with its immediate neighbors, although it supports the recording of multiple routes per destination. Table 7-6 summarizes the pairs of immediately adjacent routers illustrated in Figure 7-5.

Table 7-6   *Routers that Share Routing Information with Immediate Neighbors*

Router	A	B	C	D
A	—	Yes	Yes	No
B	Yes	—	No	Yes
C	Yes	No	—	Yes
D	No	Yes	Yes	—

The entries in Table 7-6 that contain the word *Yes* indicate a physically adjacent pair of routers that would exchange routing information. The entries that contain a dash denote the same router: A router cannot be adjacent to itself. Finally, those entries that contain the word *No* indicate nonadjacent routers that cannot directly exchange routing information. Such routers must rely on their adjacent neighbors for updates about destinations on non-adjacent routers.

From this table, it is apparent that because they are not directly connected to each other, Routers A and D must rely on Routers B and C for information about each other's destinations. Similarly, Routers B and C must rely on Routers A and D for information about each other's destinations.

Figure 7-6 shows this sharing of routing information between immediate neighbors.

The important implication in this scenario is that, because not every router is immediately adjacent to every other router, more than one routing update may be required to fully propagate new routing information that accommodates the failed link. Therefore, accommodating topological change is an iterative and communal process.

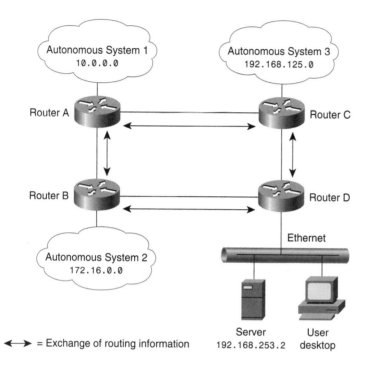

Figure 7-6
Immediate neighbors sharing routing data.

For the sake of simplicity, assume that convergence occurs within two routing table updates in this example. During the first iteration, the routers are starting to converge on a new understanding of their topology. Routers C and D, because of the unusable link between them, cannot exchange routing information. Consequently, they invalidate this route and all destinations that use it. Table 7-7 summarizes the contents of the four routers' routing tables *during* the convergence process. Note that the contents of some routing tables may reflect the mistaken belief that the link between Routers C and D is still valid.

Table 7-7 *Midconvergence Routing Table Contents*

Gateway Router	Destination	Next Hop	Number of Hops to Destination
A	`172.16.0.0`	B	1
A	`192.168.125.0`	C	1
A	`192.168.253.0`	B or C	2
B	`10.0.0.0`	A	1
B	`192.168.125.0`	A or D	2
B	`192.168.253.0`	D	1
C	`10.0.0.0`	A	1
C	`172.16.0.0`	A only (D failed)	2
C	`192.168.253.0`	D - Invalid route	Not reachable
D	`10.0.0.0`	B or C	2
D	`172.16.0.0`	B	1
D	`192.168.125.0`	C - Invalid route	Not reachable

In Table 7-7, Routers C and D have invalidated the route between them. Routers A and B, however, still believe that their routes through this link are viable. They must await a routing update from either Router C and/or D before they can recognize the change in the internetwork's topology.

Table 7-8 contains the contents of the four routers' routing tables *after* they have converged on a new topology. Remember that this is an intentionally generic depiction of the convergence process; it is not indicative of any particular routing protocol's mechanics.

Table 7-8 *Postconvergence Routing Table Contents*

Router	Destination Name	Next Hop	Number of Hops to Destination
A	172.16.0.0	B	1
A	192.168.125.0	C	1
A	192.168.253.0	B only	2
B	10.0.0.0	A	1
B	192.168.125.0	A only	2
B	192.168.253.0	D	1
C	10.0.0.0	A	1
C	172.16.0.0	A only	2
C	192.168.253.0	A	3
D	10.0.0.0	B only	2
D	172.16.0.0	B	1
D	192.168.125.0	B only	3

As evident in Table 7-8, all the routers in the internetwork eventually agree that the link between C and D is unusable, but that destinations in each autonomous system are still reachable via an alternative route.

Convergence Time

It is virtually impossible for all routers in a network to simultaneously detect a topology change. In fact, depending on the routing protocol in use, as well as numerous other factors, a considerable time delay may pass before all the routers in that network reach a consensus, or agreement, on what the new topology is. This delay is referred to as *convergence time*. The important thing to remember is that convergence is not immediate. The only uncertainty is how much time is required for convergence to occur.

Some factors that can exacerbate the time delay inherent in convergence include the following:

- A router's distance (in hops) from the point of change

- The number of routers in the network that use dynamic routing protocols

- Bandwidth and traffic load on communications links

- A router's load

- Traffic patterns vis-à-vis the topological change

- The routing protocol used

The effects of some of these factors can be minimized through careful network engineering. A network can be engineered to minimize the load on any given router or communications link, for example. Other factors, such as the number of routers in the network, must be accepted as risks inherent in a network's design. It may be possible, however, to engineer the network such that fewer routers need to converge! By using static routes to interconnect stubs to the network, you reduce the number of routers that must converge. This directly reduces convergence times. Given these factors, it is clear that the two keys to minimizing convergence times are

- Selection of a routing protocol that can calculate routes efficiently

- Designing the network properly

ROUTE CALCULATION

As demonstrated through the examples in the preceding section, convergence is absolutely critical to a network's capability to respond to operational fluctuations. The key factor in convergence is communications among the routers in the network. Routing protocols are responsible for providing this function. Specifically, these protocols are designed to enable routers to share information about routes to the various destinations within the network.

Route Flapping

One symptom of network instability that may arise is known as *route flapping*. Route flapping is just the rapid vacillation between two, or more, routes. Flapping happens during a topology change. All the routers in the network must converge on a consensus of the new topology. Toward this end, they begin sharing routing information.

In an unstable network, a router (or routers) may be unable to decide on a route to a destination. Remember that during convergence a router may alter its primary route to any given destination as a result of the last-received update. In complex, but unstable networks with redundant routes, a router may find itself deciding on a different route to a given destination every time it receives an update. Each update nullifies the previous decision and triggers another update to the other routers. These other routers, in turn, adjust their own routing tables and generate "new" updates. This vicious cycle is known as flapping. You may find it necessary to power down affected routers and slowly develop convergence in your network, one router at a time.

Unfortunately, all routing protocols are not created equal. In fact, one of the best ways to assess the suitability of a routing protocol is to evaluate its capabilities to calculate routes and converge relative to other routing protocols. It should be obvious from the previous list of factors that convergence times may be difficult for you to calculate with any degree of certainty. Your router vendor may be able to assist you with this process, even if the vendor provides you with general estimates only.

A routing protocol's convergence capability is a function of its capability to calculate routes. The efficacy of a routing protocol's route calculation is based on several factors:

- Whether the protocol calculates, and stores, multiple routes to each destination

- The manner in which routing updates are initiated

- The metrics used to calculate distances or costs

Storing Multiple Routes

Some routing protocols attempt to improve their operational efficiency by only recording a single route (ideally, the best route) to each known destination. The drawback to this approach is that when a topology change occurs, each router must calculate a new route through the network for the impacted destinations.

Other protocols accept the processing overheads that accompany larger routing table sizes and store multiple routes to each destination. Under normal operating conditions, multiple routes enable the router to balance traffic loads across multiple links. If, or when, a topology change occurs, the routers already have alternative routes to the impacted destinations in their routing tables. Having an alternative route already mapped out does not necessarily accelerate the convergence process. It does, however, enable networks to more gracefully sustain topology changes.

Initiating Updates

As you will see in Part III, some protocols use the passage of time to initiate routing updates. Others are event driven. That is, they are initiated whenever a topological change is detected. Holding all other variables constant, event-driven updates result in shorter convergence times than timed updates.

Timed Updates

A timed update is a very simple mechanism. Time is decremented in a counter as it elapses. When a specified period of time has elapsed, an update is performed regardless of whether a topological change has occurred. This has two implications:

- Many updates will be performed unnecessarily. This wastes bandwidth and router resources.

- Convergence times can be needlessly inflated if route calculations are driven by the passing of time.

Event-Driven Updates

Event-driven updates are a much more sophisticated means of initiating routing updates. Ostensibly, an update is initiated only when a change in the network's topology has been detected. Given that a topology change is what creates the need for convergence, this approach is obviously the more efficient one.

You can select an update initiator just by selecting a routing protocol; each protocol implements either one or the other. Therefore, this is one factor that must be considered when selecting a routing protocol.

Routing Metrics

The routing protocol determines another important mechanism: its metric(s). There is a wide disparity in terms of both the number and the type of metrics used.

Quantity of Metrics

Simple routing protocols support as few as one or two routing metrics. More sophisticated protocols can support five or more metrics. It is safe to assume that the more metrics there are, the more varied and specific they are. Therefore, the greater the variety of available metrics, the greater your ability to tailor the network's operation to your particular needs. For example, the simple distance-vector protocols use a euphemistic metric: distance. In reality, that distance is not related at all to geographic mileage, much less to the physical cable mileage that separates source and destination machines. Instead, it usually just counts the number of hops between those two points.

Link-state protocols may afford the capability to calculate routes based on several factors:

- Traffic load

- Available bandwidth

- Propagation delay

- The network cost of a connection (although this metric tends to be more of an estimate than an actual value)

Most of these factors are highly dynamic in a network; they vary by time of day, day of week, and so forth. The important thing to remember is that as they vary, so does the network's performance.

Therefore, the intent of dynamic routing metrics is to allow optimal routing decisions to be made using the most current information available.

Static Versus Dynamic Metrics

Some metrics are simplistic and static, whereas others are highly sophisticated and dynamic. Static metrics usually offer the capability to customize their values when they are configured. After this is done, each value remains a constant until it is manually changed.

Dynamic protocols enable routing decisions to be made based on real-time information about the state of the network. These protocols are supported only by the more sophisticated link-state or hybridized routing protocols.

SUMMARY

One of the most important decisions in the development of an internetwork is the selection of a routing protocol or protocols. Such selection should be done carefully and with an appreciation for the long-term implications of your decisions. This chapter provides a generic overview of the various ways that routing can be performed, as well as the benefits and limitations of each. Part III builds on this overview with specific details about how the more commonly encountered routing protocols operate.

PART III

Routing Protocols

CHAPTER 8

Routing Information Protocol

The Routing Information Protocol, or RIP as it is commonly called, is one of the most enduring of all routing protocols. RIP is one of a class of protocols that is based on distance-vector routing algorithms that predate ARPANET. These algorithms were academically described between 1957 and 1962. Throughout the 1960s, these algorithms were widely implemented by different companies and marketed under different names. The resulting products were highly related but, because of proprietary enhancements, couldn't offer complete interoperability.

This chapter traces the evolution of the various distance-vector algorithms and delves into the details, mechanics, and uses of today's open standard RIP.

NOTE

An *open standard* is one that is defined in a collaborative effort and published openly. This enables virtually any interested parties to develop products to a consistent standard. Such consistency makes possible the interoperability of products manufactured by different entities.

THE ORIGINS OF RIP

One of the oldest routing protocols is RIP. RIP uses distance-vector algorithms to calculate routes. This type of algorithm has been used to calculate network routes, in numerous variations, for decades. In fact, the distance-vector algorithms used in today's open standard RIP are based directly on those algorithms used to calculate routes across the ARPANET as far back as 1969.

> **NOTE**
>
> *ARPANET* was the predecessor to the Internet. It was named after the U.S. Department of Defense's (DoD's) Advanced Research Projects Agency (ARPA). ARPA's name vacillated between ARPA and DARPA as the agency struggled with whether to focus exclusively on defense-oriented research.

One of the more persistent misperceptions about RIP is that it was originally designed and developed at the University of California at Berkeley. It was not. Although today's RIP is related to the Berkeley distance-vector routing protocol, *routed* (pronounced "route-dee"), its origins are quite a bit more obfuscated than this simple explanation indicates.

Distance-vector algorithms were originally described academically (and supported with calculations and research) by R. E. Bellman, L. R. Ford Jr., and D. R. Fulkerson. Princeton University Press published their research in at least two books. These algorithms set the standard for route calculation in small networks that would withstand the test of time.

Distance-Vector Algorithms

Distance-vector algorithms are sometimes referred to as Bellman-Ford or Ford-Fulkerson algorithms. L. R. Ford, Jr. and D. R. Fulkerson published the earliest known description of a distance-vector algorithm in *Flows in Networks*, which was published by the Princeton University Press in 1962.

Bellman-Ford algorithms refer to distance-vector algorithms that utilize R. E. Bellman's dynamic programming equation. Bellman's work, *Dynamic Programming*, was published by the Princeton University Press in 1957.

These books formed the foundation for the development of myriad RIP-like distance-vector routing protocols during the 1960s and 1970s.

Xerox's RIP

The first organization, commercial or academic, to successfully implement a distance-vector routing protocol was Xerox. Its protocol was designed to fit a niche in the Xerox Network Systems (XNS) architecture. The XNS architecture already included a proprietary gateway routing protocol, the Gateway Information Protocol (GIP). GIP was designed to exchange routing information among nonadjacent networks or autonomous systems. Xerox rounded out its networking architecture by adding a simple protocol for calculating routes within autonomous systems. This new routing protocol was based on the works of Bellman, Ford, and Fulkerson. This new protocol was called Routing Information Protocol—a logical name for GIP's interior complement.

Figure 8-1 illustrates how GIP and RIP would work together to calculate routes within, and across, autonomous systems.

Xerox's RIP was revolutionary in that it allowed routing tables to be constructed and updated dynamically without human intervention. These updates were made based on a series of distance-vector metrics that allowed routers to share their perspective with other routers. Each router would compare its routing table with updates received from other routers to automatically, and dynamically, maintain a relatively up-to-date routing table.

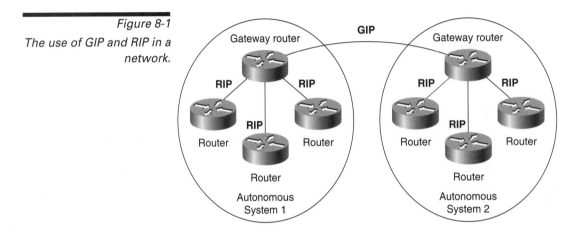

Figure 8-1

The use of GIP and RIP in a network.

routed

The University of California at Berkeley was another pioneer of distance-vector routing protocols. Its variant was called *routed*. *routed* was developed for Release 4.3 of Berkeley UNIX. *routed* was closely modeled after Xerox's RIP, but it incorporated some important distinctions.

Some of the most critical distinctions between *routed* and Xerox's RIP include the following:

- *routed* eschewed the Xerox-proprietary XNS addressing architecture in favor of a more flexible address format. This new format could accommodate IP as well as XNS and other internetwork address formats.

- *routed* limited routing updates to a maximum of once every 30 seconds. Xerox's RIP did not have this feature.

Thus, *routed* was more network friendly and could scale upward more gracefully.

- *routed* was distributed as part of the Berkeley UNIX system instead of tightly integrated into a proprietary hardware/software bundled solution.

Over time, thanks to its more open nature and its free distribution with the Berkeley UNIX system, *routed* became a de facto standard for interior routing.

NOTE

It should be obvious from this brief description that these early variations of distance-vector routing algorithms were very closely related. Their similarities resulted in some confusion as to exactly what RIP meant! At that time, RIP was generally accepted to mean either the Xerox RIP protocol or the distance-vector route calculation algorithm used by *routed*.

RFC 1058

As similar as their algorithms were, *routed* and Xerox RIP (not to mention the numerous other, minor, RIP-like protocols that appeared contemporaneously [such as the AppleTalk Routing Table Maintenance Protocol, better known as RTMP]) were different enough to make them less than completely interoperable. Therefore, the Internet Engineering Task Force (IETF) moved to standardize a routing protocol, loosely based on *routed*, that would be backward compatible with all preexisting variants.

In June 1988, Request for Comments (RFC) 1058 was released. This RFC described a new and truly open form of distance-vector routing protocol. To add to the confusion, the RFC 1058 protocol was also called RIP. This resulted in the term *RIP* having four distinct definitions:

- The routing protocol specified in RFC 1058

- Xerox's proprietary routing protocol

- Novell's proprietary version of RIP, which was also called RIP

- The distance-vector algorithms used by *routed*

Despite its name, RFC 1058's RIP was really just a modestly modified version of *routed*. *routed* was already remarkably open, especially compared to Xerox's RIP and other proprietary RIP-like variants. The IETF's open standard added only minor modifications to *routed*. These enhancements were designed to provide backward compatibility with other known RIP-like and *routed*-like protocols.

RFC 1058 SPECIFICATIONS

RFC 1058 specified an open standard RIP. This RIP, like its proprietary ancestors, was designed as a simple distance-vector routing protocol. It was specifically designed for use as an Interior Gateway Protocol (IGP) in small, simple networks.

RIP Packet Format

RIP uses a special packet to collect and share information about distances to known internetworked destinations. This packet contains the following structure:

- A 1-octet command field

- A 1-octet version number field

- A 2-octet zero field

- A 2-octet Address Family Identifier (AFI) field

- Another 2-octet zero field

- A 4-octet Internetworking Address (i.e., IP Address) field

- A 4-octet zero field

- Another 4-octet zero field

- A 4-octet metric field

Figure 8-2 illustrates the RIP packet format.

1-octet command field	1-octet version number field	2-octet zero field	2-octet AFI field	2-octet zero field	4-octet IP Address field	4-octet zero field	4-octet zero field	4-octet metric field

Figure 8-2
The RIP packet format.

NOTE

Examining the RIP packet structure reveals the lack of a conventional data field. RIP is a routing protocol, not a *routed* protocol. As such, application data is not passed in a RIP packet. Such data must use a *routed* protocol suite, such as TCP/IP, regardless of which routing protocol was used to calculate its route.

Figure 8-2 illustrates a RIP packet with routing information fields for just a single destination. RIP packets can support up to 25 occurrences of the AFI, IP Address, and Metric fields within a single packet. This enables one RIP packet to be used to update multiple entries in other routers' routing tables. RIP packets that contain multiple routing entries just repeat the packet structure from the AFI through the Metric field, including all Zero fields. The repeated structures are appended to the end of the structure depicted in Figure 8-2. Figure 8-3 shows a RIP packet with two table entries.

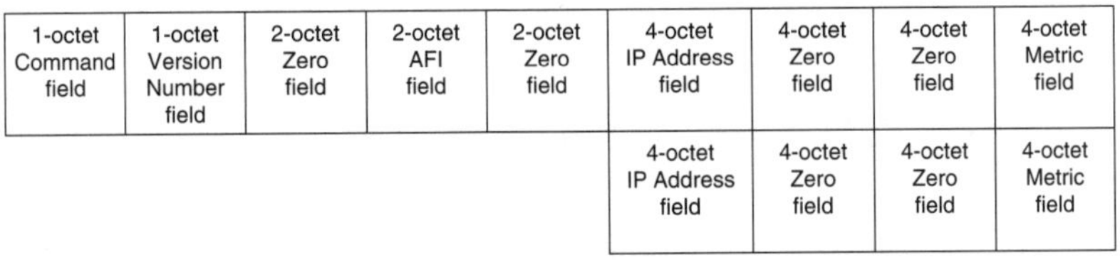

Figure 8-3
The RIP packet format with
two table entries.

1-octet Command field	1-octet Version Number field	2-octet Zero field	2-octet AFI field	2-octet Zero field	4-octet IP Address field	4-octet Zero field	4-octet Zero field	4-octet Metric field
					4-octet IP Address field	4-octet Zero field	4-octet Zero field	4-octet Metric field

The IP Address field can contain either the address of its originator or a series of IP addresses that the originator has in its routing table. Request packets contain a single entry and include the originator's address. Response packets can include up to 25 entries of a RIP router's routing table.

The overall size limitation of a RIP packet is 512 octets. Therefore, in larger RIP networks, a request for a full routing table update may require the transmission of several RIP packets. No provisions were made for the resequencing of the packets on arrival at their destination; individual routing table entries are not split among RIP packets. The contents of any given RIP packet are complete unto themselves, even though they may only be a subset of a complete routing table. The recipient node is free to process the updates as the packets are received without having to resequence them.

A RIP router may contain 100 entries in its routing table, for example. Sharing its routing information with other RIP nodes would require four RIP packets, each one containing 25 entries. If a receiving node received packet number 4 first (containing entries numbered 86 through 100), it could just update that portion of its routing table first. There are no sequential dependencies. This allows RIP packets to be forwarded without the overheads of a fully featured transport protocol such as TCP.

The Command Field

The Command field indicates whether the RIP packet was generated as a request or as a response to a request. The same frame structure is used for both occurrences:

- A request packet asks a router to send all, or part, of its routing table.

- A response packet contains routing table entries that are to be shared with other RIP nodes in the network. A response packet can be generated either in response to a request or as an unsolicited update.

The Version Number Field

The Version Number field contains the version of RIP that was used to generate the RIP packet. Although RIP is an open standard routing protocol, it is not frozen in time. The architects of RFC 1058 anticipated this and provided a field that RIP nodes could use to specifically identify the newest version that they conform to. RIP has been treated to updates over the years, and these updates are reflected in a version number. To date, only two version numbers have been assigned—numbers 1 and 2. The version of RIP described in this chapter uses version number 1. RIP 2, explored in the next chapter, uses version number 2 in this field.

The Zero Fields

The numerous Zero fields embedded in each RIP packet are silent testimony to the proliferation of RIP-like protocols before RFC 1058. Most of the Zero fields were contrived as a means of providing backward compatibility with older RIP-like protocols, without supporting all their proprietary features.

Two such obsolete mechanisms are traceon and traceoff, for example. These mechanisms were abandoned by RFC 1058, yet the open standard RIP needed to be backward compatible with the proprietary RIP-like protocols that did support them. Therefore, RFC 1058 preserved their space in the packet but required this space to always be set to zeros. Packets that are received with these fields set to something other than zeroes are just discarded.

Not all the Zero fields originated in this manner. At least one of the Zero fields was reserved for an unspecified future use. Reserving a field for an unspecified future use is what usually happens when a committee cannot reach consensus on how to use that space. This is particularly true in cases, such as RIP, where backward compatibility required conformance to a predetermined header size. Therefore, reserving a field for future use accomplishes two things:

- It creates future flexibility for the protocol.

- It provides a noncommittal means of creating consensus where none previously existed.

The AFI Field

The AFI field specifies the address family that is represented by the IP Address field. Although the RFC 1058 RIP was created by the IETF, which would imply the use of the Internet Protocol (IP), it was explicitly designed to provide backward compatibility with previous versions of RIP. This meant that it had to provide for the transport of routing information of a wide variety of internet-working address architectures or families. Consequently, the open standard RIP needed a mechanism for determining which type of address was being carried in its packets.

The IP Address Field

The 4-octet IP Address field contains an internetwork address. This address can be a host, a network, or even a default gateway address code. The following are two examples of how this field's contents can vary:

- In a single-entry request packet, this field would contain the address of the packet's originator.

- In a multiple-entry response packet, this field would contain the IP addresses stored in the originator's routing table.

The Metric Field

The last field in the RIP packet, the Metric field, contains the packet's metric counter. This value is incremented as it passes through a router. The valid range of metrics for this field is between 1 and 15. The metric can actually be incremented to 16, but this value is associated with invalid routes. Consequently, 16 is an error value for the Metric field and not part of the valid range.

The RIP Routing Table

RIP hosts communicate the routing information that they have tabulated using the RIP packet described in the previous section. This information is stored in a routing table. The routing table contains *one* entry for each known, reachable destination. The one entry per destination is the lowest-cost route to that destination.

NOTE

This section specifically describes RFC 1058 RIP. It is quite common, however, for router manufacturers to add features to this specification. Consequently, RIP might not behave exactly as this section describes in your network. Cisco routers running RIP may simultaneously track up to four routes to a single destination, for example.

Each routing table entry contains the following fields:

- The Destination IP Address field

NOTE

The Destination IP Address can identify either a network, a default route, or a specific host. Although RIP supports routing to individual hosts, this capability is seldom actually used. In practice, it is far more likely that RIP will summarize routes to all hosts within a common network number and calculate routes to just that network address rather than individual host addresses. Despite this, it is useful to examine the processes that support host routes before adding the conceptual complexity of route summarization. Consequently, the following examples assume routing to specific hosts.

- The Distance-Vector Metric field
- The Next Hop IP Address field
- The Route Change Flag field
- Route timers

NOTE

Although RFC 1058 RIP is an open standard that can support a variety of internetwork address architectures, it was designed by the IETF for use in autonomous systems within the Internet. As such, it was tacitly assumed that IP would be the internetworking protocol used by this form of RIP.

The Destination IP Address Field

The most important piece of information contained in any routing table is the IP address of the known destination. Whenever a RIP router receives a data packet, it looks up its destination IP address in its routing table to determine where to forward that packet.

The Metric Field

The metric contained in the routing table represents the total cost of moving a datagram from its point of origin to its specified destination. The Metric field in the routing table contains the sum total of the costs associated with the network links that comprise the end-to-end network path between the router and the specified destination. Typically, the metric or cost associated with a link is equal to 1. Therefore, the number of hops in a route is usually equal to the total cost of that route.

The Next Hop IP Address Field

The Next Hop IP Address field contains the IP address of the next router interface in the network path to the destination IP address. This field is populated in a router's table only if the destination IP address is on a network not directly connected to that router.

The Route Change Flag Field

The Route Change Flag field is used to indicate whether the route to the destination IP address has changed recently. The architects of RFC 1058 deemed this field important because RIP records only one route per destination IP address. Specific implementations of RIP may not limit themselves in this fashion, but they still use the Route Change Flag to identify changes in routes to specific destinations.

Route Timers

The two timers associated with each route are the route timeout and the route-flush timers. These timers work together to maintain the validity of each route stored in the routing table. The routing table maintenance process is described in more detail in the section titled "Updating the Routing Table."

OPERATIONAL MECHANICS

As explained in Chapter 7, "The Mechanics of Routing Protocols," routers using a distance-vector routing protocol periodically pass copies of their routing tables to their immediate network neighbors. A router's routing table contains information about the distance between itself and known destinations. These destinations can be individual host computers, printers, or other networks.

Each recipient adds a distance vector—that is, its own distance "value"—to the table and forwards the modified table to its *immediate neighbors*. This process occurs in an omnidirectional manner among immediately neighboring routers. Figure 8-4 uses a simple RIP internetwork to illustrate the concept of immediate neighbors.

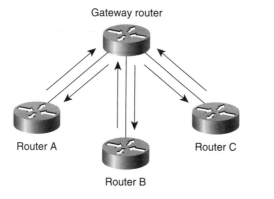

Gateway router

Router A

Router B

Router C

Figure 8-4
Each RIP node advertises the contents of its routing table to its immediate neighbors.

In Figure 8-4, there are four routers. The gateway router is interconnected with each of the other three. It must exchange its routing information with these routers. Routers A, B, and C have only one connection to the gateway. Consequently, they can only exchange their information with the gateway directly. They can learn about each other's hosts through the information shared with the gateway. Table 8-1 shows the abbreviated contents of each of the three routers' routing tables. This information is shared with the gateway router. For the sake of simplicity, this example uses fictitious and generic network addresses. This generic addressing is intended to help you understand the mechanics of routing without the complexity of IP addressing. Examples with IP addresses are presented later in this chapter, as well as throughout the remainder of the book.

Table 8-1 *Routing Table Contents*

Router Name	Host Name	Next Hop
A	A.10	Local
	A.15	Local
B	B.2	Local
	B.9	Local
C	C.5	Local
	C.20	Local

The gateway router uses this information to build its own routing table. Table 8-2 presents the abbreviated contents of this table.

Table 8-2 *Gateway Router Routing Table Contents*

Router Name	Host Name	Next Hop	Number of Hops
Gateway	A.10	A	1
	A.15	A	1
	B.2	B	1
	B.9	B	1
	C.5	C	1
	C.20	C	1

The routing information in Table 8-2 is then shared via routing information update packets with each of the other routers in the network. These routers use this information to round out their own routing tables. Table 8-3 shows the abbreviated contents of Router A's routing table after it has shared routing information with the gateway router.

Table 8-3 *Router A Routing Table Contents*

Router Name	Host Name	Next Hop	Number of Hops
A	A.10	Local	0
	A.15	Local	0
	B.2	Gateway	2
	B.9	Gateway	2
	C.5	Gateway	2
	C.20	Gateway	2

Router A knows that the gateway router is one hop away. Therefore, seeing that the B.x and C.x hosts are also one hop away from the gateway, it adds the two numbers together, for a total of two hops to each machine.

This highly simplified step-by-step process results in each router's learning about other routers and developing a cumulative perspective of the network as well as the distances between source and destination devices.

Calculating Distance Vectors

Distance-vector routing protocols use metrics to keep track of the distance separating it from all known destinations. This distance information enables the router to identify the most efficient next hop to a destination that resides in a nonadjacent autonomous system.

In RFC 1058 RIP, there is a single distance-vector metric: hop count. The default hop metric in RIP is set to 1. Therefore, for each router that receives and forwards a packet, the hop count in the RIP packet metric field is incremented by one. These distance metrics are used to construct a routing table. The routing table identifies the next hop for a packet to take to get to its destination at a minimal cost.

The earlier, proprietary RIP-like routing protocols typically used 1 as the only supported cost per hop. This convention was preserved as a default in RFC 1058 RIP, but provisions were made for the router's administrator to select higher cost values. Such values would be beneficial in discriminating between links of differing performance capabilities. These capabilities could be the bandwidths available on different network links (that is, 56 kbps versus T1 private lines) or even the performance difference between a new router versus an older model.

Typically, a cost of 1 is assigned to each of a router's ports that connect to other networks. This is apparently an artifact from RIP's pre-RFC 1058 days, when the cost per hop defaulted to 1 and was not modifiable. In a relatively small network that consisted of homogeneous transmission technologies, setting all ports to a cost of 1 would be reasonable. Figure 8-5 illustrates this.

Figure 8-5

A homogeneous network with equivalent costs.

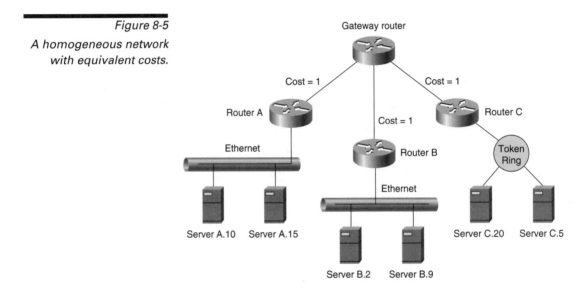

A router's administrator can change the default metric. An administrator may increase the metric for slower-speed links to other routers, for example. Although this might more accurately represent the costs or distances to a given destination, this practice is not recommended. Setting the metric to a value greater than 1 makes it correspondingly easier to reach the packet's maximum hop count of 16! Figure 8-6 demonstrates how quickly routes can become invalid if route metrics are increased.

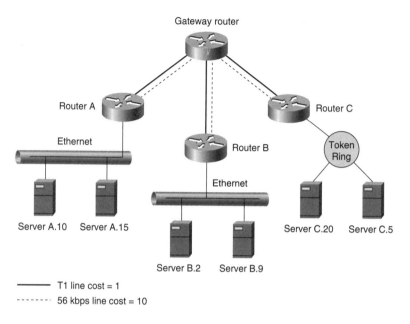

Figure 8-6 presents a slightly modified version of the WAN depicted in Figure 8-5. This illustration adds low-bandwidth redundant links to the topology depicted in Figure 8-5. The network administrator, to ensure that the alternate routes remained alternate routes, set the metric value of these alternate routes to 10. These higher costs preserve the bias toward the higher-bandwidth T1 transmission facilities. In the event of a failure of one of those T1 lines, the internetwork can continue to function normally; although there may be some degraded performance levels due to the lower available bandwidth on the 56 kbps backup facility. Figure 8-7 illustrates how the internetwork will react to a failure of a T1 line between the gateway and Router A.

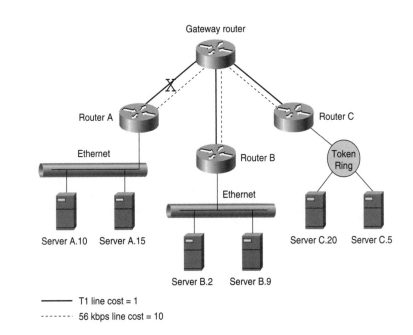

Figure 8-7
Hop counts add up quickly,
but the network remains
functional.

The alternative 56 kbps transmission facility becomes the only way for A and the rest of the network to communicate. Router A's routing table, after the network converges upon a common understanding of this new topology, is summarized in Table 8-4.

Table 8-4   *Router A Routing Table Contents with a Link Failure*

Router Name	Host Name	Next Hop	Number of Hops
A	A.10	Local	0
	A.15	Local	0
	B.2	Gateway	11
	B.9	Gateway	11
	C.5	Gateway	11
	C.20	Gateway	11

Although a higher route cost is a more accurate reflection of the lower bandwidths offered by these alternative routes, it can introduce unwanted routing problems. In Figure 8-8, both of the T1 lines have failed and, therefore, cause both of the alternative routes to become active simultaneously.

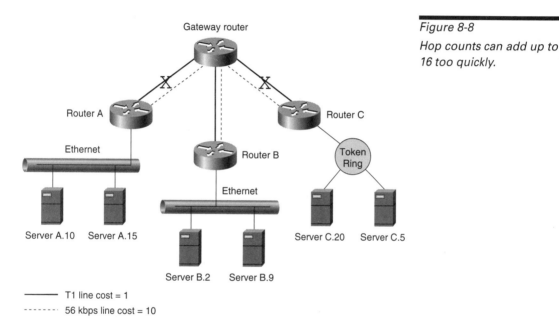

Gateway router

Router A

Router C

Ethernet

Router B

Token Ring

Server A.10   Server A.15

Ethernet

Server C.20   Server C.5

Server B.2   Server B.9

——— T1 line cost = 1
- - - - - 56 kbps line cost = 10

Figure 8-8

Hop counts can add up to 16 too quickly.

Because both alternative links had a cost metric of 10, their simultaneous activation results in a route cost of greater than 16. The valid range for RIP's hop counter is from 0 through 16, with 16 representing an unreachable route. RIP ceases calculating routes above 15. Routes whose total cost would exceed 16 are declared invalid. Consequently, a notification (a triggered update) is sent to all immediately neighboring routers.

Obviously, this problem can be avoided by leaving the default cost equal to 1. If it is absolutely necessary to increment the cost metric of a given hop, the new cost value should be selected with great care. The sum total of the route between any given pair of source and destination addresses in a network should never exceed 15. Table 8-5 demonstrates the impacts of a second link failure on Router A's routing table.

Table 8-5   *Router A Routing Table Contents with Two Link Failures*

Router Name	Host Name	Next Hop	Number of Hops
A	A.10	Local	0
	A.15	Local	0
	B.2	Gateway	11
	B.9	Gateway	11
	C.5	Gateway	16
	C.20	Gateway	16

As is evident in Table 8-5, the cost of the route between A and C exceeds 16, and all entries are declared invalid. Router A can communicate with B, however, because the total cost of that route is only 12.

Updating the Routing Table

The fact that RIP records only one route per destination requires RIP to aggressively maintain the integrity of its routing table. It does so by requiring all active RIP routers to broadcast their routing table contents to neighboring RIP routers at a fixed interval. All updates received automatically supercede previous route information that was stored in the routing table. Each RIP router's timers are activated independently of the other RIP routers in the network. Therefore, it is highly unlikely that they will attempt to broadcast their routing tables simultaneously.

RIP relies on three timers to maintain the routing table:

- The update timer
- The route timeout timer
- The route-flush timer

The update timer is used to initiate routing table updates at the node level. Each RIP node only uses one update timer. Conversely, the route timeout timer and the route-flush timer are kept for each route.

As such, separate timeout and route-flush timers are integrated in each routing table entry. Together, these timers enable RIP nodes to maintain the integrity of their routes as well as to proactively recover from failures in the network by initiating activity based on the passing of time. The following sections describe the processes used to maintain the routing tables.

Initiating Table Updates

A table update is initiated approximately every 30 seconds. The update timer is used to track this amount of time. Upon the expiration of this amount of time, RIP launches a series of packets that contain the entire routing table.

These packets are broadcast to each neighboring node. Therefore, each RIP router should receive an update from each of its neighboring RIP nodes approximately every 30 seconds.

NOTE

In larger RIP-based autonomous systems, these periodic updates can create unacceptable levels of traffic. Therefore, it is desirable to stagger the updates from node to node. This is done automatically by RIP; each time the update timer is reset, a small, random amount of time is added to the clock.

If such an update fails to occur as expected, it indicates a failure or error somewhere in the internetwork. The failure may be something as simple as a dropped packet that contained the update. The failure could also be something as serious as a failed router, or virtually anything in between these two extremes. Obviously, the appropriate course of action to take differs greatly along this spectrum of failures. It would be unwise to invalidate a series of routes just because the update packet was lost. (Remember that RIP update packets use an unreliable transport protocol to minimize overheads.) Therefore, it is not unreasonable to not take corrective action based on a single missed update. To help discriminate between magnitudes of failures and errors, RIP uses timers to identify invalid routes.

Identifying Invalid Routes

Routes can become invalid in one of two ways:

- A route can expire.

- A router can be notified by another router of a route's unavailability.

In either event, the RIP router needs to modify its routing table to reflect the unavailability of a given route.

A route can expire if a router doesn't receive an update for it within a specified amount of time. The route timeout timer is usually set to 180 seconds, for example. This clock is initialized when the route becomes active or is updated.

One hundred and eighty seconds is approximately enough time for a router to receive six routing table updates from its neighbors (assuming that they initiate table updates every 30 seconds). If 180 seconds elapses and the RIP router hasn't received an update on that route, the RIP router assumes that the destination IP address is no longer reachable. Consequently, the router marks that routing entry in its table as invalid. This is done by setting its routing metric to 16 and by setting the *route change flag*. This information is then communicated to the router's neighbors via the periodic routing table updates.

Earlier in this chapter, RIP's valid range of cost metrics was established at 0 through 15, with 16 equaling an error condition. To be more precise, a RIP node considers 16 to be infinity. It is impossible to count to infinity. In RIP's case, it is an artificial and arbitrary limitation that precludes it from being able to count beyond 15. Therefore, setting the cost metric to 16 in a RIP routing table entry can invalidate a route.

Neighboring nodes that receive notification of the route's new invalid status use that information to update their own routing tables. This is the second of the two ways that routes can become invalid in a routing table.

An invalid routing table entry is not automatically purged from the routing table. Instead, that invalid entry remains in the table for a brief amount of time, just in case the route really is still viable. A RIP node cannot send datagrams to an invalid destination address, however, regardless of whether that address is actually reachable. The process by which invalid routes are actually purged from the routing table is examined in the following section.

Purging Invalid Routes

When a router recognizes a route as invalid, it initializes a second timer: the route-flush timer. Therefore, 180 seconds after the last time the timeout timer was initialized, the route-flush timer is initialized. This timer is usually set for 90 seconds.

If the route is still not received after 270 seconds (180 second timeout timer plus the 90-second route-flush timer), the route is removed (that is, flushed) from the routing table. The timer responsible for counting down the time to route flush is known as the route flush timer. These timers are absolutely essential to RIP's capability to recover from network failures.

Active Versus Passive Nodes

It is important to note that for a RIP internetwork to function properly, every gateway within the network must participate. Participation can be active or passive, but all gateways must participate. Active nodes are those that actively engage in the sharing of routing information. They receive updates from their neighbors, and they forward copies of their routing table entries to those neighboring nodes.

Passive nodes receive updates from their neighbors and use those updates to maintain their routing table. Passive nodes, however, do not actively distribute copies of their own routing table entries.

The capability to passively maintain a routing table was a particularly useful feature in the days before hardware routers, when *routed* was a daemon that ran on UNIX processors. This kept routing overheads on the UNIX host to a minimum.

Addressing Considerations

The IETF ensured that RIP was fully backward compatible with all known RIP and *routed* variants. Given that these were highly proprietary, it was necessary that the open standard RIP not dictate an address type. Therefore, the field labeled Address in a RIP packet may contain the following:

- The host address

- The subnet number

- The network number

- A 0, which indicates a default route

Implicit in this flexibility is the fact that RIP permits calculating routes to either individual hosts or to networks that contain numerous hosts. To accommodate this address flexibility in operation, RIP nodes use the most specific information available when they forward datagrams. When a RIP router receives an IP packet, for example, it must examine the destination address. It attempts to match this address with a destination IP address in its routing table. If it cannot find an entry for that specific host address, it then checks whether that destination address matches a known subnet or network number. If it cannot make a match at this level, the RIP router uses its default route to forward the datagram.

Routing to a Gateway

Up to this point in the chapter, entries in the RIP routing table have been assumed to be routes to individual hosts. This was a simplifying assumption designed to facilitate your understanding of routing tables and table updates. This is not indicative of how routing really works, however.

In reality, many networks are set up such that routes do not have to be calculated to each individual host. In larger networks, this can be an onerous task that only inflates the size of routing tables and slows down routing across the internetwork.

In real-world networks, it is almost always preferable to summarize routes instead of explicitly identifying each potential destination. If each host on any given network (or subnet) is accessible through the same gateway(s), for example, the routing table can just define that gateway as a destination IP address. All datagrams addressed to hosts within that network or subnetwork will be forwarded to that gateway. That gateway will then assume responsibility for forwarding it on to its ultimate destination. Figure 8-9 illustrates this point; it preserves the topology of the previous few illustrations, but uses more conventional IP addresses.

Figure 8-9
RIP can deliver datagrams
to gateways.

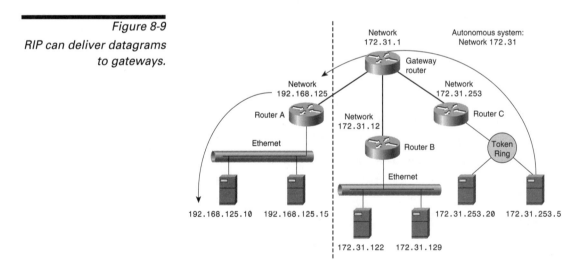

In Figure 8-9, host 172.31.253.5 needs to transmit an IP packet to host number 192.168.125.10. This address is unknown to Router C. The router checks the subnet mask and finds it set to 255.255.255.0. From this, it is easy to deduce that 192.168.125 is a network number. More importantly, Router C knows a route to that subnet. Router B assumes that the gateway router at that subnet knows how to reach that host. Consequently, Router C forwards the packet to that gateway. This approach requires hosts to be known only to the router that is closest and not known throughout a network. The finely dotted lines in Figure 8-9 illustrate the two parts of the IP packet's journey: Its trip from Router B to the Router A and from A to host 192.168.125.10.

NOTE

This section assumes that there is only one subnet mask for each network. This is a simplifying assumption. It is quite likely that a network may contain multiple networks, each with its own subnet mask.

Routing Between Gateways

In the case presented in the preceding section, a potential routing problem exists. If Router C did not know the subnet mask of the destination IP address and the host part of the address was not zero, it wouldn't be able to determine whether the address was a subnet number or a host address. Therefore, the packet would be discarded as undeliverable.

To help avoid the ambiguity, routes to a subnet are not advertised outside the network that contains the subnet. The router at the border of this subnet functions as a gateway; it treats each subnet as an individual network. RIP updates are performed between immediate neighbors within each subnet, but the network gateway advertises a single network number only to its neighboring gateways in other networks.

The practical implication of this is that a border gateway will send different information to its neighbors. Immediate neighbors within the subnetted network will receive updates containing lists of all subnets directly connected to that gateway. The routing entries will list the number of each subnet.

Immediate neighbors outside the network will receive a single routing entry update that encompasses all the hosts on all the subnets contained within that network. The metric passed would be that associated with reaching the network, not including the costs of hops within the network. In this fashion, distant RIP routers assume that datagrams addressed to any host number within that subnet are known to, and reachable through, the network's border gateway router.

Default Routes

The IP address 0.0.0.0 is used to describe a default route. Much like the way subnets can be summarized by routing to a network gateway, a default route can be used to route to multiple networks without explicitly defining and describing them. The only requirement is that there be at least one gateway between these networks that is prepared to handle the traffic generated.

To create a default route, a RIP entry needs to be created for the address 0.0.0.0. This special address is treated just like any other destination IP address. The next hop should be the destination IP address of the neighboring gateway router. This routing entry is used just like every other entry, with one important exception: The default route is used to route any datagram whose destination address doesn't match any other entries in the routing table.

Table 8-6 demonstrates the abbreviated contents of Router A's
routing table with a default route. In this table, the two local hosts
are the only ones explicitly identified. Any other locally generated
transmission requests are automatically forwarded to the gateway
router.

Table 8-6   *Router A Routing Table Contents with a Default Route*

Router Name	Host Name	Next Hop
A	192.168.125.10	Local
	192.168.125.15	Local
	0.0.0.0	Gateway

TOPOLOGY CHANGES

Up to this point, RIP's fundamental mechanisms and specifications have been examined in a rather static fashion. A deeper
appreciation for RIP's mechanics, however, can be gained by looking at how these mechanisms interact to accommodate changes in
network topology.

Convergence

The most significant implication of a topology change in a RIP
internetwork is that it changes the solution set of neighboring
nodes. This change may also result in different results the next
time the distance vectors are calculated. Therefore, the new sets of
neighboring nodes must then converge, from different starting
points, on a consensus of what the new topology looks like. This
process of developing a consensual perspective of the topology is
known as *convergence*. In simple terms, the routers develop an
agreement of what the network looks like *separately, together*.

Figure 8-10 illustrates convergence; it demonstrates the following four possible routes to Router D:

- From Router A, to Router B, to Router D

- From Router A, to Router C, to Router D

- From Router A, to Router B, to Router C, to Router D

- From Router A, to Router C, to Router B, to Router D

Vendor-specific implementations of RIP that can remember multiple routes can use these four possible routes to reach Router D. Such route diversity affords protection from failures in the network. Of these four routes, the two that use the link between Routers B and D are the least desirable. This is because that link has a metric cost of 10, compared to a cost of 1 for the other routes.

Implementations of RIP that adhere rigidly to RFC 1058 will only remember one of these routes. Ostensibly, this will be the least-cost route that it learns about. For the sake of this example, the primary route to Router D's network is via Router C. If this route were to fail, it would take some time for all the routers to converge on a new topology that didn't include the link between Routers C and D.

As soon as the C–D link fails, it is no longer usable, but it may take a little time for this fact to become known throughout the network. The first step in convergence is for D to realize that the link to C has failed. This assumes that Router D's update timer elapses before Router C's timer. As this link was the one that should have carried updates from Router D to Router C, no updates can be received. Consequently, C (as well as A and B) is still unaware that the C–D link has failed. All routers in the internetwork will continue to forward datagrams addressed to Router D's network number, through that link. Figure 8-11 illustrates this first stage in convergence.

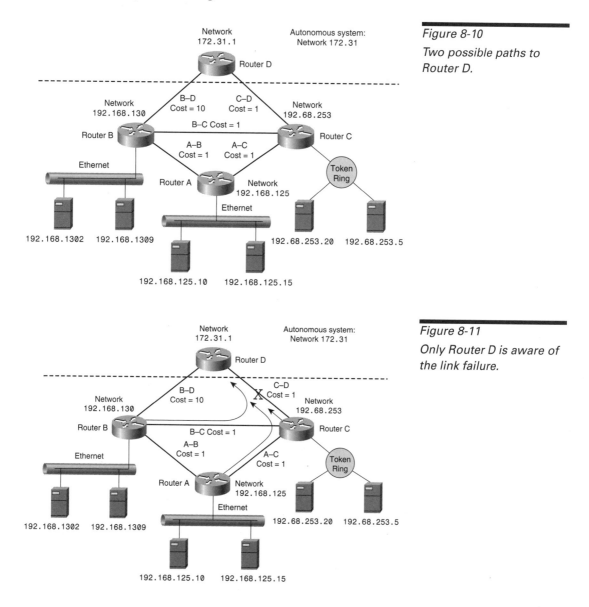

Figure 8-10

Two possible paths to Router D.

Figure 8-11

Only Router D is aware of the link failure.

Upon expiration of its update timer, Router D will attempt to notify its neighbors of its perception of the change in the network's topology. The only immediate neighbor that it will be able to contact is B. Upon receiving this update, B will update its routing table to set the route from B–C to infinity for all destination addresses in the 172.31 network, which is the network connected via Router D. This will allow it to resume communications with D, albeit via the B–D link. After B has updated its table, it can advertise its newfound perception of the topology to its other neighbors, A and C.

NOTE

Remember that a RIP node invalidates a route by setting its metric to 16, the RIP equivalent of infinity.

As soon as A and C have received updates, and have recalculated network costs, they can replace their obsolete entries that used the C–D link with the B–D link. The B–D route was previously rejected by all nodes, including B, as being more expensive than the C–D link. Its cost metric of 10 compared unfavorably with the C–D cost of 1 for each node. Now, with the failure of the C–D link, the B–D link features the lowest cost. Therefore, this new route replaces the timed-out route in the neighbors routing tables.

When all routers agree that the most efficient route to D is via B, they have converged. Figure 8-12 illustrates this.

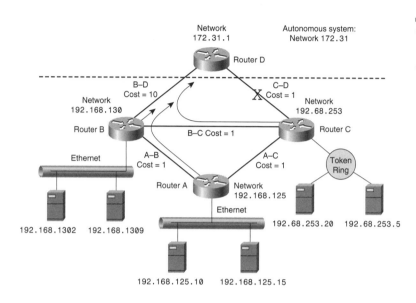

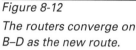

Figure 8-12

The routers converge on B–D as the new route.

The amount of time that will elapse before convergence completes is not easy to determine. It will vary greatly from network to network, based on a wide variety of factors that include the robustness of the routers and transmission facilities, amount of traffic, and so on.

Counting to Infinity

In the example presented in the preceding section, the only failure was the transmission facility connecting C and D. The routers were able to converge on a new topology that restored access to gateway Router D's network via an alternative path. A much more disastrous failure would have been if D itself had failed. Remember that the convergence process in the preceding example started when D was able to notify B of the link failure. If D, rather than its link to C, had failed, neither B nor C would have received an update informing them of the change in topology.

Converging on a new topology given this type of failure can result in a phenomenon known as *counting to infinity*. When a network becomes completely inaccessible, updates between remaining routers can steadily increment routing metrics to the inaccessible destination based on the mistaken belief that another router can access the lost destination. Left unchecked, the routers in that scenario will literally count to their interpretation of infinity.

To illustrate the dangers from a routing perspective inherent in this type of catastrophic failure, reconsider the topology presented in the convergence illustrations. In Figure 8-13, Router D has failed.

Figure 8-13
Router D has failed.

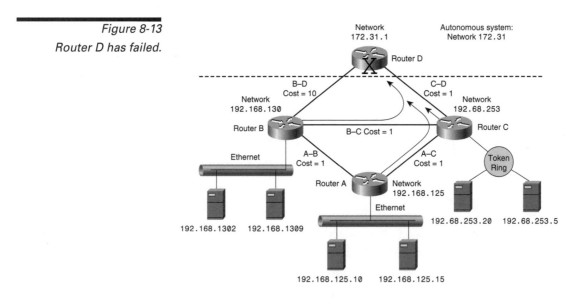

With the failure of Router D, all the hosts within its network are no longer accessible from the outside. Router C, after missing six consecutive updates from D, will invalidate its C–D route and advertise its unavailability. Figure 8-14 illustrates this. Routers A and B will remain ignorant of the route's failure until notified by C.

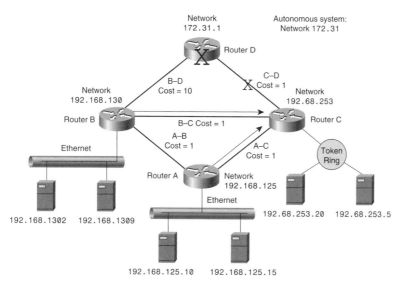

Figure 8-14
Router C invalidates its C–D route.

At this point, both A and C believe that they can get to D via B. They recalculate their routes to include the higher costs of this detour. Figure 8-15 illustrates this.

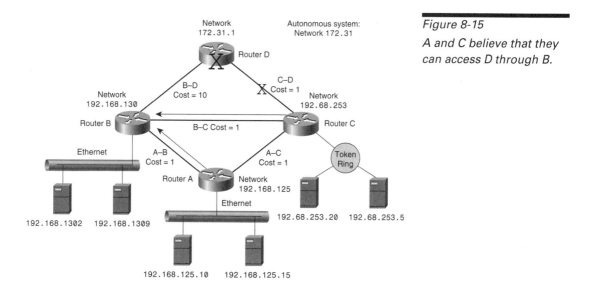

Figure 8-15
A and C believe that they can access D through B.

These routers send their next updates to B, an immediate neighbor of both routers. Router B, having timed out its own route to D, believes it can still access D through either A or C. Obviously, it cannot because those routers are relying on the link that B just invalidated. In essence, a loop is formed between A, B, and C that is fed by the mistaken belief that both A and C can still reach the unreachable Router D through each other. This is because both have a connection to B, which has the connection to D.

With each iteration of updates, the cost metrics are incremented to account for the next extra hop that is added to the loop already calculated. This form of looping is induced by the time delay that characterizes independent convergence through neighbor-transmitted updates.

In theory, the nodes will eventually realize that D is unreachable. It is virtually impossible, however, to tell how much time would be required to achieve this convergence. This example illustrates precisely why RIP's interpretation of infinity is set so low! Whenever a network becomes inaccessible, the incrementing of metrics through routine updates must be halted as soon as practical. Unfortunately, this means placing an upper limit on how high the nodes will count before declaring a destination unreachable. Any upper limit directly translates into a limitation on the maximum size of the routed network's diameter. In the case of RIP, its original designers felt that 15 hops were more than adequate for an autonomous system. Systems larger than this could utilize a more sophisticated routing protocol.

RIP supports two means of avoiding the count to infinity loop problem:

- Split horizon with poisoned reverse

- Triggered updates

Split Horizon

It should be fairly obvious that the looping problem described in the "Counting to Infinity" section could be prevented with the application of logic. The term used to describe this logic is *split horizon*. Although RFC 1058 RIP doesn't support split horizon, understanding it will facilitate understanding its somewhat more complicated variant, *split horizon with poisoned reverse*. The essence of split horizon is the assumption that it is not useful to advertise routes learned from an interface back out to the network attached via that interface. Figure 8-16 illustrates this point.

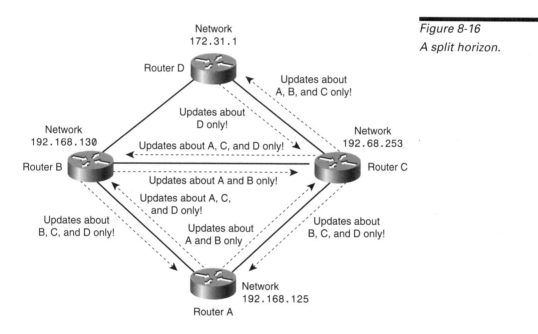

Figure 8-16

A split horizon.

In Figure 8-16, the routers support the split horizon logic. Therefore, Router C (which supports the only path to Router D) cannot receive updates from Router A about Network D. This is because A relies on C (and even B) for this route information. Router A must omit from its routing table information about routes learned from C. This simple approach to splitting loops can be relatively effective, but it does have a serious functional limitation: By omitting reverse routes from advertising, each node must wait for the route to the unreachable destination to timeout. In RIP, a timeout occurs only after six update messages fail to update a route. Therefore, a misinformed node has five opportunities to misinform other nodes about an unreachable destination. It is this time delay that creates the opportunity for invalid routing information to start the loop.

Due to this limitation, RIP supports a slightly modified version known as Split Horizon with Poisoned Reverse.

Split Horizon with Poisoned Reverse

The simple split horizon scheme attempts to control loops by ceasing to propagate information back to its originator. Although this can be effective, there are more effective ways to stop a loop. Split horizon with poisoned reverse takes a much more proactive approach to stopping loops: This technique actually poisons the looped route by setting its metric to infinity! This is illustrated in Figure 8-17.

As illustrated in Figure 8-17, Router A can provide information to Router B about how to reach Router D, but this route carries a metric of 16. Therefore, Router B cannot update its routing table with information about a better way to reach the destination. In fact, A is advertising that it cannot reach D, which is a true statement. This form of route advertising effectively breaks loops immediately.

Generally speaking, split horizon with poisoned reverse is much safer in distance-vector networks than just split horizon. However, neither is perfect. Split horizon with poisoned reverse will effectively prevent routing loops in topologies with just two gateways. In larger internetworks, however, RIP is still subject to the counting to infinity problem. To ensure that such infinite loops are caught as early as possible, RIP supports a triggered update.

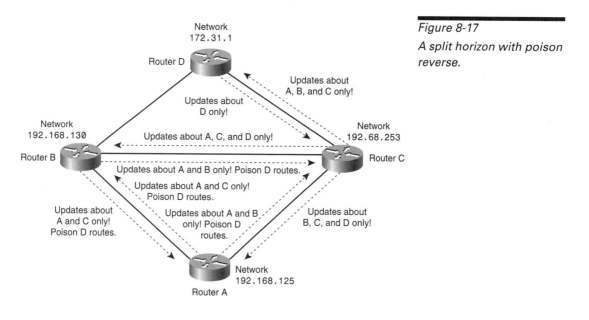

Figure 8-17
A split horizon with poison reverse.

Triggered Updates

Networks that feature three gateways to a common network are still susceptible to loops caused by mutual deception of the gateways. Figure 8-18 illustrates this point. This diagram features three gateways to Router D: A, B, and C.

In the event that Router D fails, Router A may believe that B can still access D. Router B may believe that C can still access D, and C may believe that A can still access D. The net effect is a continuous loop to infinity. Figure 8-19 illustrates this.

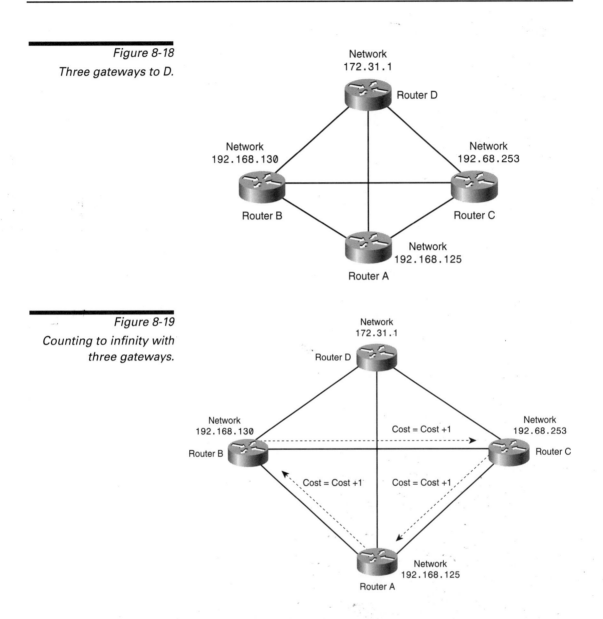

Figure 8-18
Three gateways to D.

Figure 8-19
Counting to infinity with three gateways.

Split horizon logic would be ineffective in this scenario due to the time delay before routes can be invalidated. RIP uses a different technique, known as a *triggered update*, to accelerate convergence. A triggered update is a rule in the protocol that requires gateways to immediately broadcast an update message whenever it changes a route metric, regardless of how much time remains in the 30-second update timer.

The previous sections demonstrated how time is the Achilles heel of split horizons, with or without reverse poisoning. Triggered updates are designed to overcome this vulnerability by reducing time delay to an absolute minimum.

Hold-Down Timers

Triggered updates are not a panacea! Updates are not propagated instantaneously throughout a network. Therefore, it is possible (however unlikely) that another gateway could have just transmitted a periodic update before receiving a triggered update from another gateway. In this scenario, vestiges of an invalid route could repropagate throughout the network. Although the likelihood of this occurring is extremely low, it is still possible for counting to infinity loops to occur within a RIP network despite the use of triggered updates.

The solution to this potential problem is the use of a hold-down timer. A hold-down timer works in conjunction with the triggered update logic. In essence, as soon as a triggered update has been made, a clock starts counting down to zero. Until it decrements to zero, the router will not accept any updates from any neighbors for that route or destination.

This prevents a RIP router from accepting updates for a route that has been invalidated for a configurable amount of time. This prevents a router from being misled into believing that another router may have a viable route to an otherwise invalid destination.

LIMITATIONS OF RIP

Despite its lengthy heritage, RIP isn't perfect. Although it was marvelously suited to calculating routes during the early days of internetworking, technological advance has radically changed the way that internetworks are built and used. Consequently, RIP is rapidly approaching obsolescence in today's internetwork.

Some of RIP's greatest limitations are its

- Inability to support paths longer than 15 hops

- Reliance on fixed metrics to calculate routes

- Network intensity of table updates

- Relatively slow convergence

- Lack of support for dynamic load balancing

Hop Count Limit

RIP was designed for use in relatively small autonomous systems. As such, it enforces a strict hop count limit of 15 hops, assuming that the default values for cost metrics aren't modified. As packets are forwarded by a routing device, their hop counters are incremented by the cost of the link that it is being transmitted over. If the hop counter hits 15, and the packet isn't at its addressed destination, that destination is considered unreachable and the packet is discarded.

This effectively fixes maximum network diameter at 15 hops. Therefore, if your network has a diameter of more than 15, RIP probably isn't the right routing protocol to use.

Fixed Metrics

The discussion about hop counts nicely sets the stage for an examination of RIP's next fundamental limitation: its fixed cost metrics. Although the administrator can configure cost metrics, they are static in nature. RIP cannot update them in real-time to accommodate changes it encounters in the network. The cost metrics defined by the administrator remain fixed until updated manually.

This means that RIP is particularly unsuited for highly dynamic networks where route calculations must be made in real-time in response to changes in the network's condition. If a network supports time-sensitive applications, for example, it is reasonable to use a routing protocol that can calculate routes based on the measured delay of its transmission facilities or even the existing load on a given facility. RIP uses fixed metrics. Therefore, it cannot support real-time route calculation.

Network Intensity of Table Updates

A RIP node broadcasts its routing tables omnidirectionally every 30 seconds. In large networks with many nodes, this can consume a fair amount of bandwidth.

Slow Convergence

In human terms, waiting 30 seconds for an update is hardly inconvenient. Routers and computers, however, operate at much faster speeds than humans. Therefore, having to wait 30 seconds for an update can have demonstrably adverse effects. This point is demonstrated in the section titled "Topology Changes" earlier in this chapter.

Much more damaging than merely waiting 30 seconds for an update, however, is having to wait up to 180 seconds to invalidate a route. And this is just the amount of time needed for just one router to begin convergence. Depending on how many routers are internetworked, and their topology, it may take repeated updates to completely converge on a new topology. The slowness with which RIP routers converge creates a wealth of opportunities for vestiges of invalid routes to be falsely advertised as still available. Obviously, this compromises the performance of the network, both in the aggregate and in the perception of individual users.

This chapter should have amply demonstrated the dangers inherent in RIP's slow convergence.

Lack of Load Balancing

Another of RIP's significant limitations is its inability to dynamically load balance. Figure 8-20 illustrates a router with two serial connections to another router in its internetwork. Ideally, the router in this illustration would split the traffic as evenly as possible between the two serial connections. This would keep congestion to a minimum on both links and would optimize performance.

Figure 8-20

A router with redundant serial connections.

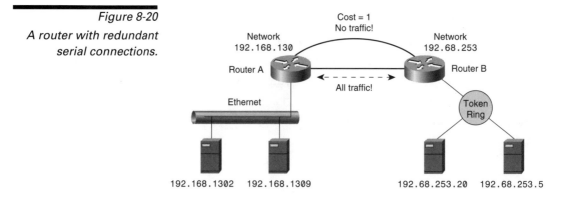

Unfortunately, RIP cannot perform such dynamic load balancing. It would use whichever of the two physical connections that it knew about first. RIP would forward all its traffic over that connection even though the second connection was available for use. This scenario would change only if the router in Figure 8-20 received a routing update informing it of a change in the metrics to any given destination. If this update meant that the second link was the lowest-cost path to a destination, it would begin using that link and cease using the first link.

RIP's inherent lack of load-balancing capability reinforces its intended use in simple networks. Simple networks, by their very nature, tend to have few (if any) redundant routes. Consequently, load balancing was not perceived as a design requirement, and support for it was not developed.

SUMMARY

RIP's ease of configuration, flexibility, and ease of use have made it a highly successful routing protocol. Since its development, there have been tremendous advances in both computing, networking, and internetworking technologies. The cumulative effects of these advances have taken their toll on RIP's popularity. In fact, many other routing protocols in use today are technically superior to RIP. Despite the success of these protocols, RIP remains a highly useful routing protocol, provided you understand the practical implications of its limitations and use it accordingly.

CHAPTER 9

Routing Information Protocol Version 2

Routing Information Protocol version 2, or RIP-2 as it is more commonly called, was first proposed as an update to RIP in RFC 1388 in January 1993. This RFC was later superseded by RFC 1723 in November 1994. Neither of these RIP-2 proposals was intended to be a replacement for RIP. Instead, they both designed RIP-2 as an extension of RIP that provided additional functionality. These extensions were concentrated on RIP's message format, and provided support for new networking functions such as subnetting, authentication, and multicasting.

Given that RIP-2 is an extension of RIP, it is not surprising that the two routing protocols remain remarkably similar in their operational mechanics and characteristics. Rather than repeat this material, this chapter focuses on the differences between RIP and RIP-2. This includes an examination of the RIP-2 message format and the functionality gained through its extensions.

THE NEED TO UPDATE RIP

RIP was one of the earliest and most successful of the distance-vector routing protocols. Its success was based on its ease of use and supportability in small networks. Over time, the Internet and its protocol (IP) grew and matured. With maturation

277

came increased functionality. RIP lacked the basic mechanisms to cope with some of these increasingly important features. Perhaps its greatest limitation was its inability to recognize subnet masks.

Subnetting was not even defined when RFC 1058 was being developed. Despite this, RIP was able to apply heuristics to determine whether a subnet mask was actually a subnet route or a host route provided that those masks remained constant, of fixed-length, and were well known throughout the network. These conditions were necessary due to RIP's inability to advertise subnet information to neighboring RIP nodes. If these conditions weren't satisfied, subnets couldn't be supported across a routed link.

Introduction of classless interdomain routing (CIDR), variable-length subnet masks, and supernetting, however, rendered RIP incapable of differentiating between network routes, subnet routes, and host routes.

Despite its functional limitations, RIP remained solidly entrenched in small networks and autonomous systems. Part of the reason for its persistence in the face of obsolescence can be found in the emerging crop of competitor routing protocols. These included Open Shortest Path First (OSPF) and Intermediate System to Intermediate System (IS-IS). As powerful and feature-rich as these new protocols were, they were not easy to use, implement, or manage. Consequently, there was reluctance to migrate, especially within smaller networks.

Another reason for its persistence was the inertia of its tremendous installed base. Many of the extant RIP nodes couldn't be upgraded, nor could they support any other routing protocols. Consequently, RIP soldiered on.

Given this backdrop, the IETF commissioned a technical committee, the RIP-2 working group, to examine the possibilities for updating RIP to include support for subnet masks and other new features.

RIP-2: RFC 1723

The culmination of the RIP-2 working group's efforts was RFC 1723. This RFC was only a modest revision of the previous RIP-2 proposal contained in RFC 1388. Both proposals sought to add functionality primarily by better utilizing the Must Be Zero (MBZ, or Zero) fields that were so prevalent in the RIP version 1 packet. These fields provided backward compatibility between RFC 1058 RIP and the myriad proprietary RIP-like routing protocols that had been spawned by the works of R. E. Bellman, L. R. Ford, Jr., and D. R. Fulkerson. RFC 1058 was successful enough that by 1993 backward compatibility with these proprietary RIP variants was no longer necessary.

NOTE

The only significant difference between RFC 1388 and RFC 1723 was the deletion of 1388's 2-octet Domain field in the protocol's message format. Consensus couldn't be reached as to how to actually use that field, so the idea was scrapped. Its space was designated unused by 1723. For more details about the RFC 1723 RIP-2 message format, refer to the section in this chapter titled "RIP-2 Message Format."

Reusing these Zero fields could enable RIP to support some of the much-needed functionality without changing the size of the RIP-2 message structure. Changing the size of the message structure would make it easier to integrate support for new functions, but would also compromise backward compatibility with RIP. This was unacceptable. Backward compatibility was deemed paramount to the success of RIP-2. Remember, RIP-2 was an extension to RIP, not a replacement for it. Consequently, backward compatibility was of primary importance.

This priority would result in the abandonment of at least one other highly desired proposed feature: extending hop count beyond 15. Adding the capability to count beyond 15 would enable RIP-2 to support much larger networks and autonomous systems. Unfortunately, it would also make RIP-2 less than completely backward compatible with RIP. Any routing information shared by a RIP-2 node with a RIP node that contained a metric greater than 16 would be interpreted by that RIP node as an invalid route!

RFC 1723 SPECIFICATIONS

RIP-2, like its predecessor, was specifically designed for use as an Interior Gateway Protocol (IGP) in small networks. Its capability to support subnet masks, however, meant that it would accommodate a degree of network addressing complexity that RIP couldn't.

RIP-2 Message Format

RIP-2 uses a special message format, or packet, to collect and share information about distances to known internetworked destinations. This packet contains the following structure:

- A 1-octet Command field

- A 1-octet Version Number field

- A 2-octet Unused field

- A 2-octet Address Family Identifier (AFI) field

- A 2-octet Route Tag field

- A 4-octet Networking Address (that is, IP address) field

- A 4-octet Subnet Mask field

- A 4-octet Next Hop field

- A 4-octet Metric field

Of these fields, only the Command, Version, and Unused fields are considered header fields. The remainder are routing data fields. Figure 9-1 illustrates the RIP-2 message format.

1-octet Command field	1-octet Version Number field	2-octet Unused field	2-octet AFI field	2-octet Route Tag field	4-octet Network Address field	4-octet Subnet Mask field	4-octet Next Hop field	4-octet Metric field

Figure 9-1
The RIP-2 message format.

The Command Field

The Command field remained unchanged from RIP. It indicates whether the RIP-2 message was generated as a *request*, or a *response* to a request. The same frame structure is used for both occurrences:

- A request message asks a RIP-2 node to send all, or part, of its routing table. Setting this octet to a value of 1 indicates that the message contains a request for routing information.

- A response message contains routing table entries that are to be shared with other RIP or RIP-2 nodes in the network. A response message can be generated either in response to a request, or as an unsolicited update. Setting this octet to a value of 2 indicates that the message contains a response replete with routing data.

The Version Number Field

The Version Number field contains the version of Routing Information Protocol that was used to generate the RIP packet. RIP-2 always sets this field equal to 2.

The Unused Field

The Unused field is an artifact of a lack of consensus about how to recognize domains. RFC 1388 allocated two octets for a Domain field in the RIP-2 message header. Despite the agreement to support domain recognition, there was no clear agreement on how to use that field. Consequently, in RFC 1723, this field was redesignated as Unused. The contents of this field are ignored by RIP-2 nodes and must be set to zeros by RIP version 1 nodes.

The AFI Field

The AFI field is the start of the payload or data field in the RIP-2 message. The AFI field serves several purposes:

- Each routed protocol has its own address architecture, or family. Therefore, it is necessary to indicate which routed protocol's address architecture is contained in the Network Address field. A value of 2, for example, indicates the address family of the network address is IP.

- Setting AFI equal to 1 indicates the recipient should send a copy of its entire routing table to the requesting node.

- The AFI can also contain a special character sequence, 0xFFFF. This sequence identifies the contents of the AFI's row as authentication data, not routing data. Authentication was one of the features added to RIP-2. For more information on RIP-2 authentication, refer to the section in this chapter titled "Authentication."

The Route Tag Field

RIP-2 also provided a mechanism for differentiating between internal and external routes. This mechanism is the 2-octet route tag. An internal route is one that was learned by the RIP-2 protocols within confines of the network or autonomous system. External routes are those that were learned from other routing protocols, such as the various Border Gateway Protocols (BGPs).

In cases where the AFI is set to 0xFFFF, the Route Tag field is used to identify the type of authentication being performed. This is more closely examined in the section entitled "Authentication."

The Network Address Field

This 4-octet field contains a network (IP) address. The use of this field did not vary from the RFC 1058 RIP. This address can be a host, a network, or a default gateway address code. Two examples of how this field's contents can vary are as follows:

- In a single-entry request message, this field would contain the address of the packet's originator.

- In a multiple-entry response message, this field(s) would contain the IP addresses stored in the originator's routing table.

The Subnet Mask Field

The single most important change made to the RIP-2 message structure was the creation of a 4-octet subnet mask. This field contains the subnet mask of the network address. If the network address does not have a subnet mask, this field is set to zeros.

The Next Hop Field

The next field in the message structure is the 4-octet Next Hop field. This field contains the IP address of the next hop in the route to the destination as specified in the Network Address field.

The Metric Field

The last field in the RIP-2 packet contains its metric counter. The Metric field, too, remained the same as its RFC 1058 antecedent. The metric's value is incremented as it passes through a router. The valid range of metrics for this field is between 1 and 15. The Metric field can actually be incremented to 16, but this value is associated with invalid routes. Consequently, 16 is an error value for the Metric field and not part of the valid range used to calculate and compare routes.

Using RIP-2 Messages

The basic RIP-2 message format can be for two specific purposes. It can be used to request a routing update, or it can be used to respond to such a request. The message size can vary considerably between these two functions. More importantly, the contents and uses of certain fields will also vary. The following two sections detail the differences between these two types of RIP-2 messages.

RIP-2 Request Message

The RIP-2 Request Message is used by a RIP-2 node to request its neighbors to send a routing update. To create a request message, a RIP-2 node must set the contents of the Command field and the Network Address field properly.

The Command field of the request message is set to 1. This value is interpreted as a request by other RIP and RIP-2 nodes. The Network Address field is set to the IP address of the request message's originator.

RFC 1723 provides for the simultaneous transmission of a requesting node's routing table entries with a request message. Consequently, a requesting node may actually forward up to 25 of its routing table's entries along with a request for a routing update from its neighbor(s).

NOTE

Setting the AFI equal to 2 indicates that the address family is IP.

RIP-2 Response Message

The RIP-2 response message is generated either by a timing mechanism (as described in Chapter 8, "Routing Information Protocol") or in response to a neighboring node's request for an update. Each entry in the response message contains the routing information for a single network address, although this address may belong to a network or a subnet, rather than a single host.

RIP-2 packets can support from 1 to 25 occurrences of the Network Address, Subnet Mask, Next Hop, and Metric fields within a single packet. This enables one RIP Response Message to be used to update multiple entries in other routers' routing tables. RIP packets that contain multiple routing entries just repeat the packet structure from the AFI through the Metric fields. The repeated structures are appended to the end of the structure depicted in Figure 9-1. Figure 9-2 illustrates a RIP-2 packet with two table entries.

Figure 9-2
The RIP-2 packet format
with two table entries.

1-octet Command field	1-octet Version Number field	2-octet Unused field	2-octet AFI field	2-octet Route Tag field	4-octet Network Address field	4-octet Subnet Mask field	4-octet Next Hop field	4-octet Metric field
			2-octet AFI field	2-octet Route Tag field	4-octet Network Address field	4-octet Subnet Mask field	4-octet Next Hop field	4-octet Metric field

In larger RIP-2 networks, a request for a full routing table update may require the transmission of several response messages. As with version 1 of RIP, no provisions were made for the resequencing of the response messages upon arrival at their destination; individual routing table entries are not split between messages. Therefore, the contents of any given message are complete unto themselves, even though they may only be a subset of a complete routing table. The recipient node is free to process the updates as the packets are received, without having to resequence them.

RIP-2'S NEW FEATURES

The following four features are the most significant new features added to RIP-2:

- Authentication of the transmitting RIP-2 node to other RIP-2 nodes

- Subnet masks

- Next hop IP addresses

- Multicasting RIP-2 messages

Together, these changes represented a significant increase in the sophistication and capability of RIP-2 over RIP, without a commensurate decrease in its usability, manageability, or ease of implementation. There were other features as well, including enhanced Management Information Blocks (MIBs) and support for tagging external routes, but these held relatively minor implications for the operational functionality of a RIP-2 network.

Authentication

The RIP-2 working group added support for the authentication of the node that is transmitting response messages. The need for this is rather simple. Response messages are used to propagate routing information throughout a network. Authenticating the initiator of a response message was intended to prevent routing tables from being corrupted with spurious routes from a fraudulent source.

The RIP-2 working committee recognized the need for adding authentication to RIP-2 but were operating under stringent space constraints. The only available space in the RIP-2 message format was the 2-octet unused field. Unfortunately, two octets are hardly adequate for any rigorous authentication mechanism.

Given that authentication needs to be performed only once per message, it was reasoned that the function could take the place of one routing entry. This would allow 16 octets for authentication rather than just 16 bits. Substituting an authentication mechanism for a routing entry meant that there had to be some way to discern authentication data from routing entries within the message.

Authentication Conventions

The RIP-2 working group settled on the following conventions:

- The header structure of the authenticated response message would be unaltered. It would continue to feature a 1-octet Command field, a 1-octet Version Number field, and a 2-octet Unused field. These fields would adhere to all the standard conventions governing their use.

- The first, and only the first, routing entry in an authenticated response message would be used to transport authentication data.

- The AFI of that first record in an authenticated message would be set to 0xFFFF. This reduces the maximum amount of routing entries that can be passed in an authenticated message to just 24.

- The Route Tag field following the AFI in this authentication entry would be converted to a field that identified the type of authentication being performed. Implicit in this definition is that multiple forms of authentication can be supported by RIP-2, although RFC 1388 specified only a fairly rudimentary authentication mechanism.

- The last 16 octets—normally used for the Network Address, Subnet Mask, Next Hop, and Metric fields—would be used to carry the password.

Authenticated Message Format

Given these conventions, a RIP-2 message with authentication activated would have the following structure:

- A 1-octet Command field

- A 1-octet Version number

- A 2-octet Unused field

- A 2-octet AFI field set to `0xFFFF`

- A 2-octet Authentication Type field

- A 16-octet Password field

Figure 9-3 illustrates the authentication message.

2-octet AFI = 0xFFFF field	2-octet Authentication Type field	16-octet Password field

Figure 9-3

The RIP-2 authentication message.

To this structure could be added up to 24 RIP-2 routing entries, which contain the following:

- A 2-octet AFI field

- A 2-octet Route Tag field

- A 4-octet Networking Address (that is, IP address) field

- A 4-octet Subnet Address field

- A 4-octet Next Hop field

- A 4-octet Metric field

Figure 9-4 illustrates a RIP-2 message with authentication and one routing entry.

1-octet Command field	1-octet Version Number field	2-octet Unused field	2-octet AFI = 0xFFFF field	2-octet Authentication Type field	16-octet Password field				
			2-octet AFI field	2-octet Route Tag field	4-octet Network Address field	4-octet Subnet Mask field	4-octet Next Hop field	4-octet Metric field	

Figure 9-4

The RIP-2 packet format with one routing entry and authentication activated.

RIP-2 nodes that receive a response message with authentication must verify that the password is valid before accepting the routing entries contained in that message.

Authentication Concerns

The only authentication type defined for RIP-2 was a simple, unencrypted, 16-octet password. This type, identified as Type 2 in the Authentication Type field, affords minimal protection. Although a 16-octet password, mathematically speaking, can pose a formidable challenge to would-be crackers, it is transmitted in the clear. Worse, there are no provisions for enforcing a 16-octet password. Administrators can select passwords of less than 16 octets.

CAUTION

The authentication mechanism of RIP-2 does not encrypt any part of the response message's payload, including the password contained in the Authentication field. The Authentication password and all routes are transmitted in clear text. Consequently, RIP-2 networks that use authentication remain very vulnerable to attack by anyone with direct physical access to the network.

The native authentication mechanisms supported in RIP-2 are hardly robust or foolproof. The only protection they afford is the prevention of fraudulent routing information by persons outside the network. The only redeeming quality of the RIP-2 authentication mechanism is that it reserved space in the message structure for the authentication function. This space can be used to support more sophisticated authentication mechanisms. For example, Cisco routers can be configured to use MD5 encrytion with RIP-2.

Subnet Masks

RIP-2 was born of the need to support subnet masks in small, relatively homogeneous networks that were using RIP. RIP-2 allocated a 4-octet field to correlate a subnet mask to a destination IP address. This field lies directly behind the IP address in the packet. Therefore, a full 64 bits of the RIP-2 routing entry is dedicated to identifying a destination.

Used in tandem, the IP address and its subnet mask enable RIP-2 to specifically identify the type of destination that the route leads to. RIP-2 can, by reading the contents of these two fields, discern network from subnet from host. This permits RIP-2 to be used in network environments that require support of subnet masks on a route-by-route basis. Therefore, RIP-2 can route to specific subnets, regardless of whether the subnet mask is fixed or of variable length!

Next Hop Identification

The inclusion of a Next Hop identification field helped make RIP-2 more efficient than RIP by preventing unnecessary hops. This feature is particularly effective for network environments using multiple routing protocols simultaneously. This is because with multiple, dissimilar routing protocols, it is possible that some routes may never be discovered.

Consider a scenario in which there is a large-sized company with a corporate data center and an internal IP WAN (an intranet), for example. Instead of examining the entire intranet, an example using just two work locations within this intranet should suffice. Each location has its own LAN and router. (Router 1 connects network 193.168.125.0 to the company's IP WAN, and Router 2 connects network 193.168.124.0.) These two routers are interconnected via a T1 to an older router (Router 3) in the intranet's backbone. This company has elected to use RIP-2 between the work location routers and the backbone. EIGRP is used for route calculations between the backbone routers and the data centers. The older backbone router, Router 3, is being phased out. This router is connected to the intranet backbone with an ancient 56 kbps leased line. Although originally a wise and economical selection, this transmission facility is now obsolete and impedes traffic flows in the intranet. The new router, Router 4, is physically co-located with Router 3, and the two are interconnected via a FDDI ring. Router 4 is also connected to the backbone router with a T3 leased line. Figure 9-5 illustrates this network.

Figure 9-5

A network diagram for a
next hop example.

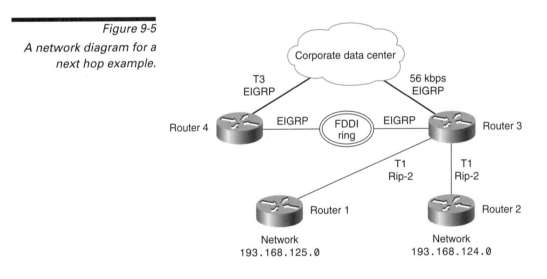

The company's use of two different routing protocols creates the potential for routing problems during the migration to Router 4 and its T3. This router connects only to other routers in the intranet's backbone. Therefore, all its ports have been configured to use EIGRP. Because it is not running RIP-2, or even RIP, the work location Routers 1 and 2 can't learn of its existence. As a result, the T3 route won't be discovered or used by the networks connected to Routers 1 and 2.

Figure 9-6 depicts this.

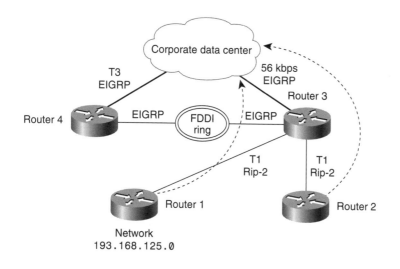

Network
193.168.125.0

Figure 9-6

The T3 route cannot be discovered by routers 1 and 2.

The problem is that Router 4 has a vastly superior connection to the data center than does Router 3. As such, Router 4 should be the next hop to the data center from Router 3, even though this router has its own direct connection! This dilemma can be solved in several ways. One obvious approach would be to violate the company's network architecture rules by configuring RIP-2 for the interfaces connecting Routers 3 and 4. This would enable end systems in networks 193.168.124.0 and 193.168.125.0 to discover routes through Router 4. RIP-2 is still a simple routing protocol that uses one, dimensionless routing metric, however: hop count. To end systems in these two networks, the data center would appear further away using the T3 route through Router 4 than it would using the

56 kbps link via Router 3. Therefore, merely configuring Router 4 for the RIP-2 protocol wouldn't bias traffic heading to the data center to use this router.

The architects of RIP-2 understood that this could pose problems. Their answer was to develop a mechanism that would force "next hops" regardless of metrics. This metric would enable a RIP-2 node (Router 3, in this example) to inform end systems on other RIP-2 nodes of the presence of a superior path that it would otherwise not be able to discover.

The IP address of the next hop router would be passed to the neighboring routers via routing table updates. These routers would force datagrams to use a specific route, regardless of whether that route would have been calculated to be optimal using available metrics. RIP-2 nodes would check the Next Hop field of an inbound datagram. If unpopulated, it would be forwarded along the path determined by that router to be optimal. If the Next Hop field was populated with an IP address, however, that datagram would be forwarded according to this Next Hop information.

NOTE

This type of mechanism is frequently called source routing in the context of other protocols. The difference between RIP-2's Next Hop field and source routing is that source routing is performed by end systems. RIP-2's Next Hop field is populated by a RIP-2 node as it forwards datagrams on behalf of end systems.

Figure 9-7 illustrates the impact of this use of the Next Hop field.

Figure 9-7
Using the Next Hop field.

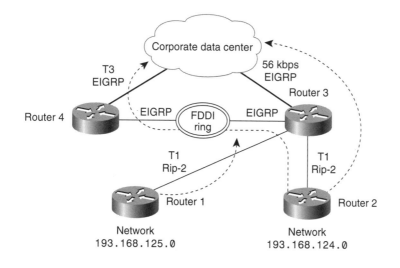

Multicasting

Multicasting is a technique for simultaneously advertising routing information to multiple RIP or RIP-2 devices. Multicasting is beneficial whenever multiple destinations must receive the identical information. The conventional solution to this problem would be to generate separate packets containing identical payloads specifically addressed to each machine. Multicasting enables packets to be simultaneously delivered to multiple machines. This reduces overall network traffic and reduces the processing load of the source machine.

RIP-2 multicasting also supports a filter that can be used to prevent a RIP router from receiving a RIP-2 routing update. Initially, this would seem contrary to the goal of backward compatibility. Although there is some truth to this, it is needed whenever it is necessary to route to a specific subnet. As the Subnet Mask field corresponds to a Zero field in RIP, RIP nodes would either discard such updates as invalid, or accept the route but ignore the subnet mask. Therefore, this form of filtration is a feature, not a flaw.

LIMITATIONS OF RIP-2

Despite its overhaul, RIP-2 couldn't compensate for all its predecessors' limitations. In fairness to the creators of RIP-2, they didn't seek to make RIP-2 anything but a modernized RIP. This included maintaining its original purpose as an IGP for use in small networks or autonomous systems. Therefore, all the original functional limitations designed into RIP also apply to RIP-2. The critical differences are that RIP-2 can be used in networks that require either support for authentication and/or variable-length subnet masks.

Some of the more salient limitations that were inherited by RIP-2 include the following:

- *15-hop maximum*—Perhaps the single greatest limitation that RIP-2 inherited from RIP is that its interpretation of infinity remained pegged at 16. In other words, after a route's cost is incremented to 16, that route becomes invalid, and the destination is considered unreachable.

  Any attempt to increase infinity in RIP-2 would have compromised its backward compatibility with RIP. Consequently, RIP-2 remains limited to use in networks with a maximum diameter of 15 or fewer hops.

NOTE

A maximum network diameter of 15 hops assumes that the cost metric remains fixed at 1 per hop. Configuring RIP-2 for higher costs will directly reduce the maximum network diameter.

- *Counting to infinity*—RIP-2 continues to rely on counting to infinity as a means of resolving certain error conditions within the network. One such error condition would be a routing loop. RIP-2 remains dependent on timers to generate updates. Therefore, it is also relatively slow to converge on a consensus of the network's topology following any change to that topology. The more time that it takes to converge, the greater the opportunity for obsolete information to be mistakenly propagated as current information. The result could be a routing loop.

  RIP-2 continues to support counting to infinity as a means of breaking such loops. Counting to infinity just means incrementing the metric until it reaches 16, the threshold at which a route is considered invalid and the destination unreachable.

  Counting to infinity is considered problematic because it permits a routing loop to continue for a potentially lengthy amount of time.

- *Static distance-vector metrics*—Yet another inherited limitation is found in RIP-2's static cost metrics. RIP-2 selects optimal routes based on a fixed cost metric. The default value, just like RIP, is 1—although this may be manually adjusted by the network's administrator. This metric remains constant, and can only be changed by the administrator.

  Therefore, RIP-2 remains unsuited for network environments that require routes to be selected in real-time based on either delay, traffic loads, or any other dynamic network performance metric.

- *Lack of alternative routes*—RIP-2 continues to maintain a single route to any given destination in its routing tables. In the event a route becomes invalid, the RIP-2 node does not know any other routes to the destination of the failed route. Consequently, it must await a routing update before it can begin to assess potential alternative routes to that destination. This approach to routing minimizes the size of routing tables but can result in the temporary unreachability of destinations during a link or router failure.

SUMMARY

RIP was a highly successful, simple, and easy-to-use routing protocol that found great acceptance within small networks and autonomous systems. Over time, RIP began to experience the technological obsolescence that inevitably comes with the passage of decades. RIP-2 was designed as an update to RIP that would enable its tremendous embedded base a graceful way to support new networking features without the pain and suffering that would otherwise accompany a routing protocol migration.

RIP-2 was intended as a means of staving off a forced migration to a more complex, link-state protocol (such as OSPF) in smaller networked environments. This new protocol offered support for many new features, including subnet masking, but retained many of RIP's fundamental limitations.

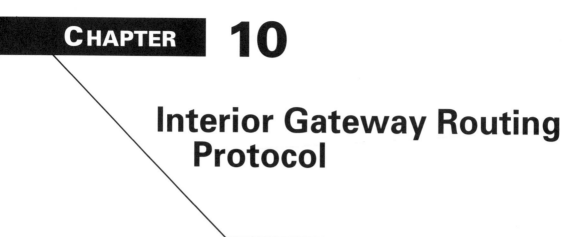

Interior Gateway Routing Protocol

Routing Information Protocol's (RIP's) success proved the viability of using distance vectors to calculate routes within autonomous systems. Unfortunately, as more (and larger) organizations embraced routing, and the Internet Protocol (IP), the limitations of RIP became increasingly apparent. During the early 1980s, Cisco Systems saw an opportunity in the marketplace for an improved distance-vector routing protocol, one that was simultaneously more scalable and feature-rich than RIP.

Cisco's response to this market need was the development of Interior Gateway Routing Protocol (IGRP). IGRP was explicitly designed to be as easy to use as RIP, yet without any of RIP's operational limitations. IGRP proved so successful that it established Cisco Systems as the vendor of choice for routing technologies. This chapter examines the details, mechanics, and uses of IGRP.

THE ORIGINS OF IGRP

Until the early 1980s, internetworking was not broadly required by commercial organizations. They relied extensively on a hard-wired infrastructure, populated with dumb terminals, cluster controllers, and mainframes. Some organizations required internetworking capabilities—research groups or universities, for example—as did some commercial entities. The limited market requirements for internetworking technologies meant that the vast majority of existing networks were relatively small. Therefore, RIP enjoyed immense popularity.

The 1980s, however, witnessed several significant technological advances. Two of the most significant of these were the development of a standardized platform for desktop computing (a PC) and the emergence of local-area networks. Together, PCs and LANs formed a new paradigm of inexpensive distributed computing. The dispersion of computational power within, and across, organizations resulted in an increased need for internetworking. RIP, which had served the needs of the internetworking community for so long, began to exhibit the symptoms of its advanced age.

Perhaps the most obvious limitation of RIP was that it was designed for use only in small autonomous systems. In the early days of internetworking, this wasn't deemed much of a limitation. By the middle of the 1980s, however, small autonomous systems were becoming the exception rather than the rule. This size limitation, however, wasn't the only limitation that was causing operational difficulties in RIP internetworks. Internetworks, in addition to growing larger were also becoming much more complex. They were being constructed with an ever-increasing variety of technologies and transmission facilities and protocols, and were taking on interesting topological patterns.

Cisco Systems, Inc. saw the need for a robust routing protocol that could gracefully scale upward and that could accommodate the increased complexity of internetworks.

Needed Capabilities

Developing a new routing protocol is not a trivial undertaking. Success requires carefully identifying requirements and developing capabilities to satisfy those requirements. Cisco was able to use RIP's functional limitations as requirements for its new routing protocol.

In addition to RIP's relatively low hop-count limit (a maximum of 15 countable hops—with hop 16 constituting unreachable) were other limitations. RIP could not balance traffic loads across multiple redundant links because it remembered only a single route per destination, for example. Worse, this route was calculated using a single, static metric. Therefore, RIP could calculate routes based only on the number of routers in between a source and destination machine. RIP could not differentiate between types of links, nor make intelligent route selections based on actual performance characteristics of different links.

Translating RIP's limitations into requirements for a new protocol was relatively easy. Some of the specific internetwork attributes that needed to be supported included the following:

- Moderate to large-sized autonomous systems

- Complex topologies

- Dynamic load balancing (which implied tracking multiple routes per destination)

- Calculating routes using dynamic metrics

- Rapid convergence after a topology change

- The capability to select optimal routes despite having an internetwork constructed of widely divergent transmission technologies, such as Ethernet, FDDI, ATM, fractional T1s, Frame Relay, and T3s

This last item, supporting a diverse collection of transmission technologies, means that each link would have vastly different propagation delay, bandwidth, and other characteristics. Therefore, selecting an "optimal" route is far from a trivial endeavor. Just counting the number of hops between any two points is inadequate. Instead, the emphasis would have to be placed on the transmission facilities themselves rather than on the routers that interconnect transmission facilities.

Cisco's Solution

Cisco Systems had a solution that could satisfy the ever-growing and ever-divergent demands for internetworking. The answer was a homegrown distance-vector routing protocol called IGRP. IGRP was designed to be easy to configure and use; in operation, it minimized operational overheads without exacerbating convergence times. It also leveraged many of the features that made RIP so useful. This would enable a relatively graceful migration, because most network administrators were quite familiar with RIP.

Despite retaining many of RIP's better features, IGRP was carefully crafted to avoid the RIP's limitations. The end result was that network administrators found IGRP to be vastly superior to RIP, yet familiar enough to mitigate the migration.

An Overview of IGRP

IGRP is a distance-vector protocol designed for use on interior gateway routers within an autonomous system. As explained in Chapter 7, "The Mechanics of Routing Protocols," routers that use distance-vector routing protocols regularly forward all, or part, of their routing tables to their immediate neighbors. This process recurs periodically, and recursively throughout the AS until all the nodes in that system agree on its topology and distances to known destinations.

IGRP was given an expanded capability set relative to RIP and other distance-vector protocols. One of the more revolutionary new features was the way it calculated distance vectors. Unlike previous distance vector protocols that used a single metric for calculating routes, IGRP has a series of metrics, each with a wide range of possible values. Each of these metrics can be hashed against a mathematical value, or weight. This enables network administrators to customize the route calculation algorithm according to their specific needs. These metrics, and their weights, are used to calculate a single, composite routing metric. This composite metric is used to mathematically compare potential routes to destinations.

Additionally, IGRP could support multipath routing. RIP, and its myriad RIP-like variants, could only remember a single route to any given destination. These routing protocols were, inherently, unable to conduct multipath routing. IGRP can remember up to four routes to any given destination. This enables it to support multipath routing in a distance-vector network. The practical implications of multipath routing are two new capabilities:

- Load balancing across two, three, or four links

- Automatic recovery from a failed link

These features are examined in more detail in the section titled "Multipath Routing."

Despite its tremendous success in the market and internetworks around the world, IGRP remains a proprietary routing protocol. The ubiquity of Cisco routers may make IGRP appear open, but it is not. No other router manufacturer besides Cisco Systems supports it. Cisco has not published the details of IGRP's internal mechanisms, nor is it likely to. Therefore, it is not possible to examine IGRP to the same extent that openly specified routing protocols can be examined. Despite this handicap, it is still possible to gain an appreciation for IGRP by examining some of its configurable attributes, as well as its functional mechanics.

Metrics

One of the areas in which IGRP excels is its high degree of flexibility. This flexibility is afforded via its routing metrics. Unlike RIP—which has a single, static metric—IGRP uses six metrics:

- Hop count

- Packet size (described as Maximum Transmission Unit—MTU)

- The link's bandwidth

- Delay

- Loading

- Reliability

IGRP nodes share information pertaining to all six metrics during table updates, but not all six metrics are used to calculate routes. In fact, only bandwidth, delay, load, and reliability can be used to calculate routes. The other two, hop count and MTU, facilitate routing in other ways.

The flexibility of IGRP extends beyond a mere increase in the number of metrics. Additional flexibility is afforded in the range of values that each of these metrics can support. The administrator can define each of these metrics. IGRP also allows the administrator to establish the default weights for these metrics, which are also factored into route calculation.

Hop Count

Consistent with its heritage, IGRP supports the incrementing of a hop counter as one means of determining how far away specific destinations are. Each router in a path counts as a single hop. Unlike RIP, IGRP does not cap this value at 16. The default maximum hop count is 100; this may be increased, however, up to 255. This enables IGRP to be used in substantially larger networks than RIP can support.

It is important to note that although IGRP maintains a hop counter, it does not use this value to determine optimal paths. Instead, hop counting is just a means of protecting against routing loops. Routes with a hop count in excess of the stated maximum are automatically invalidated by IGRP. Routes whose hop counts exceed this diameter are considered invalid and are not advertised to neighboring nodes via table updates.

This fundamental difference in the use of hop counts between RIP and IGRP demonstrates just how different these protocols are. RIP is a simple, if not crude, distance-vector protocol. It determined network distances only by counting the number of routers separating a source and destination machine. Rather than focus on the number of routers in its route calculations, IGRP focuses on the attributes of the transmission facilities that interconnect the routers. Properly configured, IGRP can discriminate between the performance attributes of different types of transmission facilities.

MTU

MTU identifies the largest-size datagram that an IGRP router will accept. This value is not used to calculate routes, nor is it factored into IGRP's composite metric. IGRP nodes communicate with other IGRP nodes the maximum size of the datagram that they can accommodate. Datagrams larger than a router's MTU size must be split into two or more datagrams that comply with this size limitation.

Very large MTUs may result in a performance penalty, because routers must buffer incoming datagrams until they can determine where to forward them. The larger the datagrams, the more buffer space must be used. Conversely, very small MTUs may also result in a performance penalty, because they unnecessarily compromise the header-to-payload ratio of datagrams. Both of these are relatively minor concerns because routers have grown tremendously in both speed and processing capacity over the last few years. Therefore, the MTU can best be thought of as a way of fine-tuning the performance of your network. Ideally, this value will be set to a value consistent with user requirements and consistent across all the routers in an autonomous system.

Bandwidth

Bandwidth identifies the speed of the transmission facility that is connected to a given I/O port on the router. Values for this field can range from 1,200 bps up to 10 Gbps. It is important to note that, unless explicitly set to a different value, the Cisco IOS will assume that the link is a T1 and will default the bandwidth metric to 1.544 Mbps.

It is important to note that, even though the default is for 1.544 Mbps of bandwidth, interface ports will not attempt to use more bandwidth than is actually available. These ports are connected to a line driver device such as a CSU/DSU. It is these physical layer devices that actually place data on the transmission facility.

Using default values effectively nullifies the bandwidth metric for the purposes of route calculation, however. Therefore, it is usually preferable to define the bandwidth actually available, per interface port, instead of just accepting the default values. Defining actual bandwidth values, per link, improves IGRP's capability to calculate and select optimal routes.

Bandwidths can be intentionally understated to reduce the use of specific transmission facilities. Ostensibly, this can allow dial-on-demand, as well as other types of transmission facilities, to be reserved for use in emergencies or during periods of peak traffic loads.

For the purposes of metric calculation, IGRP looks at the defined bandwidth on all the outbound interface ports in a given route and selects the smallest of these numbers—which is the bandwidth limit for that route. This number is then divided by 10,000,000, which results in the bandwidth being expressed as kilobits per second.

Delay

Delay measures the approximate amount of time needed to traverse a link in the network, assuming the link is otherwise unused. The aggregate delay of a route in an IGRP network is the sum of the delays attributed to each outbound router interface in a route. This sum is divided by 10 to express the result in microseconds. This metric can have any value, from 1 up to 16,777,215.

> **NOTE**
>
> Additional delay may be incurred as a result of congestion. The effects of congestion, or even moderate traffic levels, can also be factored into the IGRP composite metric through the use of the load metric. Load measures the delays incurred as a result of bandwidth utilization levels.

Rather than develop an algorithm that calculated actual delay (per route) on-the-fly, IGRP uses an average delay value for each transmission technology. A T1 private line defaults to a delay factor of 21,000 μs, for example. This simplifying assumption reduces the CPU-intensity of IGRP, yet still provides flexibility in calculating routes in a heterogeneous network.

IGRP automatically populates the delay metric for each defined transmission facility according to its defined bandwidth and transmission technology. A 10 Mbps Ethernet link has 10 times the average delay of a 100 Mbps Ethernet link, for example. Network administrators can also change this value to any other value in the supported range to reflect specific conditions in their network. This enables an IGRP router to differentiate between a T1 terrestrial circuit and a T1 with a satellite uplink. Although both offer identical bandwidths, the terrestrial circuit will feature noticeably less delay.

The delay of a circuit also varies with its distance. A terrestrial T1 circuit that stretches from San Francisco to Boston inherently has a higher propagation delay than a similar circuit of the same bandwidth that runs from Boston to New York City, for example. A network administrator can manipulate route calculation toward shorter circuits by lowering their delay rating, or increasing the delay rating of longer circuits. Great care should be exercised when modifying metrics; you may not always achieve the results that you expect! If you insist on modifying these metric weights, test the new settings in a laboratory or test environment first. After you have achieved the desired results and are convinced the modifications won't jeopardize the stability of the network, proceed cautiously with the modification of the metric weights in your IGRP network.

Load

Whereas delay measures just the innate delay of a given transmission facility, load adds a dimension of realism to the composite metric. The load factor measures the amount of bandwidth currently available across a given link. The more heavily utilized a link is, the more time is needed to traverse that link. IGRP's load metric enables it to factor current utilization levels into the calculation of optimal routes in the network.

In theory, basing route calculation on the load levels of individual links is a good idea. It enables the routing protocol to route around congestion. In practice, however, network loads can be far too transient to warrant recalculation of routes or any other action by the routing protocol. A user with a robust LAN connection to a router can easily consume all the available bandwidth on a serial link with nothing more than a simple File Transfer Protocol (FTP) session, for example. In such cases, an IGRP network that actually uses Load in its route calculation would perceive that link as suddenly unacceptable. This would cause IGRP to take corrective actions, including holding down any routes that use that link, and possibly even attempt convergence on a new network topology. The FTP session could, quite conceivably, end before the network routes around the problem that session caused.

Consequently, the default value for the constant used to weight this metric effectively cancels it out of the calculation of IGRP's composite metric. It is there, and can be used; however, you must explicitly modify the value of this metric's constant before Load will be factored into the IGRP composite metric. Should you choose to throw caution to the wind, the supported range of values for this metric is from 1 to 255. The network administrator can manipulate both this metric's value, as well as its weight, so that their typical loads can be factored into route calculations. Extreme care should be used whenever modifying any metrics or their weights. Load, however, can be particularly dangerous to experiment with in a real network because the effects of your change might not become apparent until the network experiences heavy loads.

Reliability

Another way for a network administrator to bias the outcomes of IGRP route calculations is through the use of the reliability metric. Reliability tracks the current error rate, per transmission facility. An error rate is just the ratio of packets that arrive undamaged.

This metric, like Load, can have any value between 1 and 255. By default, reliability is set to 1 for all types of transmission facilities. Over time, this value will likely increase as the IGRP node factors in the actual error rates incurred, per transmission facility. High-reliability metrics indicate unreliable or problematic links.

Using the Metrics

The key to IGRP's flexibility does not lie in any of its metrics but in what IGRP *does* with these metrics. Unlike RIP and most other routing protocols, IGRP does not just compare metric values of potential routes. Instead, IGRP uses the metric values, as well as the default or administrator-defined weightings, to develop a single, composite metric that mathematically describes potential routes. This composite metric can be used to compare potential routes through the network, even though the routes vary widely in reliability, bandwidth, delay, and utilization rates.

The obvious benefit to such a large metric, developed using so many different weighted variables, is that it is possible to more accurately describe a route's performance potential. The network administrator can use these variables to influence the route selection process within the autonomous system.

The limitation to IGRP's implementation of metrics is that it is easy to nullify them. By accepting all the defaulted values, for example, all the metrics for all the routes are equal. Therefore, mathematically, they cancel out. The route calculation process would then be little more than an obfuscated comparison of the number of hops in each potential route. It is clearly in your best interest to customize these routing metrics, particularly bandwidth. You may even find it useful to alter their weighting factors to more closely resemble conditions encountered in your network and/or your users' requirements.

Calculating Vectors

IGRP uses a composite metric to calculate the optimality of routes. This metric is 24 bits long and can range in value from 1 to 16,777,215. For the purposes of route calculation, the lower the number, the better the route.

In essence, the value of the composite metric reflects the weighted sum of the delays and bandwidths along a given route. Therefore, if all the default metrics and weights were accepted and a network were constructed of strictly homogeneous media (for example, all

T1s), this metric would amount to little more than just a hop count. In networks constructed of diverse media (for example, Ethernets and Fractional T1s), the benefits of such a mathematical comparison of delays and bandwidths becomes apparent.

The general formula for calculating composite vectors is as follows:

Metric = K1 × Bandwidth + (K2 × Bandwidth)/(256 − Load) + K3 × Delay

In this formula, K1, K2, and K3 are constants used to weigh the effect of the routing metrics. The default values for K1 and K3 are = 1, and the default value for K2 is 0. Additionally, two other constants can be used to bias the route calculation: K4 and K5. Both of these constants are also defaulted to 0 and are not used if left at this default value. The network's administrator can modify all these constants. The processes by which IGRP derives the values of Bandwidth, Load, and Delay were described in the preceding sections.

Breaking the original equation into individual operations reveals why this is so:

- The first operation is to multiply Bandwidth by 1, which does not change the value of Bandwidth.

- The second part of the equation multiplies Bandwidth by 0 and then divides this result by 256 − Load. Load can have a maximum value of 255, so this operation will always yield a positive number between 255 and 1.

- The result of the preceding operation is divided into the result of the second operation (K2 * Bandwidth, which equals 0 when using the default constant values). Dividing 0 by anything results in 0. Therefore, if you accept all the default constant values, you effectively nullify the effects of Load in the calculation of the IGRP metric.

- The result of the preceding operation, which is always 0 if you accept the default constant values, is added to the result of the first operation.

- The last operation in the basic metric calculation, is to multiply Delay by K3, which defaults to a value of 1. The result, if you accept the default constant values, is the preservation of the original Delay value. This amount is then added to the result of the previous operations.

Therefore, mathematically, the basic metric calculation reduces to just this:

Metric = Bandwidth + Delay

Conspicuously absent from this mathematical process was IGRP's fourth routing metric: Reliability. Reliability is used only if the network's administrator modifies the values of constant K5. If this is changed to any number greater than 0, an additional operation is performed using the metric that resulted from the previous equation. This operation is as follows:

Metric = Metric × *[K5/(reliability + K4)]*

Given K5's default value of 0, this formula would always return a zero for the entire IGRP composite metric. Therefore, it is only performed if K5 > 0. As is evident in this formula, both K5 and K4 are used to weight the effect that reliability has on the composite metric. Having seen the complexity of this formula, it should be self-evident why it is dangerous to arbitrarily manipulate constant values without thorough testing in a laboratory or test environment first.

Regardless of whether you use the default values, the result of the IGRP metric calculation is a composite metric that can fairly evaluate potential routes through a highly diverse network. The value of this composite metric is frequently described as the *cost* of a route. The route with the lowest cost is the best route.

IGRP's Mechanisms

In addition to its large, composite routing metric, IGRP also relies on a series of mechanisms to function properly and maintain a stable internetworking environment. These mechanisms fall into two broad categories: timing mechanisms and convergence mechanisms. In operation, the distinction between these two blurs, because there is considerable interdependence between them. This will become more obvious as you more closely examine these mechanisms in this section.

Timing Mechanisms

As with other distance-vector routing protocols, IGRP maintains the integrity of its routing tables by requiring routers to share their routing information. Each IGRP router sends updates of its routing table information to its immediate neighbors at fixed intervals. All updates received automatically supersede previous route information that was stored in the routing table.

IGRP relies on four timers to maintain the routing table:

- Update timer

- Hold timer

- Route invalid timer

- Route-flush timer

These timing mechanisms operate in much the same manner as RIPs timing mechanisms.

Update Timer

The update timer is used to initiate routing table updates at the node level. Each IGRP node uses only one update timer and tracks it as a system-level resource. The other timers, however, are specific to individual routes. Separate hold, route-flush, and route invalid timers are integrated in each routing table entry.

The default for the IGRP update timer is 90 seconds, although a network administrator can adjust this value. Unless modified, IGRP nodes will attempt to update their routing tables by sharing their routing information with their neighboring nodes every minute and a half.

Hold Timer

As with its antecedent, IGRP uses a hold timer. This timer tracks the amount of time that IGRP nodes hold down routing table updates. The default hold-down time for IGRP nodes is three times the maximum value of the update timer plus 10 seconds. If the update timer were left at its default value of 90 seconds, the hold timer would be set to 280 seconds.

Intentionally delaying such updates helps prevent accidentally reinstating routes to unreachable destinations. This process is examined in more detail in the section titled "Hold-Downs."

Route Invalid Timer

The route invalid timer specifies how long a router should wait, in the absence of routing update messages about a specific route, before declaring that route invalid. The IGRP default for this variable is three times the update period. Assuming the default value for the update timer, the route invalid timer is set to 270 seconds. If an IGRP node does not receive updated information about any route in that time, it declares that route to be inaccessible.

Route-Flush Timer

The route-flush timer indicates how much time should pass before a route should be flushed from the routing table. The IGRP default is seven times the routing update period, or 630 seconds if the default update timing value is used. This mechanism is used to purge, or flush, invalid routes from IGRP routing tables.

Convergence Mechanisms

IGRP includes several features designed to both reduce convergence times and improve the stability of IGRP networks:

- Flash update

- Hold-downs

- Split horizons

- Poison reverse updates

Flash Update

IGRP has a rather simple mechanism for improving convergence times. This mechanism is known as a flash update. Rather than waiting for the update timer to elapse before sending routing information, an IGRP node can flash an update to its neighbors. By effectively reducing the time that must elapse before convergence begins, the network can converge much more rapidly. The quicker the nodes in the network can agree on the network's new topology, the less opportunity there is for routing problems to arise.

Hold-Downs

One of the convergence features that IGRP borrowed from RIP is the hold-down. As explained in Chapter 8, "Routing Information Protocol," routing table updates are not propagated instantaneously throughout a network. The time delay inherent in the distance-vector convergence process creates the possibility that invalid routes can be wrongly resurrected through nonsimultaneous sharing of routing table information. This could happen if a router that has not yet learned about a failure that changes the network's topology transmits a scheduled table update to its neighbors. Its neighbors, who may already have invalidated affected routes, would see that this router still has valid routes to those destinations. Therefore, they would restore those invalid routes to service.

The solution to this potential problem is the use of the hold-down timer. The hold-down timer, known as a hold timer in IGRP, is usually set to a value slightly greater than the amount of time needed for all the routers in a network to converge on a mutual understanding of the network's topology. When a router receives an update that affects its routing table, it begins decrementing its hold timer. Until it decrements to zero, the router will not accept any updates from any neighbors for that route or destination. This prevents an IGRP router from accepting updates for a route that has been invalidated for a configurable amount of time. This prevents a router from being misled into believing that another router may have a viable route to an otherwise invalid destination.

While a route is being held down, it cannot be used. Under certain circumstances, this can be problematic for a network's users. With this in mind, IGRP developers established a way for hold-downs to be disabled. Although disabling hold-downs further improves convergence times by removing a waiting period, it can destabilize routing in the network by wrongly restoring invalid routes to service. Carefully evaluate the practical implications of your actions before you disable this mechanism.

Split Horizons

Another convergence-enhancing feature borrowed from RIP is the split horizon. Split horizons operate on the assumption that it is never a good idea to send routing information received from a given source back to that source. Figure 10-1 illustrates this point.

Figure 10-1
A split horizon scheme.

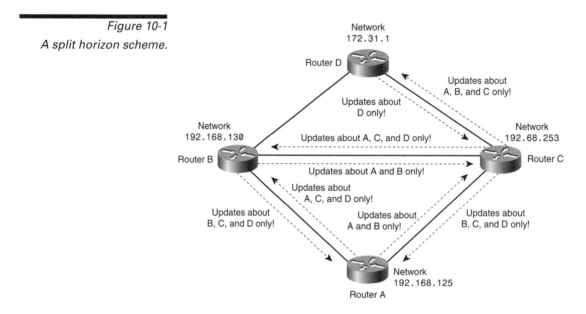

In Figure 10-1, the routers support the split-horizon logic. Therefore, Router C (which supports the only path to Router D) cannot receive updates from Router A about Network D. This is because Router A relies on Router C (and even Router B) for this route information. Router A must omit information about routes learned from Router C from its routing table updates to Router C. Advertising routing information about a specific route back to the source from which it was originally learned is known as *reverse routing*. This simple technique prevents routing loops by splitting the network's "horizon." In other words, advertising reverse routes is not permitted.

Although split horizons can be relatively effective, this technique does have a serious functional limitation. When you omit reverse routes from advertising, each node must wait for the route to the unreachable destination to expire. In IGRP, routes expire only after seven update messages fail to update a route. Therefore, there are six opportunities for a misinformed node to misinform other nodes about an unreachable destination. This time delay creates the opportunity for invalid routing information to start the loop. Using hold-downs, in conjunction with split horizons, should prevent the routing instability that can occur when neighboring routers misinform each other.

Poison Reverse Updates

One more mechanism that IGRP can employ to improve convergence is the poison reverse update. The poison reverse update is a relatively simple mechanism that enables an IGRP node to poison, or invalidate, a route learned from a neighbor (a reverse route) if that node believes the route to be looping. When an IGRP node receives a table update from a neighbor, it compares its route information with the information received from the neighboring node. If the updated information includes a route whose routing metric has increased by 10% or more since the last update, that route is assumed to be invalid. This assumption is based on the generalization that increases in routing metrics are caused by routing loops.

It is not always safe to make such an assumption. Therefore, rather than flush the route in question, IGRP just places that route in a hold-down state, and then informs its neighbors. Neighboring nodes, upon receiving this poison reverse update, also update their own routing tables, placing the route in question into a hold-down. This prevents users from using the route in question until new routing information can be obtained and a clearer consensus of the network's topology is reached.

Whereas split horizons are intended to prevent loops between adjacent routers, poison reverses are designed to guard against routing loops in larger networks. Large networks can feature multiple paths to any given destination. This creates an opportunity for looping to occur, despite a split horizon. To reduce the possibility of this occurring, IGRP uses a poison reverse update.

OPERATIONAL MECHANICS

Routers using a distance-vector routing protocol converge on a mutual understanding of the network's topology by sharing what they know about the network. Such routers periodically pass copies of their routing tables to their immediate network neighbors. Each recipient adds its distance-vector information to the table and forwards the modified table to its immediate neighbors. This process occurs omnidirectionally between immediately neighboring routers. Figure 10-2 uses a simple IGRP internetwork to illustrate the concept of immediate neighbors.

In Figure 10-2, there are four routers in an autonomous system. The gateway router is interconnected with each of the other three. It must exchange its routing information with these routers. Routers A, B, and C only have one connection each: to the gateway.

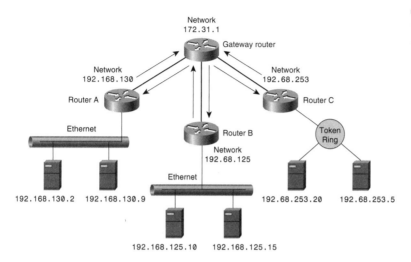

Figure 10-2

Each IGRP node advertises the contents of its routing table to its immediate neighbors.

Consequently, they can only exchange their information with the gateway directly. They can learn about each other's hosts through the information shared with the gateway.

Table 10-1 shows the abbreviated contents of each of the three routers' routing tables. This information is shared with the gateway router.

Table 10-1   *Initial State of Routing Table Contents*

Router Name	Network Address	Next Hop	Cost
A	192.168.130.0	E0	500
B	192.168.125.0	E0	500
C	192.68.253.0	T0	350

The gateway router received this information via scheduled updates from Routers A, B, and C. The gateway router uses this information to build its own routing table, the abbreviated and summarized contents of which is presented in Table 10-2. The local hosts on Router C enjoy a local cost metric from that router as they are connected via a Token-Ring network. IGRP's composite cost metric uses both Bandwidth and Delay. Therefore, it shouldn't be surprising that a deterministic 16 Mbps LAN enjoys a lower cost than a 10 Mbps contention-based LAN.

NOTE

It is virtually impossible to provide actual valuations for the composite cost metrics in an IGRP network. This is due to the dynamic nature of some of its components, notably Load and Reliability, as well as the highly customizable constants K1 through K5. Consequently, the routing costs presented in this chapter's illustrations are fictitious. They are presented for illustrative purposes only and are not indicative of actual values that may occur.

Table 10-2 *Gateway Router Routing Table Contents*

Router Name	Destination	Next Hop	Number of Hops	Cost Metric
Gateway	Network 192.168.130	A	1	1500
	Network 192.168.125	B	1	1500
	Network 192.68.253	C	1	1350

Rather than maintain an entry for each host number within a given network number, routers will summarize routing information. This is done to conserve memory and CPU utilization within the router. In this example, the gateway router shares the routing information in Table 10-2 with each of the other routers in the network. These routers use this information to complete their own routing tables. Table 10-3 shows the abbreviated contents of Router A's routing table after it has shared routing information with the gateway router.

Table 10-3 *Router A Routing Table Contents*

Router Name	Destination	Next Hop	Number of Hops	Cost Metric
A	Host 192.168.130.2	Local	0	500
	Host 192.168.130.9	Local	0	500
	Network 192.168.125	Gateway	2	2500
	Network 192.68.253	Gateway	2	2350

Router A knows that hosts 192.168.130.2 and 192.168.130.9 are local. Datagrams addressed to these devices that are received via its serial port to the gateway router are just placed on to the Ethernet for delivery via the LAN's broadcast mechanisms. The cost metric associated with the local hosts reflects the performance of the LAN. Remember that every link has costs associated with it regardless of whether that link connects to another router!

Router A also knows that the gateway router is one hop away. Therefore, seeing that the 192.168.125.x and 192.68.253.x hosts are also one hop away from the gateway, it adds the two numbers together for a total of two hops to each machine. Each of these hops, however, has a different cost metric. This cost is IGRP's calculated composite routing metric. In a multihop route, the total cost of a route is the sum of the costs of each link in the route. Therefore, the cost of the route from 192.168.130.9 to 192.68.253.20 is 2350. This sum includes 1000 for each of the two serial links, and 350 for the LAN that the end system is connected to.

This is a highly simplified overview of the iterative process by which IGRP routers develop a consensual perspective of the network, as well as the distances between source and destination devices. If there were more than just one router interconnecting the remainder of the network's routers, convergence would require multiple iterations of this process. Needless to say, the more iterations are required to fully propagate routing information, the greater the amount of time that will elapse before all routers converge on a mutual understanding of the network's topology and distances. The network cannot be considered stable until after convergence is complete. The next section, "Topological Changes," describes some of the ways that IGRP attempts to improve stability by minimizing convergence times.

Topological Changes

Whenever a topological change occurs in a network based on distance vectors, the routers within that network gradually learn about the impact. Routers closest to the point of that change learn about the change, and its impacts, long before other, more distant routers. Through an iterative process of sharing routing information, all the routers in the network will gradually converge on a consensus of the network's new topology. This section examines how IGRP maintains its routing tables and converges after topological changes.

Routing Table Deletions

IGRP relies on its four timing mechanisms to proactively maintain the integrity of routes. IGRP can also use these timers to recover from failures in the network that prevent neighboring nodes from passing updates to each other. The processes used to maintain the routing tables are described in the following sections.

IGRP routing table updates are initiated every 90 seconds. The update timer is used to track this amount of time. Upon the expiration of this amount of time, IGRP launches a series of packets that contain its entire routing table. These packets are broadcast to each neighboring node. Therefore, each IGRP router should receive an update from each of its neighboring IGRP nodes approximately every 90 seconds. This process is remarkably similar to the update process used by RIP. The major difference is the amount of time that must elapse between updates. RIP posts its updates every 30 seconds—a brief enough period of time that table updates can compromise network performance.

Such an update failing to occur as expected indicates a failure or error somewhere in the internetwork. As with RIP, failure to complete an update can be caused by a number of different events. The simplest and easiest to recover from is that the packet containing the update was either damaged in transit or discarded. Alternatively, the failed update could have been as a result of a transmission facility or router failure. These types of changes would actually change the topology of the internetwork. For the internetwork to return to stability, the surviving routers must identify the lost resources and agree on the network's new topology.

Given the extreme variance between possible causes of failed updates, it is important to take the time needed to understand the cause of the problem. The appropriate course of action differs greatly along this spectrum of failures. If the update failed to occur because the update packet was discarded, for example, acting too quickly might result in wrongly invalidating dozens of routes. Alternatively, if the update failed to occur because a router became disabled, not acting quickly enough would result in a noticeable loss of service. IGRP uses its timers to invalidate routes that have failed.

Identifying Invalid Routes

Routes can become invalid in one of two ways:

- A route can expire.

- A router can be notified by another router of a route's unavailability.

Regardless of the cause, the IGRP router needs to modify its routing table to reflect the unavailability of a given route.

A route can expire if a router doesn't receive an update for it within a specified amount of time. IGRP uses the route invalid timer to elapse this amount of time. As explained earlier in this chapter, the default for this timer is three times the update period. The default value for the update period is 90 seconds. Therefore, a route becomes invalid 270 seconds after updates for it have ceased being received.

This information is then communicated to the router's neighbors via the periodic routing table updates. Neighboring nodes that receive notification of the route's new invalid status use that information to update their own routing tables. This is the second of two ways that routes can become invalid in a routing table.

An invalid route remains in the routing table long enough for the IGRP nodes to decide what to do with it. If the route really is valid, and its destinations still reachable, the IGRP nodes will detect this and converge on this understanding. Otherwise, if the route really is invalid, it remains in the routing table until the route flush timer expires.

Purging Invalid Routes

An IGRP node purges invalid routes from the routing table if they remain invalid for an interval equal to seven times the routing update period. If the default update timing value is used, this equals 630 seconds. Only routes that have become invalid and have then endured the route-flush interval can be purged. This provides an effective double layer of protection against hastily deleting routes.

MULTIPATH ROUTING

One of the most important features of IGRP is its capability to perform multipath routing. Unlike RIP, which only remembers a single route to any given destination, IGRP can remember up to four different routes to any given destination! This allows IGRP to balance traffic loads across multiple routes, while protecting against the impacts of link failures.

Redundant routes may be of equal or different costs. Therefore, IGRP can support two types of load balancing:

- Equal-cost load balancing

- Unequal-cost load balancing

Equal-Cost Load Balancing

Equal-cost load balancing, as its name implies, is the balancing of a traffic load across redundant links of equal cost. Figure 10-3 illustrates this in a small network, and the contents of Router A's routing table are presented in Table 10-4. In this table, you can see that there are multiple ports that Router A can use to get to the gateway router. These ports are called S0 and S1, or serial ports 0 and 1.

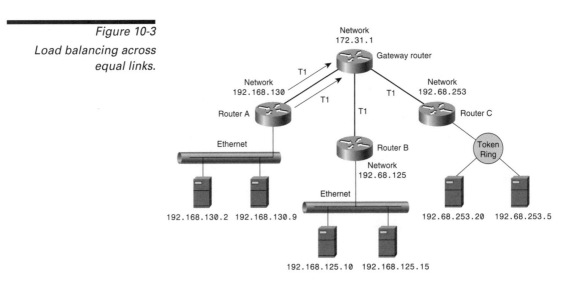

Figure 10-3
Load balancing across
equal links.

Table 10-4   *Router A Routing Table Contents*

Router Name	Destination	Next Hop	Number of Hops	Cost Metric
A	Host 192.168.130.2	Local	0	500
	Host 192.168.130.9	Local	0	500
	Network 192.168.125	Gateway—Port S0	2	2500
	Network 192.68.253	Gateway—Port S0	2	2350
	Network 192.168.125	Gateway—Port S1	2	2500
	Network 192.68.253	Gateway—Port S1	2	2350

In Figure 10-3, Router A has two, equal-cost, serial connections (both T1s) to the gateway router. Given that the two paths are of equal cost, IGRP should be indifferent between which of them is used. In practice, IGRP will split the traffic equally between these two paths. Balancing loads across equal-cost paths can be done in two different ways:

- Per packet
- Per destination

Balancing traffic on a per-packet basis means that sequential packets in a stream, bound for the same destination, may be sent out to different interfaces. This can result in data being received late, or out of sequence, which can cause application problems.

Balancing traffic on a per-destination basis means that all the packets in a stream that are bound for the same destination will be forwarded via the same route. This alleviates the potential for problems caused by per-packet load balancing but can result in a somewhat less than perfect distribution of traffic across equal-cost links.

IGRP will determine which of these approaches to use based on its capability to perform *route caching*. Route caching is a relatively simple technique for keeping a route cached in memory. Therefore, the route is already calculated and stored in memory before a packet is received. The router uses this cached route to ship the next inbound packet in a stream over the same route that the preceding one took. The obvious drawback to supporting route caching is that it can be memory intensive. If you disable route caching, load balancing will automatically be performed per packet.

Regardless of your preference for or against route caching, one of the most endearing aspects of multipath routing is the capability to automatically recover from network failures. In the event of a failure that impacts one of the paths in a multipath arrangement, traffic is automatically shunted over to the surviving paths. Figure 10-4 demonstrates the results of a link failure in the network shown in Figure 10-3.

In Figure 10-4, the dual T1 lines interconnecting Routers A and the gateway router were used to support communications in a round-robin fashion. Datagrams are alternated between the two available equal-cost paths. When one of the links fails, as illustrated in Figure 10-4, Router A would invalidate the failed link's routing entry and use the surviving link for all the traffic to that destination. Table 10-5 summarizes the effects of this occurrence on Router A's routing table.

Figure 10-4

Automatic recovery from a failed route.

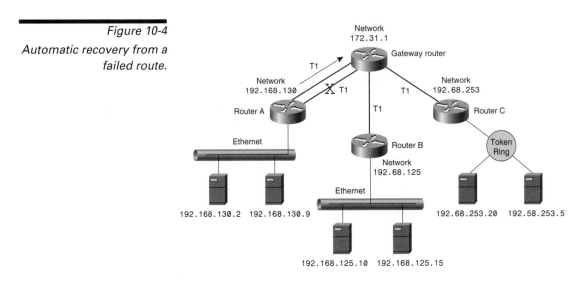

Table 10-5   *Router A Routing Table Contents After a Link Failure*

Router Name	Destination	Next Hop	Number of Hops	Cost Metric
A	Host 192.168.130.2	Local	0	500
	Host 192.168.130.9	Local	0	500
	Network 192.168.125	Gateway—Port S0	2	2500
	Network 192.68.253	Gateway—Port S0	2	2350
	Network 192.168.125	Gateway—Port S1	2	Invalid route
	Network 192.68.253	Gateway—Port S1	2	Invalid route

This recovery is automatic; users are not adversely affected, nor is any manual intervention required. Automatic recovery is not limited to just equal-cost links. Redundant links of unequal costs may also automatically recover from failures.

Unequal-Cost Load Balancing

As beneficial as equal-cost load balancing is, it suffers from a fundamental problem: It is based on dynamic metrics. Over time, normal operating conditions may result in the composite cost metrics of equivalent paths becoming unequal. Error conditions, in particular, can increase the costs of individual links. The designers of IGRP realized this and developed a mechanism for balancing traffic loads across unequal cost paths.

The way that unequal-cost load balancing works is relatively simple. Traffic can be balanced across up to four paths of unequal cost. The link with the lowest cost becomes the primary path. The other, higher-cost, paths can be used as alternatives. Alternative paths provide redundant connectivity to a common destination (or set of destinations).

The issue for network administrators is how to best use this bandwidth without incurring performance penalties. Clearly, the optimal route is the least-cost route. Nevertheless, the performance of routing to a given destination can be improved by using other, higher-cost routes to augment the primary route. The key to success in balancing traffic across links of unequal cost is to meter traffic onto each of the possible links in direct proportion to their relative costs. If the cost of a primary path were half the value of its alternative, for example, it would make sense to use that primary path twice as frequently.

Given that the IGRP composite metric has a range of more than 16,000,000 possible values, it was necessary to establish some mechanism for defining an acceptable range of cost metrics for balancing traffic over unequal cost routes. This mechanism is known as *variance*.

Defining Variance

The key to the success of load balancing in an IGRP network is variance. Variance is a user-modifiable attribute that specifies the percentage by which the performance of different links can vary, yet still be considered viable paths to the same destination. This attribute applies to the entire IGRP network rather than individual links.

The Cisco IOS defaults variance equal to one, but this can be customized according to your needs. If you establish a variance of two, for example, routes with cost metrics up to two times the cost of the best route can be accepted, up to a maximum of four routes.

 NOTE

Setting variance equal to one precludes unequal cost load balancing. Variance must be set greater than one, or there can be no variance! In such cases, load balancing is limited to just those paths whose cost metrics equal the best route.

Given that IGRP was explicitly designed to support a network with a wide diversity of transmission technologies, routes can consist of virtually any number and combination of transmission facilities. Therefore, their paths will likely have very different composite metrics. Use of IGRP's variance feature enables the IOS to automatically balance traffic loads across all feasible paths that fall within the specified variance range (refer to the section titled "Unequal-Cost Load Balancing").

To better illustrate the concept of variance and load balancing, consider the network diagram shown in Figure 10-5.

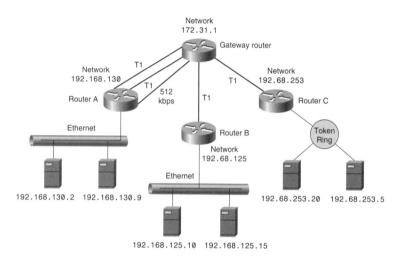

Figure 10-5

IGRP network with multiple paths of unequal costs.

In Figure 10-5, Router A has three possible paths to the gateway router. Two of these are T1 leased lines, and the third is a 512 Kbps Frame-Relay connection.

Table 10-6 summarizes the contents of Router A's routing table. Assuming that bandwidth was the only user-defined routing metric that was modified, two routes between Routers A and the gateway are of equal cost. These two paths are T1s. The third path, the 512 kbps Frame-Relay connection, has a higher cost that reflects its lower bandwidth. The T1s enjoy almost three times the usable bandwidth of the Frame-Relay connection.

The contents of Router A's routing table, given the scenario presented in Figure 10-5, are summarized in Table 10-6. As is evident by these entries, there are three serial links interconnecting Router A and the gateway router: S0, S1, and S2. S0 and S1 are the T1 lines, and S2 is the 512 kbps Frame-Relay circuit.

Table 10-6 *Router A Routing Table Contents with Three Links to the Gateway*

Router Name	Destination	Next Hop	Number of Hops	Cost Metric
A	Host 192.168.130.2	Local	0	500
	Host 192.168.130.9	Local	0	500
	Network 192.168.125	Gateway—Port S0	2	2500
	Network 192.68.253	Gateway—Port S0	2	2350
	Network 192.168.125	Gateway—Port S1	2	2500
	Network 192.68.253	Gateway—Port S1	2	2350
	Network 192.168.125	Gateway—Port S2	2	4500
	Network 192.68.253	Gateway—Port S2	2	4350

IGRP automatically balances the load across the two equal-cost T1 links. Given a default variance of 1, however, IGRP shuns the higher-cost Frame-Relay link as an undesirable route. Setting variance equal to 2, however, will qualify the Frame-Relay link for use in an unequal-cost load-balancing arrangement. Traffic is split across the three links connecting Router A and the gateway in a ratio commensurate with their cost.

Although variance is the key attribute that enabled this unequal-cost load balancing, it is not the only attribute. Alternative paths must also pass a series of other feasibility tests before they can be used in a multipath routing arrangement. These feasibility tests are intended to maintain the stability of the network.

Testing for Feasibility

Any alternative path through a network must first prove to be feasible for use in an unequal-cost load-balancing arrangement before it can be used. Feasibility, in this context, means that each path conforms to three basic principles:

- Alternative path metrics must be within the specified variance range of the local best metric.

- The best local metric must be greater than the metric for the same destination that is learned from the next router. In other words, the next hop must be closer to the destination than the current router.

- The variance value, multiplied against the best local metric for a destination, must be greater than or equal to the cost metric for that destination on the next router.

Additionally, up to a maximum of four paths may be used for load balancing. Alternative routes that satisfy these four criteria are deemed to be feasible alternatives to the local best-cost path. Unfeasible routes, as per these criteria, may not be used to balance the traffic load to a given destination.

In general, unequal-cost load balancing provides greater overall throughput and reliability. Although these attributes are generally of value universally, the four feasibility criteria tends to limit your ability to use unequal-cost load balancing. This limitation is necessary to ensure the stability of an IGRP network in operation.

Feasible Successors

IGRP can be used to establish a hierarchy of feasible succession in a multipath routing environment. Feasible successors are routes whose costs are greater than the specified variance from the optimal route to a given destination. As such, they are unfeasible for unequal-cost load balancing. Such routes can still serve as feasible successors to that optimal route, however, should it become unusable. In Figure 10-5, the 512 kbps Frame-Relay circuit would be considered a feasible successor to the two T1 circuits interconnecting Router A and the gateway router. Therefore, if both T1s failed, Router A would automatically try using the Frame-Relay circuit on its S2 port.

The Dangers of Multipath Routing

Despite the benefits of multipath routing, there are some subtle dangers. By enabling datagrams bound for a common destination to be split across multiple paths through the networks (with different performance characteristics), you practically guarantee that a session's datagrams will be delivered out of order. Given that transport layer mechanisms exist that should, in theory, automatically detect and correct sequencing errors, this shouldn't be a problem. If you establish a variance that is too large, however, it is possible that application performance will suffer noticeably due to the increased need for managing the sequencing of incoming datagrams. This impact is particularly acute for time-sensitive applications.

Another, much more subtle, potential danger in multipath routing is that datagrams may be forwarded upstream. *Upstream*, in this context, means that datagrams may be forwarded away from their intended destination rather than toward it. IGRP is not supposed to allow this to happen. In fact, its four feasibility criteria for developing unequal-cost multipath routes disallow such an event. Nevertheless, in a dynamic network with dynamic routing metrics it is virtually impossible to guarantee that upstream forwarding won't occur.

Although these two potential risks are relatively minor, they can affect performance across your network. As with any other metric or weight, great care should be taken when attempting to modify the variance. Leaving it set to its default precludes unequal-cost load balancing, but enabling this form of load balancing is not risk-free. Understand the potential implications of unequal-cost load balancing in your network *before* you enable it.

SUMMARY

Despite its proprietary status, IGRP has proven to be one of the most successful routing protocols of all time. No small part of its success has been due to its functional similarity to RIP, a simple yet highly successful and widely deployed routing protocol. Cisco took great pains to carefully preserve many of the effective features of RIP, while greatly expanding its capabilities.

Cisco Systems built upon this legacy of success by further enhancing IGRP in the early 1990s. This enhancement was dubbed *Enhanced Interior Gateway Routing Protocol* (EIGRP, or Enhanced IGRP). This protocol is examined in Chapter 11, "Enhanced Interior Gateway Routing Protocol."

CHAPTER 11

Enhanced Interior Gateway Routing Protocol

Enhanced Interior Gateway Routing Protocol, also known as either EIGRP or Enhanced IGRP, is a relatively new innovation from Cisco that is based on IGRP. EIGRP shares its predecessor's distance-vector technology, but differs greatly in its operational mechanics. Additionally, EIGRP features several important new features. Some of these features were designed to expand the market potential for EIGRP. Unlike its predecessor, for example, EIGRP supports both classless and class-based IP addresses, as well as other network protocols. This allows networks using CIDR-compliant IP addresses and/or VLSM to use Cisco's distance-vector routing technology.

Other updates were designed to reduce convergence times and improve network stability. One such update was a new algorithm, the *Diffusing Update Algorithm* (DUAL), which enables EIGRP routers to determine whether a path advertised by a neighbor is looped or loop free and allows a router running EIGRP to find alternative paths without waiting for updates from other routers. This helps EIGRP networks converge, without incurring any significant risk of introducing or propagating routing loops. Other measures were also introduced that reduced the network intensity of convergence. This chapter examines the architectural framework of EIGRP, its operational mechanics, and the similarities and differences between EIGRP and IGRP.

EIGRP BACKGROUND

The Internet is a highly dynamic network. Consequently, its protocol, IP, must be equally dynamic. The IETF, it seems, never ceases upgrading, modifying, and extending the IP specification. One of the unfortunate consequences of this sort of activity is that many other IP-centric technologies are forced to either keep the same pace of innovation or fall into obsolescence. Frequently, such technologies opt for some point in between these two extremes. IGRP, despite its success in the market, began to demonstrate some of the effects of obsolescence relative to the ever-evolving IP.

IGRP is still a highly useful routing protocol, but it just can't support some of the more complex changes made to IPv4. IGRP is, for example, inherently a classful IP routing protocol. Therefore, it can't support classless interdomain routing (CIDR), or even variable-length subnet masks (VLSM).

Rather than modify IGRP, which may have caused migration issues for its customers, Cisco Systems decided to implement the needed modifications in a new proprietary, distance-vector routing protocol. This strategy held many benefits for Cisco's customers. For example, Cisco could offer customers a modern and robust routing protocol, EIGRP, which was based on IGRP's proven distance-vector technology.

Equally important, developing EIGRP separately from IGRP offered Cisco the opportunity to make fundamental improvements to the operational efficiency of the new routing protocol. Had Cisco attempted to make such changes to IGRP, the result may have been two very different versions of IGRP. The last benefit of Cisco's strategy was that there was no impact on any of the existing IGRP customer networks; IGRP soldiered on, unaffected by the development of EIGRP.

Backward Compatibility with IGRP

Although EIGRP was developed as a more up-to-date and efficient alternative to IGRP, it was also explicitly an extension of IGRP. Consequently, the two are designed to be completely compatible. These two routing protocols even share the same distance-vector routing technology: EIGRP uses the same composite routing metric as IGRP. EIGRP also supports all the same distance vectors, and their mathematical weights, as does IGRP. EIGRP also uses IGRP's Variance feature to provide unequal-cost load balancing.

NOTE

There are strong similarities between many of IGRP and EIGRP's basic components. These include the formula for calculating their respective composite metrics, as well as equal or unequal-cost load balancing using the Variance mechanism. If you would like more information on any of these topics, refer to Chapter 10, "Interior Gateway Routing Protocol."

There is only one minor difference in the algorithm that calculates the composite metric: The IGRP metric is 20 bits long, whereas the EIGRP metric is 32 bits long. This difference results in the EIGRP metric being larger by a factor of 256 than a comparable IGRP metric for any given route. The larger metric allows a better and finer mathematical comparison of potential routes.

This minor difference is easily and automatically compensated for by EIGRP. EIGRP automatically adjusts the composite metric of IGRP routes and adjusts its own metric on routes being redistributed to IGRP routers. IGRP's and EIGRP's metrics are directly comparable. Therefore, they can be used interchangeably after translation. EIGRP does, however, track the translated IGRP routes as external routes.

NOTE

IGRP doesn't have any concept of internal and external routes. Consequently, EIGRP routes that are translated and redistributed into an IGRP network are treated as IGRP routes.

Automatic redistribution between IGRP and EIGRP will only occur if the two protocols are configured with the same autonomous system (AS) number. If they have different AS numbers, they will assume that they are part of different networks (that is, autonomous systems).

EIGRP's automatic metric adjustment mechanism enables IGRP and EIGRP to be fully integrated in a network via a simple mathematical function. External IGRP routes that are automatically adjusted by EIGRP can be directly compared to internal EIGRP routes. Cisco routers will always select the route with the best metric (adjusted or otherwise) rather than automatically select the route of any particular protocol. Therefore, an EIGRP router might decide that the best route is actually an external IGRP route rather than an internal EIGRP route.

Migration from IGRP to EIGRP can be done gradually without incurring any network downtime. EIGRP can be introduced into strategic areas of the network such as the backbone. Its automatic metric translation mechanism would enable the network administrator to replace IGRP with EIGRP in those strategic areas. Support for IGRP is integral to EIGRP so the network's functionality isn't compromised. The network administrator can then selectively extend its use in the network, until the migration to EIGRP is complete. At this point, some of the more advanced IP architectures, such as VLSM and classless addressing, can be implemented.

EIGRP's Improvements

Cisco also instituted several changes in EIGRP that were designed to improve its operational efficiency relative to IGRP. These two protocols are interoperable thanks to their mutual distance vectors, but they operate in very different ways. EIGRP reacts to topological change differently, advertises routes differently, and even has a different approach to updating entries in routing tables. In many ways, EIGRP behaves more like a link-state routing protocol than it does a traditional distance-vector protocol. Yet, EIGRP uses the distance vectors and composite metric of IGRP. Consequently, EIGRP is sometimes referred to as a *hybrid routing protocol* (or an *advanced distance-vector protocol*). It combines the best features of link-state routing with the best features of distance-vector routing. Properly designed and implemented, an EIGRP network is extremely stable and efficient and converges rapidly after any topological change.

Some of the specific advantages of EIGRP include the following:

- *Minimal consumption of bandwidth when the network is stable*—During normal, stable network operation, the only EIGRP packets exchanged between EIGRP nodes are hello packets. This simple handshake enables the EIGRP routers to know that all remains well in the network.

- *Efficient use of bandwidth during convergence*—EIGRP only propagates changes to the routing table, not the entire routing table. Also, updates are advertised only after a topological change rather than on a strict, periodic basis. These updates are also only transmitted to those EIGRP routers that need to know of the change. This is known as a *partial, bounded update*.

- *Rapid convergence*—EIGRP routers store every path they have learned to every destination in the network. Therefore, a router running EIGRP can quickly converge on an alternative route after any topological change.

- *Support for VLSM and CIDR*—EIGRP supports the definition of network and host numbers on any bit boundary, per interface, for both IP addresses and subnet masks.

- *Complete independence from routed protocols*—EIGRP is designed to be completely independent of routed protocols. Support for routed protocols is via individual, protocol-specific modules. Therefore, evolution of a protocol, such as IP, won't threaten EIGRP with obsolescence. Nor will such technological advances force a painful revision of EIGRP.

The features highlighted in this list are examined in more detail throughout this chapter. Combined, they make a compelling case for migrating to EIGRP.

NEW FEATURES FOUND IN EIGRP

EIGRP enjoys many new technologies, each of which represents an improvement in operating efficiency, rapidity of convergence, or feature/functionality relative to IGRP and other routing protocols. These technologies fall into one of the following four categories:

- Neighbor discovery and recovery

- Reliable Transport Protocol

- DUAL finite-state machine

- Protocol-specific modules

In addition to these categories of technological improvements, EIGRP was also treated to some other substantial enhancements relative to IGRP. These enhancements may defy easy categorization, but were needed to keep pace with the ongoing evolution of IP as well as other routing protocols. EIGRP enhances the security of a network, for example, by permitting authentication to be used between routers. This function is very similar to the authentication supported by OSPF and can be used in conjunction with any routed protocol. Other innovations such as support for VLSM and CIDR are specific only to IP. As such, they are integrated in a protocol-specific module rather than included in EIGRP itself.

Neighbor Discovery and Recovery

EIGRP, unlike virtually every other distance-vector routing protocol, does not rely exclusively and rigidly on the use of timers for maintaining its routing table. Instead, the basis for maintaining routing tables is a periodic communication between EIGRP routers. They use this process to

- Dynamically learn of new routers that may join their network

- Identify routers that become either unreachable or inoperable

- Rediscover routers that had previously been unreachable

The basic neighbor discovery/recovery process consists of periodically transmitting a small hello packet to neighbors. The hello packet establishes the relationship between immediate neighbors (known as an adjacency). This relationship is used to exchange routing metrics and information.

An EIGRP router can safely assume that, as long as it is receiving hello packets from known neighbors, those neighbors (and their routes) remain viable. If an EIGRP router ceases to receive such greetings from a neighbor, however, it can assume that something is amiss. That router will enter the DUAL process for those routes. These processes are examined in more detail in the section titled "Hello Packets."

Reliable Transport Protocol

One of EIGRP's more important new features is its capability to provide guaranteed, reliable delivery of its various packets. Other protocols eschew reliable delivery and rely on other mechanisms such as the passing of time to determine whether a packet needs to be retransmitted. Unfortunately, the fundamental flaw in such an approach is that it aggravates the convergence process. The longer it takes a network to converge, the greater the opportunity for disrupting service across the network. EIGRP was given a new protocol, the Reliable Transport Protocol (RTP), to provide reliable delivery of its own packets.

RTP is a transport layer protocol that correlates to the functionality identified by Layer 4 of the OSI reference model. RTP is a private innovation of Cisco Systems, however, and is not an open standard. IP uses two similar transport protocols: TCP and UDP. In fact, RTP embodies some of the functionality of each TCP and UDP. TCP—as was explained in Chapter 5, "Internet Protocol Versions,"—provides reliable delivery of IP datagrams and can resequence datagrams received out of order. UDP provides a more efficient, but unreliable, delivery of IP datagrams. RTP can support both reliable and unreliable, delivery of datagrams. It can even support both transport types simultaneously and resequence packets received out of order.

Instead of creating a new transport protocol, the designers of EIGRP could have used TCP and/or UDP as the transports for EIGRP messages. However, this would have made EIGRP distinctly IP specific. The designers' goal was a truly protocol-independent routing protocol that could easily be extended to support any new routing protocols, such as IPv6, that may be developed in the future. Consequently, a new transport protocol was needed: RTP. RTP was specifically developed to meet these requirements.

RTP is used to transport all EIGRP message types through a network. However, not every EIGRP packet requires reliable delivery! Some functions, such as the exchanging of hello packets, just don't warrant the overhead of acknowledging receipt. RTP can deliver hello packets (and other packet types) in an unreliable manner.

RTP can also support both multicasting and unicasting. Multicast packets are delivered to multiple, specific destinations simultaneously using a group address. Unicast packets are explicitly addressed to a single destination. RTP can even support both multicast and unicast transmissions simultaneously for different peers.

The Distributed Update Algorithm

The centerpiece of EIGRP's new technologies is DUAL, EIGRP's route-calculation engine. The full name of EIGRP's engine is DUAL Finite-State Machine. This engine contains all the logic used to calculate and compare routes in an EIGRP network. DUAL tracks all the routes advertised by neighbors and uses the composite metric of each route to compare them. Selected paths must be loop-free paths and have the lowest cost. Such routes are inserted by the DUAL protocol into a routing table for use in forwarding datagrams.

Routes selected for insertion in a routing table are also evaluated on the basis of feasible succession. A *feasible successor* is a neighbor router that is the next hop in a least-cost path to any given destination. A feasible successor is a path that is loop-free according to the DUAL FSM.

Protocol-Specific Modules

As indicated earlier in the chapter, one of the key design principles guiding the development of EIGRP was complete independence from routed protocols. Therefore, EIGRP implemented a modular approach to supporting routed protocols. Many other protocols are either specifically designed for a single routed protocol—such as IP, AppleTalk, and so on—or have mechanisms for supporting multiple protocols. EIGRP has such native mechanisms, but they are completely modular. In theory, EIGRP can be easily retrofitted to support any new routed protocols that may be developed by just adding another protocol-specific module.

Each protocol-specific module is responsible for all functions related to its specific routed protocol. The IP-EIGRP module is responsible for the following, for example:

- Sending and receiving EIGRP packets that bear IP data

- Notifying DUAL of new IP routing information that is received

- Maintaining the results of DUAL's routing decisions in the IP routing table

- Redistributing routing information that was learned by other IP-capable routing protocols

IP-EIGRP can redistribute routes learned from other IP-capable routing protocols, including OSPF, RIP, Integrated Intermediate System-Intermediate System (IS-IS), Exterior Gateway Protocol (EGP), and Border Gateway Protocol (BGP). EIGRP has comparable modules for supporting both AppleTalk and IPX. The AppleTalk module (AT-EIGRP) can redistribute routes learned from the Routing Table Maintenance Protocol (RTMP). IPX-EIGRP can redistribute routing information from Novell's proprietary version of RIP as well as that company's Service Advertisement Protocol (SAP) and Novell Link State Protocol (NLSP).

EIGRP's IP-EIGRP module brought support for many of the updates to IP that Cisco's IGRP customer base had been clamoring for. Specifically, IP-EIGRP introduced support for VLSM as well as CIDR. IGRP did not support either of these features.

EIGRP Data Structures

EIGRP is a fairly information-intensive routing protocol; it must keep track of the current state (or nearly current state) of many different facets of the network. This information is organized into collections of related information, which are stored in tables. EIGRP maintains the currency of these tables via a series of specialized packet types. Each packet type is used for a specific function. This section examines the basic functionality and use of each of EIGRP's tables and packet types.

EIGRP Tables

EIGRP uses many different tables, each dedicated to organizing and storing data pertinent to a specific facet of the network. The proprietary nature of EIGRP precludes an exhaustive survey of these tables as well as their structures. It is possible, however, to examine the role of some of the more important EIGRP tables, including the following:

- The neighbor table

- The routing table

- The topology table

There are other tables, but these three should adequately convey the bulk of EIGRP's internal mechanics.

The Neighbor Table

The single most important table in EIGRP is the neighbor table. The neighbor relationships tracked in this table are the basis for all of EIGRP's routing update and convergence activity.

The neighbor table tracks state information about adjacent neighboring EIGRP nodes. Whenever a new neighbor is discovered, the address and interface of that neighbor are recorded in a new entry in the neighbor table. Actually, an EIGRP router may contain several neighbor tables because one is required for each protocol-dependent module. Therefore, a network that runs both Apple-Talk and IP would have two different neighbor tables. A separate EIGRP process would have to be configured for each routed protocol used in the network.

Additionally, a neighbor table is used to support reliable, sequenced delivery of packets. One field in each row of the table is populated with the last sequence number of the packet received from that neighbor. EIGRP uses this field for two purposes:

- Sequence numbers are used to acknowledge specific packets that were delivered reliably. Acknowledgments are transmitted bearing the sequence number of the packet of which they are acknowledging receipt. This enables the router that receives the acknowledgment to know which packet is being acknowledged.

- This field can also alert EIGRP to packets being received out of sequence.

For both of these reasons, EIGRP records the sequence number of the last message received from each specific neighbor.

The Routing Table

The routing table contains the least-cost routes that DUAL calculated for all known destinations. EIGRP, as with all Cisco-supported routing protocols, tracks up to six routes to each destination. Whenever a router detects a change in a single routing table entry, it must notify its neighbors of that change. These neighbors must then determine the impact that change has on their routes.

A separate routing table is maintained for each routed protocol that EIGRP is configured to support. Thus, if you are simultaneously running IP and AppleTalk, your EIGRP routers will each have two routing tables—one for each routed protocol.

The Topology Table

EIGRP uses its topology table to store all the information it needs to calculate a set of distances, and vectors, to all known and reachable destinations. This information includes the following fields:

- *Bandwidth*—The bandwidth of the slowest interface in the path to a destination. This effectively limits the performance of the route and is used in calculation of the route's composite metric. This metric is calculated the same way in both IGRP and EIGRP.

- *Total Delay*—This field contains the sum total of delay expected in that route. This sum is calculated the same way as IGRP.

- *Reliability*—The reliability of the path is also recorded in the topology table. This metric is also identical to the IGRP Reliability metric.

- *Load*—The load level of the path is another of the IGRP metrics that has been retained by EIGRP.

- *MTU*—This field contains the size of the smallest MTU supported by the router interfaces in the path. As the least-common MTU, datagrams exceeding this value will be fragmented en route to their destination. Therefore, EIGRP attempts to notify all routers, in advance, of the maximum MTU on each path to a given destination.

- *Reported Distance*—The reported distance of the path is the distance reported by an adjacent neighbor to a specific destination. This metric does not include the distance between this router and the adjacent neighbor.

- *Feasible Distance*—The feasible distance is the lowest calculated metric to each destination.

- *Route Source*—The source of the route is the identification number of the router that originally advertised that route. This field is populated only for routes learned externally from the EIGRP network. Route tagging can be particularly useful with policy-based routing. For more information on EIGRP's route tagging capabilities, refer to the sidebar titled "Route Tagging with EIGRP" later in this chapter.

Also recorded for each entry is the interface through which this destination is reachable. The topology table is sorted. Successors are at the top, followed immediately by feasible successors. EIGRP even stores routes that DUAL believes to be loops in the topology table. These routes are at the bottom of the sorted topology table. You can see the entire contents of the EIGRP topology table by executing the following command:

```
show ip eigrp topo all
```

A separate topology table is maintained for each protocol-dependent module being used by EIGRP. The information contained in a topology table is used as input to the DUAL finite-state machine.

Entries in a topology table can be in one of two states: active or passive. These states identify the status of the route indicated by the entry rather than the status of the entry itself. A passive route is one that is stable and available for use.

An active route is one currently being recomputed. *Recomputation* is the process of recalculating routes in search of new successors. This process isn't necessarily processor intensive, but it can be time intensive. Consequently, extensive recomputation can exacerbate convergence times in an EIGRP network. Recomputation is a rather resource-intensive measure. Therefore, in the event of a topology change, DUAL is designed to use any and all available feasible successors before recomputing. A recomputation will only occur if there are no successors or feasible successors to a route.

Route Tagging with EIGRP

EIGRP classifies routes as either internal or external. Internal routes are those that originated within an EIGRP network. External routes were either learned from a different routing protocol—those that lie outside of EIGRP's Autonomous System and were learned by a router on the border between the two autonomous systems—or are static routes that have been injected into EIGRP through redistribution. All external routes are tagged in the topology table and include the following information:

- The identification number (router ID) of the EIGRP router that re-distributed that route into the EIGRP network

- The number of the Autonomous System where that route's destination resides

- The protocol used in that external network

- The cost or metric received from that external protocol

- A tag that can be administratively set and used in route filtering

Route tagging gives the network administrator flexibility in establishing routing policies. This flexibility is most useful when the EIGRP network is internetworked with a policy-based routing protocol such as EGP or BGP.

EIGRP routers will reject external routes tagged with a router ID identical to their own; this prevents routing loops from occurring with external routes.

The topology table also stores the identities of neighbors that are feasible successors. The concept of feasible succession was held over from IGRP. It is important to understand, however, that EIGRP's feasible succession is very different from IGRP's feasible succession. The concepts are similar, but their implementation and mechanics are very different. The IGRP version of feasible succession was examined in the preceding chapter.

In EIGRP, all neighboring routers that have an advertised composite metric (reported distance) that is less than a router's best current metric (feasible distance) for any given route are considered feasible successors to the current successor (path currently being used). If there are multiple routes with a cost equal to the best cost, they are all considered successors and are all installed in the routing table. A destination must have at least one successor before it can be moved from the topology table to the routing table!

An EIGRP router views its feasible successors as neighbors that are downstream, or closer, to the destination than it is. Whenever a change occurs in the network, which affects either its topology or even the composite metric of a single route, the set of successors and feasible successors to the affected route(s) may have to be reevaluated.

If a router loses its route through its successor, and there are no feasible successors, the route automatically goes into the active state and triggers recomputation. The router queries its neighbors, requesting new information about possible alternative paths to the impacted route. The neighboring routers must reply. Their reply can either contain information about their successors or notification that they can no longer reach the route either.

The route can only return to the passive state after the router has received a reply from each of its neighboring routers and can select a successor or determine that the destination is no longer reachable.

EIGRP Packet Types

EIGRP uses five specialized packets to maintain its various routing tables. Each packet type performs a specific function in support of routing table maintenance. The five EIGRP packet types are

- Hello

- Acknowledgment

- Update

- Query

- Reply

Given that EIGRP is a proprietary Cisco Systems product, its detailed specifications—including the size and structure of its internal packet type—are not made public. Consequently, the following survey of the six EIGRP packet types is limited to their functional description and uses.

Hello Packets

Hello packets, as their name implies, are used to discover (or rediscover) and track other EIGRP routers in the network. Rediscovering neighbors can sometimes occur during convergence. In theory, a failure in the network changes its topology. If, during the process of convergence, neighboring routers lose contact for a moment, the hello process will eventually reestablish the relationship. Rediscovering a lost neighbor is known as *recovery* or *rediscovery*.

EIGRP nodes transmit hello packets at fixed intervals known as *hello intervals*. The default interval depends on the bandwidth available per interface. On relatively low-bandwidth (less than T1) multipoint circuits (such as multipoint Frame Relay, ATM, and X.25 circuits), EIGRP uses a 60-second hello interval. Higher-bandwidth interfaces include point-to-point serial links, multipoint circuits with bandwidth greater than or equal to T1, and LANs. EIGRP uses a 5-second hello interval on such interfaces. An EIGRP node uses its neighbor table to keep track of the other EIGRP routers in its network. Included in this table is the last time that each neighbor was heard from. Such contact may have been made via hello packets or any other EIGRP packet type. The point is that an EIGRP router considers a neighbor to be functional as long as it is capable of some form of communication.

There must be a finite period that an EIGRP router endures before concluding that a silent neighbor is actually out of service. This period is known as the *hold time*, which is tracked by the *hold timer*. If a router's hold timer counts down to zero, and a neighbor still hasn't been heard from, that router informs DUAL of the change. DUAL initiates convergence among the surviving routers in the network.

Hold time is usually defaulted to three times the hold time for an interface. Therefore, hold times are defaulted to 180 and 15 seconds respectively for low- and high-bandwidth interfaces. Both the hello interval and the hold time may be reset, per router interface, by a network administrator. Changing the hello interval does not automatically change the hold time, however. Each interval is manipulated individually. If you manually change the value of one, you should also manually change the value of the other.

NOTE

EIGRP enables a stable relationship between neighboring routers, even if they have different hold times or hello intervals! Hold time is one of the pieces of information exchanged via hello packets and stored in the neighbor table. Therefore, EIGRP routers won't prematurely assume that a neighbor is out of service just because it has a longer-than-normal hello interval or hold time. This capability is unique to EIGRP. OSPF, another protocol that uses hello intervals, requires both routers to have matching hold times and intervals.

Acknowledgment Packets

Acknowledgment packets are used to acknowledge receipt of any EIGRP packet that requires reliable delivery. As explained in the section titled "Reliable Transport Protocol," a packet's receipt must be acknowledged if it is to be delivered reliably. Otherwise, the source router would have no way of knowing whether the packet was actually delivered. EIGRP's standalone acknowledgment packet is actually a hello packet without any data. Acknowledgments (or Acks) can be differentiated from hello packets in another way, too. Hellos are always multicast, whereas acknowledgments are always sent to a single, specific IP address. This is known as *unicasting*. Hello and acknowledgment packets, incidentally, do not require acknowledgment. A router running EIGRP may also piggyback the acknowledgement information onto others' unicast packets, such as replies, being sent to the peer.

Update Packets

The update packet is used to convey routing information to known destinations. This packet type actually has two uses. The first use is to provide a complete dump of topological data to a newly discovered neighbor. Whenever a new neighbor is discovered (that is, a new router is added to an existing network), EIGRP nodes transmit update packets to this new neighbor for use in constructing its initial topology table. A series of update packets might be needed to send a complete set of topology information to the new router.

The second use of the update packet would be more typical of daily operation within an EIGRP network. Updates would be sent whenever a change in either topology or link cost occurred. These updates would be forwarded broadly to all known neighbors.

The way to differentiate between these two uses is to check the destination address of the update packets. Updates sent to a new neighbor will be directly addressed to that neighbor. Otherwise, update packets usually use an IP multicast address to forward to multiple neighbors simultaneously. The update packet is always transmitted reliably regardless of whether it is unicast or multicast.

One important improvement over virtually every other routing protocol is that EIGRP does not transmit updates of complete routing tables. Instead, EIGRP uses non-periodic, incremental routing updates. That is, EIGRP nodes convey *only the information that has changed, when it has changed.* By transmitting only the deltas, EIGRP converges more quickly and consumes much less bandwidth in the process.

Query and Reply Packets

Two of EIGRP's packet types, query and reply, are functionally interrelated. As a result, it doesn't make sense to examine them separately. Query packets are used whenever a router needs specific information from one or all of its neighbors. A reply packet is used to respond to a query.

One example showing the interaction of queries and replies is found in the process of finding an alternative route to a destination for which a router has lost its only routes. A router can send query packets to request information from neighbors about alternative paths that may be available. Neighboring routers would reply with their successor information.

Another example of the use of a query packet would be if a router receives a request for a destination that it previously didn't know about. In this case, the router receiving the query would immediately reply that it, also, doesn't know about this destination. This is one way in which queries are bounded in an EIGRP network. Unlike queries, which can be multicast, it doesn't make sense to multicast a reply. Instead, replies are unicast directly back to the originator of the query.

Queries are only sent when a destination becomes active. Otherwise, if the network is stable, and all routes are passive, there is no need to waste network bandwidth by requesting (and receiving) routing information. An additional bandwidth-conserving tactic is the capability to multicast queries. As demonstrated in the preceding two examples, queries can be both unicast and multicast. Regardless of which address type is used, queries are always transmitted reliably. Replies are also always transmitted reliably.

CONVERGENCE USING EIGRP

Convergence in an EIGRP network can be quite complicated. Part of this complexity is due to Cisco's standard of supporting up to six parallel routes to all destinations. Although this standard has helped make Cisco the market leader in internetworking products, it makes it more difficult to explain internetworking topics. For the sake of explaining the theory and mechanics of convergence, the examples in this section assume that a router remembers only a single primary route and one alternative (feasible successor) route.

The network illustrated in Figure 11-1 is a relatively small EIGRP network with five separate regions and a modest degree of route redundancy. This network is used to illustrate how EIGRP converges using its DUAL algorithm and feasible succession.

Figure 11-1
A small EIGRP network.

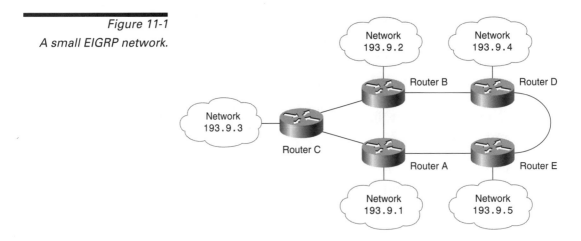

In this illustration, there are five different networks within a single EIGRP Autonomous System. The routers are labeled A through E. Another simplifying assumption in this example is that all the links are T1s. Therefore, bandwidth and delay will be constant throughout the network, and route selection becomes an obfuscated hop-counting exercise. Therefore instead of complicating the example with composite metrics, hop counts are used.

Table 11-1 contains the known distances between Router C and the other networks.

Table 11-1 *Distances from Router C in the Network*

Destination IP Address	Next Hop	Hop Count
193.9.1	A	1
193.9.2	B	1
193.9.4	B	2
193.9.5	A	2

Router C's DUAL algorithm has selected the least-cost paths from the multiple available paths to networks 193.9.4 and 193.9.5. Table 11-2 summarizes Router C's view of the network. Note that none of these routers have any feasible successors for any of these destinations. This is because the distance reported by the neighbor must be less than—not less than or equal to—the best metric available to reach that destination.

Table 11-2 *A Summary of Router C's Network Topology*

Destination IP Address	Route, from C	Hop Count	Successor or Feasible Successor?
193.9.1	A	1	Successor
193.9.2	B	1	Successor
193.9.4	B to D	2	Successor
193.9.5	A to E	2	Successor

There are other paths through the network, but their hop counts exceed both the primary route and the feasible successor. It is possible, for example, for Router C to forward datagrams to network 193.9.1 by using the route through Router B to D to E and, finally, to Router A and network 193.9.1. However, the hop count of this network (where both bandwidth and delay are equal across all links) is four. Therefore, it is unattractive as both a primary route and a feasible successor to the primary route. Such a route may become either a primary route or a feasible successor, but only if multiple network failures occurred and it were the least-cost route. However, the entire EIGRP network would have to recompute routes to known destinations for this to occur. To understand how the process of finding an alternative path works, consider Figure 11-2. In this illustration, the link between Routers B and C fails.

Figure 11-2

The link between Routers C and B fails.

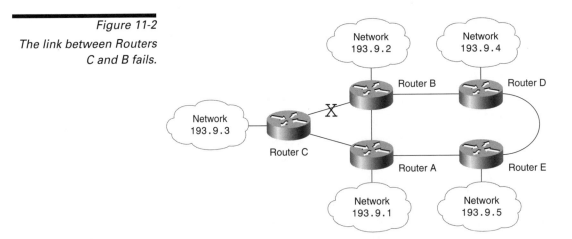

The consequences of this failure are that all routes that used B as a next hop go active in the EIGRP topology table. The effects of this failure, as documented in the topology table, are summarized in Table 11-3.

Table 11-3 *A Summary of Router C's Network Topology, after a Link Failure*

Destination IP Address	Route, from C	Route State	Successor or Feasible Successor?
193.9.1	A	Passive	Successor
193.9.2	B	Active	Successor
193.9.4	B to D	Active	Successor
193.9.5	A to E	Passive	Successor

In this example, all that used the link between Routers C and B become active in the topology table. Other routes, including those that pass through Router B via Router A, remain passive and unaffected by the topology change.

Router C responds to this topology change by sending a query to its neighbors, notifying them that it has lost two primaries. It has only two neighbors, B and A, and one of them is now unreachable.

Router A is obligated by the protocol specifications to respond to Router C's query for alternative path information. Its own topology table has not been affected by the link failure because it has a different set of neighbors. Therefore, there is hope that other routes can be discovered.

Router A's topology table, in the middle of convergence, is summarized in Table 11-4.

Table 11-4 *A Summary of Router A's Network Topology, in the Midst of Convergence*

Destination IP Address	Route, from A	Status	Successor or Feasible Successor?
193.9.2	B	Passive	Successor
193.9.3	C	Passive	Successor
193.9.4	B to D	Passive	Successor
193.9.5	E	Passive	Successor

The link failure between Routers B and C has not affected any of Router A's primary routes. They remain passive and in use. Because this is the case, Router A will respond with information on an alternative route through Router E to these destination networks.

When Router C receives the reply from Router A, it knows that all the neighbors in the network have processed the link failure and modified their tables accordingly.

Table 11-5 summarizes the results of Router C's new understanding of the network's topology.

Table 11-5   *A Summary of Router C's Network Topology, Post Convergence*

Destination IP Address	Route, from C	State	Successor or Feasible Successor?
193.9.1	A	Passive	Successor
193.9.2	A to B	Passive	Successor
193.9.4	A to B to D	Passive	Successor
193.9.5	A to E	Passive	Successor

Router C was able to identify an alternative path—that is, successor—to all the routes it had been able to reach through Router B. These alternatives are far from ideal, however: They all begin with the hop to Router A, which is also the primary route to 193.9.1. If a failure were to beset this link, Router A, or any of the router interfaces that connect this link to Routers A and C, Router C would be completely isolated from the remainder of the network.

SUMMARY

Cisco Systems' EIGRP is one of the most feature-rich and robust routing protocols to ever be developed. Its unique combination of features blends the best attributes of distance-vector protocols with the best attributes of link-state protocols. The result is a hybrid routing protocol that defies easy categorization with conventional protocols.

EIGRP is also remarkably easy to configure and use and is remarkably efficient in operation. It can be used in conjunction with IPv4, AppleTalk, and IPX. More importantly, its architecture will readily enable Cisco to add support for other routed protocols, such as IPv6, in the future.

Open Shortest Path First

As the 1980s drew to a close, the fundamental limitations of distance-vector routing were becoming increasingly apparent. One attempt to improve the scalability of networks was to base routing decisions on link states rather than hop count or other distance vectors. A *link* is the connection between two routers in a network. The status of that link can include such attributes as its transmission speed and delay levels.

This chapter provides an in-depth look at the Internet Engineering Task Force's (IETF's) version of a link-state, interior gateway routing protocol: Open Shortest Path First (OSPF). OSPF was first specified in RFC 1131. This short-lived specification was quickly made obsolete by RFC 1247. The differences between these two OSPFs were substantial enough that the RFC 1247 OSPF was called OSPF Version 2. OSPF Version 2 continued to mature and evolve. Subsequent modifications were outlined in RFCs 1583, 2178, and 2328 (which is the current version). Because the Internet and IP are both highly dynamic, it is highly likely that OSPF will continue to evolve over time to keep pace.

THE ORIGINS OF OSPF

The IETF, in response to the increased need for building larger and larger IP-based networks, formed a working group specifically to develop an open, link-state routing protocol for use in large, heterogeneous IP networks. This new routing protocol was based on the moderately successful series of proprietary, vendor-specific, Shortest Path First (SPF) routing protocols that had proliferated in the market. All SPF routing protocols, including the IETF's OSPF, were directly based on a mathematical algorithm known as the Dijkstra Algorithm. This algorithm enables the selection of routes based on link states as opposed to just distance vectors.

The IETF developed the OSPF routing protocol during the late 1980s. OSPF was, quite literally, an open version of the SPF class of routing protocols. The original OSPF was specified in RFC 1131. This first version (OSPF Version 1) was quickly superseded by a greatly improved version that was documented in RFC 1247. The RFC 1247 OSPF was dubbed OSPF Version 2 to explicitly denote its substantial improvements in stability and functionality. Numerous updates have been made to this version of OSPF. Each has been crafted as an open standard using the IETF as a forum. Subsequent specifications were published in RFCs 1583, 2178, and 2328.

The current version of OSPF Version 2 is specified in RFC 2328. The current version will only interoperate with the versions specified in RFCs 2178, 1583, and 1247. Rather than examine the iterative development of the current, open standard OSPF, this chapter focuses on the capabilities, features, and uses of the latest version specified in RFC 2328.

RFC 2328 OSPF VERSION 2

OSPF was designed specifically as an IP routing protocol for use within autonomous systems. As such, it cannot transport datagrams of other routable network protocols such as IPX or Apple-Talk. OSPF calculates routes based on the destination IP address found in IP datagram headers; and no provisions are made for calculating routes to non-IP destinations. Additionally, the various OSPF messages are encapsulated directly in IP: No other protocols (TCP, UDP, and so on) are needed for delivery.

OSPF was also designed to quickly detect topological changes in the autonomous system and converge on a new consensus of the topology after detecting a change. Routing decisions are based on the state of the links interconnecting the routers in the autonomous system. Each of these routers maintains an identical database that tracks link states in the network. Included in this database is the state of the router. This includes its usable interfaces, known-reachable neighbors, and link-state information.

Routing table updates, known as Link-State Advertisements (LSAs), are transmitted directly to all other neighbors within a router's area. The technical term for this update process is *flooding*, a rather unflattering term with a negative connotation that belies the actual performance characteristics of OSPF.

In practice, OSPF networks converge very quickly. All routers within the network run the same routing algorithm and transmit routing table updates directly to each other. This information is used to construct an image of the network and its links. Each router's image of the network uses a UNIX-like *tree* structure, with itself as the *root*. This tree, known as the *shortest-path tree*, tracks the shortest path to each destination within the autonomous system. Destinations outside the autonomous system may be acquired via border gateways to those external networks and appear as *leaves* on the shortest-path tree structure. Link-state data cannot be maintained on such destinations and/or networks just because they are outside the OSPF network. Therefore, they cannot appear as branches in the shortest-path tree.

OSPF Areas

One of the key reasons for the rapidity of OSPF's convergence is its use of areas. Remember that the two main goals that the IETF sought to achieve with OSPF were

- Improved network scalability

- Rapid convergence times

The key to both goals lies in compartmentalizing a network into smaller regions. These regions are known as *areas*. An area is a collection of networked end systems, routers, and transmission facilities. Each area is defined with a unique area number configured into each router. Router interfaces defined with the same area number become part of the same area. Ideally, these areas are not arbitrarily defined. Instead, the boundaries of an area should be selected so as to minimize the amount of traffic between different areas. In other words, each area should reflect actual traffic patterns rather than geographic or political boundaries. Of course, this is a theoretical ideal and may prove impractical in your particular environment.

The number of areas an OSPF network can support is limited by the size of its Area ID field. This field is a 32-bit binary number. Therefore, the theoretical maximum number of networks is a 32-bit binary number with all its bits equal to 1. The decimal equivalent of this number is 4,294,967,295. Obviously, the practical maximum number of areas you can support is much less than this theoretical maximum. In practice, how well designed the network is will determine the practical maximum number of areas you can support within it. Figure 12-1 illustrates a fairly simple OSPF network with just three areas, numbered 0, 1, and 2.

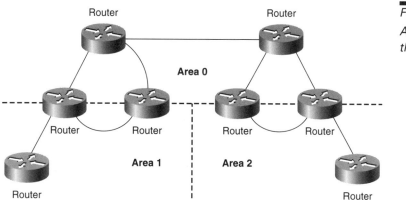

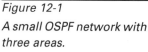

Figure 12-1

A small OSPF network with three areas.

Router Types

It is important to remember that OSPF is a link-state routing protocol. Therefore, the links and the router interfaces that they attach to are defined as members of an area. Based on area membership, there can be three different types of routers within an OSPF network:

- Internal routers

- Area border routers

- Backbone routers

Figure 12-2 uses the network depicted in Figure 12-1 to identify the three different types of routers in the network.

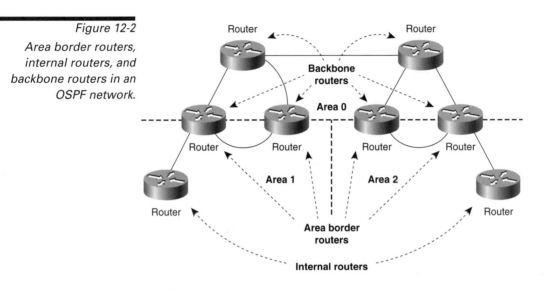

Figure 12-2

Area border routers,
internal routers, and
backbone routers in an
OSPF network.

As shown in Figure 12-2, a router with multiple interfaces may belong to two or more areas. Such routers become *area border routers*. That is, they interconnect the backbone and its area members. A *backbone* router is one that has at least one interface defined as belonging to Area 0. It is possible for an area border router to also be a backbone router. Any area border router that interconnects a numbered area with Area 0 is both an area border and a backbone router. An *internal router* features interfaces that are all defined as the same area, but not Area 0. Using these three basic types of routers, it is possible to construct highly efficient and scalable OSPF networks.

Routing Types

Given the three different types of OSPF routers illustrated in Figure 12-2, it is important to note that OSPF supports two different types of routing:

- Intra-area routing

- Inter-area routing

Their names are fairly self-evident. *Intra-area routing* is self-contained and limited to just the routers internal to a single area. Using the sample network first illustrated in Figure 12-1, Figure 12-3 demonstrates intra-area communications in an OSPF network.

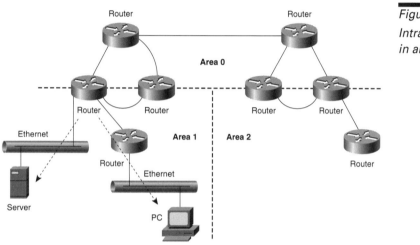

Figure 12-3
Intra-area communications in an OSPF network.

Inter-area routing requires the exchange of data between different areas. All inter-area routing must be conducted through Area 0. Nonzero area numbers are not permitted to directly communicate with each other. This hierarchical restriction ensures that OSPF networks scale gracefully without becoming confusing morasses of links and routers.

Figure 12-4 demonstrates the proper use of Area 0 to facilitate inter-area communications in an OSPF network.

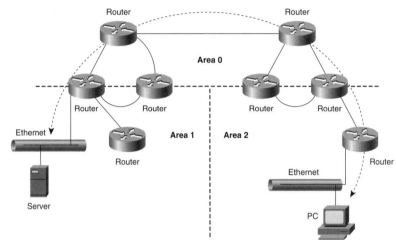

Figure 12-4
Using Area 0 to facilitate
inter-area
communications in an
OSPF network.

The preceding examples demonstrate, at a high level, how communications work within an OSPF network. However, OSPF can also be used to communicate routing information *between* OSPF networks rather than just areas within a single network. This use of OSPF is examined in the following section.

Routing Between Networks

OSPF can be used to internetwork separate networks. Such networks could be another complete OSPF network or utilize a completely different routing protocol. Internetworking an OSPF network with a different routing protocol is a complicated task and uses a technique known as *route redistribution*. Routing information from the non-OSPF network is summarized and redistributed into the OSPF network. The OSPF network tags all routes learned in this manner as *external*. For more information on route redistribution, refer to Chapter 14, "Internetworking with Dissimilar Protocols."

Internetworking two different OSPF networks is easier, because there is no need to convert one routing protocol's route cost information into a format that the other protocol can understand! Additionally, OSPF enables the creation of *autonomous systems*. An autonomous system (AS) is a self-contained network. Ostensibly, an AS would feature a single network administrator or group of administrators and use a single routing protocol.

The actual definition of an AS is somewhat fluid. In truth, it almost doesn't matter. What does matter is that OSPF permits the assignment of an AS number to a network. One very large OSPF network could be segmented into two or more autonomous systems. These systems would be interconnected via a fourth type of OSPF router, *Autonomous System Border Router* (ASBR). The ASBR summarizes all the routing information for its AS and forwards that summary to its counterpart ASBR in the neighboring AS. In this regard, the ASBR functions much like an area border router. The difference, obviously, is that they comprise the border between separate autonomous systems rather than areas within a single autonomous system or network.

Figure 12-5 demonstrates internetworking autonomous systems using ASBRs.

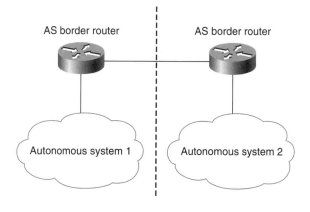

Figure 12-5

Internetworked OSPF autonomous systems.

Routing Updates

One of the reasons OSPF is so scalable is its routing update mechanism. OSPF uses an LSA to share routing information among OSPF nodes. These advertisements are propagated completely throughout an area, but not beyond an area. Therefore, each router within a given area knows the topology of their area. The topology of any given area is not known outside of that area, however. Given that there are actually four different types of OSPF routers—internal area router, area border router, ASBR, and backbone router—it is clear that each router type has a different set of peers with which LSAs must be exchanged.

Internal Area Routers

Internal area routers must exchange LSAs directly with every other router in its area. This includes every internal area router as well as any border area routers that may also be members in its area. Figure 12-6 demonstrates the forwarding, or *flooding*, of LSAs throughout Area 1 of the sample OSPF network presented in this chapter's previous illustrations. It is important to note that same-area OSPF routers needn't be directly connected to each other to share LSA information. An OSPF router directly addresses LSA packets to every known router in its area and forwards those packets using any available links.

A subtle implication of Figure 12-6 is that convergence can occur quite rapidly. There are two reasons for this. The first is that an OSPF router directly addresses and transmits LSAs to all routers in its area simultaneously (known as flooding). This is in stark contrast to the neighbor-by-neighbor approach used by RIP to drive convergence. The result is an almost instantaneous convergence on a new topology within that area.

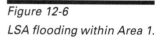

Figure 12-6
LSA flooding within Area 1.

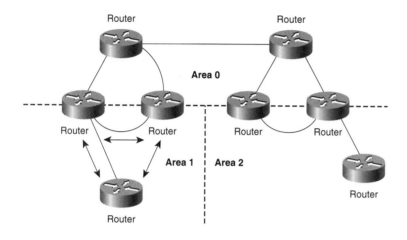

Convergence is also expedited through the definition and use of areas. Topological data is not propagated beyond an area's borders. Therefore, convergence needn't occur among all routers in the autonomous system, just the routers in the impacted area. This feature both expedites convergence and enhances the stability of the network because only a subset of the routers in the autonomous system experiences the instability that is innate in convergence.

Area Border Routers

Area border routers are responsible for maintaining topology information in their databases for each of the areas to which they contain interfaces. Therefore, if an area border router interconnects two different areas, it must exchange LSAs with peers in both networks. As with internal area routers, these LSAs are addressed and transmitted directly to its peers in each area. Figure 12-7 illustrates this.

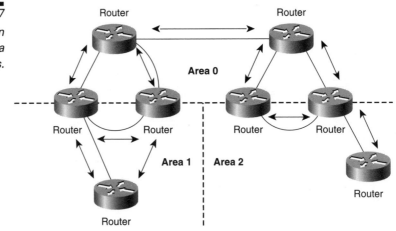

Another of the performance-enhancing features of OSPF is route summarization. Topological information about an area is not shared with other routers outside that area. Instead, the area border router summarizes all the addresses contained in all the areas to which it is connected. This summarized routing data is then shared, via Type 3 LSAs, with peer routers in each of the areas it interconnects.

In Figure 12-7, the border area router advertises this summarized data directly to all routers in Area 0. OSPF prevents areas numbered ≥1 from directly connecting to each other. All such interconnections must occur via Area 0. Therefore, it is implied that border area routers interconnect Area 0 with at least one nonzero numbered area.

Backbone Routers

Backbone routers are responsible for maintaining topology information for the backbone as well as for propagating summarized topology information for each of the other areas within the autonomous system.

Figure 12-8 illustrates the exchange of LSAs by a backbone router.

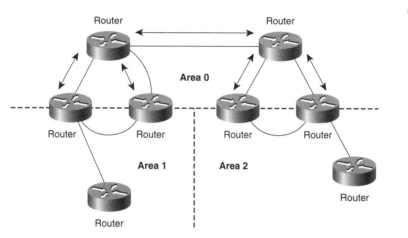

Figure 12-8
Intra-area LSA flooding in an OSPF network by backbone routers.

Although the distinctions between backbone, area border, and internal area routers may seem clear and distinct, there is room for confusion because of the capability of the router to support multiple I/O port connections to other routers. Each port, in theory, could be connected to a different area. Consequently, the router forms a border between the various areas to which its interface ports connect.

OSPF DATA STRUCTURES

OSPF is a fairly complex routing protocol with many performance- and stability-enhancing features. Therefore, it shouldn't be a surprise to find that it uses an extensive array of data structures. Each structure, or message type, is intended to perform a specific task. All of them share a common header, known as the *OSPF header*. The OSPF header is 24 octets long and has the following fields:

- *Version Number*—The first octet of an OSPF header is allocated to the identification of the version number. The current version is 2, although you may encounter older routers still running RFC 1131 OSPF Version 1. RFCs 1247, 1583, 2178, and 2328 all specify backward-compatible variations of OSPF Version 2. Therefore, no further identification is necessary.

- *Type*—The second octet identifies which of the five OSPF packet types is appended to this header structure. The five types (hello, database description, link-state request, link-state update, and link-state acknowledgment) are identified numerically.

- *Packet Length*—The next two octets of the OSPF header are used to inform the node receiving the packet of its total length. The total length includes the packet's payload as well as its header.

- *Router ID*—Each router in an area is assigned a unique, 4-octet identification number. An OSPF router populates this field with its ID number before transmitting any OSPF messages to other routers.

- *Area ID*—Four octets of the header are used to identify the area identification number.

- *Checksum*—Each OSPF header contains a two-octet checksum field that can be used to detect damage done to the message in transit. The originator runs a mathematical algorithm against each message and stores the results in this field. The recipient node runs an identical algorithm against the received message and compares its result with the result stored in the checksum field. If the message arrived undamaged, the two results will be identical. A mismatch indicates that the OSPF packet was damaged in transit. The recipient just discards any damaged packets.

- *Authentication Type*—OSPF can guard against the types of attacks that can result in spurious routing information by authenticating the originator of each OSPF message. The Authentication Type field is a two-octet field that identifies which of the various forms of authentication is being used on this message.

- *Authentication*—The last nine octets of the header are used to carry any authentication data that may be needed by the recipient to authenticate the originator of the message. OSPF enables the network's administrator to specify various levels of authentication that range from NONE, to SIMPLE, to the strong MD5 authentication mechanism.

This basic structure contains all the information an OSPF node needs to determine whether the packet should be accepted for further processing or discarded. Packets that have been damaged in transit (as indicated by the checksum field) will be discarded, as will packets that cannot be authenticated.

OSPF uses five different packet types. Each of the following five is designed to support a different, highly specific function within the network:

- Hello packets (Type 1)

- Database description packets (Type 2)

- Link-state request packets (Type 3)

- Link-state update packets (Type 4)

- Link-state acknowledgment packets (Type 5)

These five packet types are sometimes referred to by their numbers rather than by name. Therefore, an OSPF Type 5 packet is really a link-state acknowledgment packet. All these packet types use the OSPF header.

NOTE

Due to the sheer number of variations on the five basic OSPF data structures, an exhaustive review of their sizes and structures is beyond the scope of this chapter. Instead, this chapter's coverage is limited to a description of the purpose and usage of each data structure.

The Hello Packet

OSPF contains a protocol (the Hello protocol) that is used to establish and maintain relationships between neighboring nodes. These relationships are called *adjacencies*. Adjacencies are the basis for the exchange of routing data in OSPF.

It is through the use of this protocol, and packet type, that an OSPF node discovers the other OSPF nodes in its area. Its name is intentionally significant; the Hello protocol establishes communications between potential neighboring routers. The Hello protocol uses a special subpacket structure that is appended to the standard 24-octet OSPF header. Together, these structures form a *hello packet*.

All routers in an OSPF network must adhere to certain conventions that must be uniform throughout the network. These conventions include the following:

- The network mask

- The interval at which hello packets will be broadcast (the *hello interval*)

- The amount of time that must elapse before a nonresponding router will be declared dead (that is, the *router dead interval*) by the other routers in the network

All routers in an OSPF network must agree to use the same value for each of these parameters; otherwise, the network might not operate properly. These parameters are exchanged using hello packets. Together, they comprise the basis for neighborly communications. They ensure that neighbor relationships (known as *adjacencies*) are not formed between routers in different subnets and that all members of the network agree on how frequently to stay in contact with each other.

The hello packet also includes a listing of other routers (using their unique router IDs) that the source router has recently been in contact with. This field, the Neighbor field, facilitates the neighbor discovery process. The hello packet also contains several other fields such as Designated Router and Backup Designated Router. These fields are useful in maintaining adjacencies and support the operation of the OSPF network in both periods of stability and convergence. The specific roles of the designated router and backup designated router are described in later sections of this chapter.

The Database Description Packet

The database description (DD) packet is exchanged between two OSPF routers as they initialize an adjacency. This packet type is used to describe, but not actually convey, the contents of an OSPF router's link-state database. Because this database may be quite lengthy, multiple database description packets may be needed to describe the entire contents of a database. In fact, a field is reserved for identifying the sequence of database description packets. Resequencing ensures that the recipient can faithfully replicate the description of the transmitted database description.

The DD exchange process also follows a poll/response method, in which one of the routers is designated as the master. The other functions as the slave. The master router sends its routing table contents to the slave. The slave's responsibilities are just to acknowledge received DD packets. Obviously, the relationship between slave and master varies with each DD exchange. All routers within the network, at different times, will function as both master and slave during this process.

The Link-State Request Packet

The third type of OSPF packet is the link-state request packet. This packet is used to request specific pieces of a neighboring router's link-state database. Ostensibly, after receiving a DD update, an OSPF router may discover that the neighbor's information is either more current or more complete than its own. If so, the router sends a link-state request packet(s) to its neighbor (the one with the more recent information) to request more specific link-state routing information.

The request for more information must be very specific. It must specify which data is being requested by using the following criteria:

- Link-state (LS) type number (1 through 5)
- LS ID
- Advertising router

Together, these criteria identify a specific subset of an OSPF database, but not its instance. An instance is the same subset of information but with a temporal boundary. Remember that OSPF is a dynamic routing protocol: It can be expected to automatically update network perspectives in reaction to changes in the state of links in the network. Therefore, the recipient of an LS request packet interprets it to be the most recent iteration of this particular piece of its routing database.

The Link-State Update Packet

The link-state update packet is used to actually transport LSAs to neighboring nodes. These updates are generated in response to an LSA request. There are five different LSA packet types. These packet types are identified by their type number, which ranges from 1 through 5.

These packet types, and their respective LSA numbers, are as follows:

 NOTE

Potential for confusion exists because OSPF regards link-state advertisements, generically, as LSAs; however, the actual mechanism used to update routing tables is the link-state update packet (LSU). If this isn't confusing enough, there is another packet structure: the link-state acknowledgment packet (LSA). For unknown and unspecified reasons, this packet is known as *link-state acknowledgment*. Be aware, however, that *LSA* refers generically to the family of update packets.

- *Router LSA (Type 1)*—Router LSAs describe the state and costs of a router's links to the area. All such links must be described in a single LSA packet. Also, a router must originate a router LSA for each area it belongs to. Therefore, a border area router would generate multiple router LSAs, whereas an interior area router need generate only one such update.

- *Network LSA (Type 2)*—A network LSA is similar to a router LSA in that it also describes link-state and cost information for all routers attached in the network. The difference between a router and network LSA is that the network LSA is an aggregation of all the link-state and cost information in the network. Only the network's *designated router* tracks this information and can generate a network LSA.

- *Summary LSA–IP network (Type 3)*—The Type 3 LSA is somewhat awkwardly referred to as the *summary LSA–IP*, which is probably why the architects of OSPF implemented a numbering scheme for LSAs! Only border area routers in an OSPF network can generate this LSA type. This LSA type is used to communicate summarized routing information about the area to neighboring areas in the OSPF network. It is usually preferable to summarize default routes rather than propagate summarized OSPF information into other networks.

- *Summary LSA–Autonomous System Boundary Router (Type 4)*—A close relative to the Type 3 LSA is the Type 4 LSA. The distinction between these two LSA types is that Type 3 describes inter-area routes, whereas Type 4 describes routes that are external to the OSPF network.

- *AS-external LSA (Type 5)*—The fifth type of LSA is the autonomous system–external LSA. As its name implies, these LSAs are used to describe destinations outside the OSPF network. These destinations can be either specific hosts or external network addresses. An OSPF node that functions as the ASBR to the external autonomous system is responsible for propagating this external routing information throughout all the OSPF areas to which it belongs.

NOTE

OSPF supports the designation of an alternate designated router (DR). This router is known as the backup designated router (BDR). The BDR would fulfill the duties of the DR should that DR fail or become isolated from the rest of the area or network. The BDR also performs any retransmissions that may be necessary on behalf of the DR.

These LSAs are used to describe different aspects of the OSPF routing domain. They are directly addressed to each router in the OSPF area and transmitted simultaneously. This flooding ensures that all routers in an OSPF area have all the same information about the five different aspects (LSA types) of their network. A router's complete collection of LSA data is stored in a link-state database. The contents of this database, when subjected to the Dijkstra Algorithm, result in the creation of the OSPF routing table. The difference between the table and the database is that the database contains a complete collection of raw data whereas the routing table contains a list of shortest paths to known destinations via specific router interface ports.

Rather than examine the structure of each LSA type, it should be sufficient to merely examine their headers.

LSA Header

All the LSAs use a common header format. This header is 20 octets long and is appended to the standard 24-octet OSPF header. The LSA header is designed to uniquely identify each LSA. Therefore, it contains information about the LSA type, the link-state ID, and the advertising router's ID. The following are the LSA header fields:

- *LS Age*—The first two octets of the LSA header contains the age of the LSA. This age is the number of seconds that have elapsed since the LSA was originated.

- *OSPF Options*—The next octet consists of a series of flags that identify the various optional services that an OSPF network can support.

- *LS Type*—The one-octet LS type identifies which of the five possible types the LSA contains. The format of each LSA type is different. Therefore, it is imperative to identify which type of data is appended to this header.

- *Link State ID*—The Link State ID field is a four-octet field that identifies the specific portion of the network environment that the LSA describes. This field is closely related to the preceding header field, LS Type. In fact, the contents of this field directly depend on the LS type. In a router LSA, for example, the link-state ID contains the OSPF router ID of the packet's originator—the *advertising router.*

- *Advertising Router*—The advertising router is the router that originated this LSA. Therefore, the Advertising Router field contains the OSPF router ID of LSA's originator. Given that OSPF router IDs are four octets long, this field must be the same length.

- *LS Sequence Number*—OSPF routers increment the sequence number for each LSA generated. Therefore, a router that receives two instances of the same LSA has two options for determining which of the two is the most recent. The LSA Age field is four octets long and can be checked to determine how long the LSA has been traversing the network. It is theoretically possible for a newer LSA to have a greater LSA age than an older LSA, particularly in large and complex OSPF networks. Therefore, recipient routers compare the LS sequence number. The higher number was the most recently generated. This mechanism doesn't suffer from the vicissitudes of dynamic routing and should be considered a more reliable means of determining the currency of an LSA.

- *LS Checksum*—The three-octet LS checksum is used to detect damage to LSAs en route to their destination. Checksums are simple mathematical algorithms. Their output depends on their input. The input is highly consistent. Fed the same input, a checksum algorithm will always return the same output. The LS Checksum field uses part of the contents of the LSA packet (which includes the header, except for the LS Age and Checksum fields) to derive a checksum value. The source node runs an algorithm known as the Fletcher Algorithm and stores the results in the LS Checksum field. The destination node performs the same mathematical exercise and compares its result to the result stored in the Checksum field. If the values are different, it is relatively safe to assume that damage has occurred in transit. Consequently, a retransmission request is generated.

- *LS Length*—Predictably, the LS Length field informs the recipient of the LSA's length, in octets. This field is one octet in length.

The remainder of an LSA packet's body contains a list of LSAs. Each LSA describes one of the five distinct aspects of an OSPF network, as identified by the LSA number. Therefore, a router LSA packet would advertise information about routers known to exist within an area.

Processing LSA Updates

OSPF differs substantially from other routing tables in that its updates are not directly usable by recipient nodes! Updates received from other routers contain information about the network *from that router's perspective*! Therefore, the received LSA data must be subjected to a router's Dijkstra Algorithm to convert it to its own perspective before that data can be interpreted or used.

Ostensibly, LSAs are transmitted because a router detects a change in the state of a link(s). Therefore, after receiving an LSA of any type, an OSPF router must check the contents of that LSA against the appropriate portion of its own routing database. This can't be done until after the router uses the new data to form a new perspective of the network, which is done via the SPF algorithm. The result of this output is the router's new perspective of the network. These results are compared with the existing OSPF routing database to see whether any of its routes have been affected by the network's change in state.

If one or more existing routes must change as a result of the state change, the router builds a new routing database using the new information.

Duplicate LSAs

Given that LSAs are flooded throughout an OSPF area, it is possible that multiple occurrences, known as *instances*, of the same LSA type will exist simultaneously. The stability of an OSPF network, therefore, requires a router to be able to identify the most current instance of the duplicated LSA. A router that receives two or more instances of the same LSA type examines the LS Age, LS Sequence Number, and the LS Checksum fields in the LSA headers. Only the information contained in the newest LSA is accepted and subjected to the processes described in the preceding section.

The Link-State Acknowledgment Packet

The fifth type of OSPF packet is the link-state acknowledgment packet. OSPF features a *reliable* distribution of LSA packets (remember that LSA stands for *link-state advertisement*, not *link-state acknowledgement*). Reliability means that receipt of the packet must be acknowledged; otherwise, the source node would have no way of knowing whether the LSA actually reached its intended destination. Therefore, some mechanism was needed to acknowledge receipt of LSAs. This mechanism is the link-state acknowledgment packet.

The link-state acknowledgment packet uniquely identifies the LSA packet of which it is acknowledging receipt. This identification is based on the header information contained in the LSA's header, including LS sequence number and advertising router. There needn't be a one-to-one correlation between LSAs and acknowledgement packets. Multiple LSAs can be acknowledged with a single acknowledgment packet.

CALCULATING ROUTES

OSPF, despite its complexity, calculates the costs of a route in one of two remarkably simple ways:

- A non–bandwidth-sensitive default value can be used for each OSPF interface.

- OSPF can automatically calculate the cost of using individual router interfaces.

Regardless of which method is employed, the cost of any given route is calculated by summing the costs of all interfaces encountered along that route. A record is kept of the summed costs to known destination in OSPF's shortest-path tree.

Using Autocalculation

OSPF can automatically calculate the cost of an interface. This algorithm is based on the amount of bandwidth that each interface type supports. The sum of the calculated values of all interfaces in a given route forms the basis for OSPF routing decisions. These values enable OSPF to calculate routes based, at a minimum, on the bandwidth available per link in redundant routes. Figure 12-9 presents a sample network to demonstrate this point.

In Figure 12-9, the cost of the WAN route between a host in network 193.1.3.0 and an end system in network 193.1.4.0 is 138. This cost is the sum of the two T1 links between those networks, each with a cost of 64, plus the cost of the Ethernet interface to network 193.1.4.0. The cost of the Ethernet interfaces at the origination and destination points are not included in the OSPF cost calculation because the OSPF calculates only the costs of outbound router interfaces.

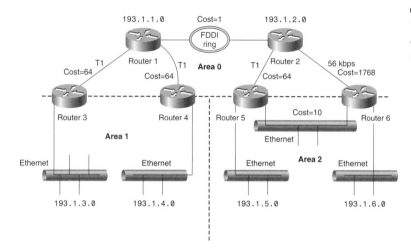

Figure 12-9
Autocalculated costs of the
links.

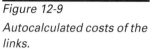

Table 12-1 summarizes the automatically calculated costs for each of the interfaces used in Figure 12-9's network diagram.

Table 12-1 *Calculated Costs Per Interface Type*

Interface Type	Calculated Cost
100-Mbps FDDI	1
10-Mbps Ethernet	10
1.544-Mbps T1 serial link	64
56-kbps serial link	1,768

Using Default Route Costs

It is usually in your best interest to have OSPF automatically calculate route costs, although this may not be possible. Older routers, for example, might not support the autocalculation feature. In such cases, all interfaces will have the same OSPF cost. Therefore, a T3 will have exactly the same cost as a 56-kbps leased line.

Clearly, these two facilities offer very different levels of performance. This disparity should form the basis of informed routing decisions.

There are, however, circumstances that may make the use of default route costs acceptable. If your network consists of relatively homogeneous transmission facilities, for example, default values would be acceptable. Alternatively, you can manually change the cost metrics for specific interfaces. This would enable you to shape traffic patterns in your OSPF network as you see fit, while still using predominantly default routing costs.

Homogeneous Networks

In a homogeneous network, all the transmission facilities are the same. All the LAN interfaces would be 10-Mbps Ethernet, for example, and all the serial WAN interfaces would be T1s. In such a scenario, using the default values would not likely cause routing problems. This would be particularly true if there were little, if any, route redundancy.

To illustrate this point, consider the network diagram in Figure 12-10.

Figure 12-10
Acceptable use of OSPF's
default interface values.

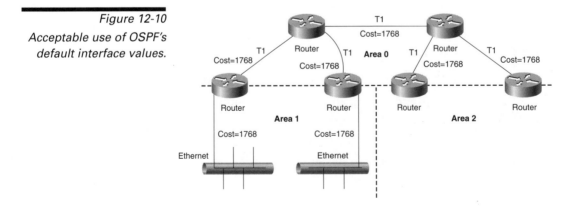

In Figure 12-10, a default value of 1,768 was assigned to each of the interfaces. All the WAN links, however, are T1s. Given that they are all the same, it doesn't matter whether the value assigned them is 1, 128, 1,768, or 1,000,000! Routing decisions, in a homogeneous network, become a simple matter of counting and comparing hops (albeit in multiples of the interface costs). This would be true regardless of how much, or how little, route redundancy existed in the network.

Obviously, in a complex network with substantial route redundancy *and* a disparity in the actual transmission technologies used, the default value would not enable selection of optimal routes to any given destination.

Manually Setting Values

In some networks, it may be desirable to accept OSPF's default costs, and then manually reset those specific links that differ the most from the default. For example, your network's default cost value might be 1,768—the calculated value for a 56-kbps serial link. If all but one or two of the links in your network offered the same bandwidth, you could accept the default values and then reset the values for those particular links.

Whether you use automatically calculated routing costs, default costs, or manually configure costs is immaterial to OSPF nodes. They will accept all such cost values and develop a shortest-path tree perspective of the network.

The Shortest-Path Tree

The purpose of the various LSA mechanisms is to enable each router to develop a perspective of the network's topology. This topology is arranged in the shape of a tree. The OSPF router forms the tree's root. The tree gives the complete path to all known destination addresses, either network or host, even though only the next hop is actually used in forwarding datagrams. The reason for this is simple: Tracking complete paths to destinations makes it possible to compare redundant paths and to select the best one to each known destination. If there are multiple paths of equal cost, they are all discovered and used by OSPF. Traffic is dynamically balanced approximately equally across all such available links.

Router 3's Perspective

To better understand the concept of the shortest-path tree, consider the network diagram presented in Figure 12-11. The simple network depicted is a small OSPF network. The administrator has enabled autocalculation of routing costs. It is important to note that the Ethernet installed between Routers 5 and 6 creates an alternate path for both networks 193.1.5.0 and 193.1.6.0 via Router 2. Therefore, it has an OSPF autocalculated cost of 10, whereas similar costs are not assigned to the other Ethernets.

The shortest-path tree for this network (illustrated in Figure 12-10) would vary from router to router. Figure 12-12, for example, presents this tree from the perspective of Router 3.

As is evident in Figure 12-12, the tree structure greatly facilitates the calculation of routing costs to any given destination. The root router (Router 3—193.1.3.0, in this case) can quickly sum the costs associated with each interface encountered along a route to a given destination. From Router 3's perspective, routing costs to each of the networks are summed for you in Table 12-2. For destinations more than one hop away, the interface costs are summed in parentheses. This will enable you to trace the path through the network in Figure 12-12.

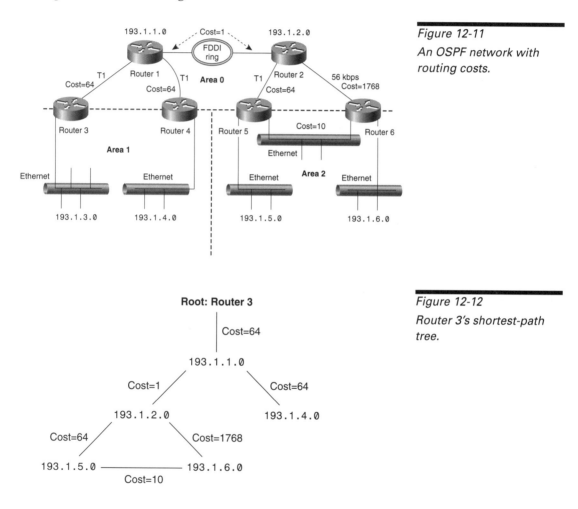

Figure 12-11
An OSPF network with routing costs.

Figure 12-12
Router 3's shortest-path tree.

Table 12-2 *Costs from Router 3 to Known Destinations*

Destination	Hops Away	Cumulative Cost
193.1.3.0	—	0
193.1.1.0	1	64
193.1.2.0	2	65 (64 + 1)
193.1.4.0	2	128 (64 + 64)
193.1.5.0	3	129 (64 + 1 + 64)
193.1.6.0	3	1,833 (64 + 1 + 1768)
193.1.6.0	4	75 (64 + 1 + 10)

In this example, there are two possible routes to network 193.1.6.0. The one route contains fewer hops, but has a much higher cost due to the low-speed serial link between Routers 2 and 6. The alternate route has a higher hop count, but a much lower overall cost. In this case, OSPF would discard the higher-cost route and use the lower-cost route exclusively. If these two redundant routes had the same overall cost, OSPF would have maintained both routes as separate entries in its routing table and balanced the traffic as equally as possible between them.

Router 2's Perspective

Each router's perspective of the network differs. Although it would be somewhat monotonous to examine each router's perspective, a second example may prove useful in demonstrating the impact that perspective has on the shortest-path tree. Figure 12-13 demonstrates the shortest-path tree for Router 2.

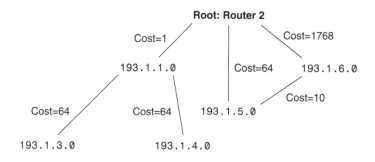

Figure 12-13

Router 2's shortest-path tree.

Table 12-3 provides the summarized routing costs to all known destinations from Router 2's perspective.

Table 12-3   *Costs from Router 2 to Known Destinations*

Destination	Hops Away	Cumulative Cost
193.1.2.0	—	0
193.1.5.0	1	64
193.1.6.0	1	1,768
193.1.6.0	2	74 (64 + 10)
193.1.1.0	1	1
193.1.3.0	2	65 (1 + 64)
193.1.4.0	2	65 (1 + 64)

Comparing Tables 12-2 and 12-3 demonstrates that the cumulative distances between a source and destination in a network can vary based on the starting point. Perspective, it seems, is everything. This is why OSPF routers use data obtained from other routers via LSA updates to develop their own perspective of the network instead of directly updating their routing tables with that information.

SUMMARY

OSPF is one of the most powerful and feature-rich open routing protocols available. Its complexity is also a source of weakness because designing, building, and operating an OSPF internetwork require more expertise and effort than a similar network using almost any other routing protocol. Accepting the default values for the routing costs will greatly simplify the design of an OSPF network. As your knowledge of both OSPF and your network's operational characteristics increases, you can slowly fine-tune its performance by manipulating the OSPF variables. Extreme care must be used in designing the areas and the network's topology. Done properly, your OSPF network will reward you and your user community with solid performance and quick convergence.

PART IV

Implementation Issues

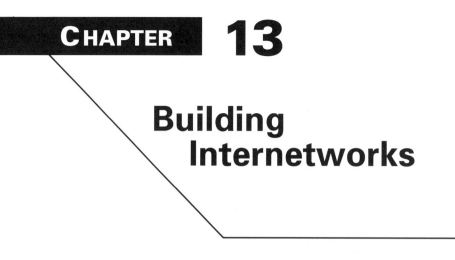

CHAPTER 13

Building Internetworks

Up to this point, this book has examined many of the underlying technologies in an internetwork. These have included routers, routing protocols, and local- and wide-area networking facilities. In this chapter, you will learn how to integrate these components into an internetwork. Internetworks can consist of LANs within a single location, or networks that are scattered across the world in a wide-area network (WAN). Of these two extremes, wide-area internetworking is the more complex. Therefore, this chapter focuses exclusively on internetworking via a WAN.

A BLUEPRINT FOR SUCCESS

The blueprint for success begins with gathering your users' requirements. These become the inputs that affect every facet of your internetwork, from the size and type of transmission technologies, to the placement of routers, to the choice of routing protocol. Planning a WAN requires the successful integration of all these technical components.

Successful integration means that the performance of the finished network meets, or exceeds, performance requirements and user expectations. Therefore, it is important that you identify and quantify (to the extent that users will cooperate) these performance criteria before you begin the design. After you have identified your users' performance expectations, you can begin planning for your WAN based on several factors:

- Scale

- Distances between user locations

- Traffic volumes

- Performance delays

- Costs of the completed WAN

Scale

The first step in planning a WAN is determining its scale. In other words, how big will it be? Although this may seem to be simple, the word *big* can have more than one meaning. In the case of a WAN, *scale* refers to the number of locations that need to be interconnected. The greater the number of locations, the larger the scale of your WAN. Large-scale WANs can impose interesting challenges for the planner. Scale may prevent you from using certain topologies, transmission technologies, and even routing protocols! Therefore, it is imperative that you understand how large your WAN will be before you start to plan it.

Distances

The next factor to evaluate is the distance between the locations that you are trying to internetwork. Many of the transmission facilities available today are priced according to distance. This is particularly true with leased private lines. If your locations are thousands of miles apart, you might find that the cost of installing a dedicated private line between them is cost prohibitive.

Fortunately, alternatives exist. Many transmission technologies are priced according to usage rather than mileage. Examples of these technologies include Frame Relay, X.25, and ATM.

NOTE

Another way to minimize the cost of transmission facilities is through careful planning of the WAN's topology. The shape of the WAN can be manipulated to accommodate the geographic distances separating the locations that are to be internetworked. Some examples of internetworking topologies are presented later in this chapter, in the sections titled "Topologies for Simple Internetworks" and "Topologies for Large Internetworks."

Traffic Volumes

One of the most important factors to consider when designing an internetwork is the traffic volumes that it will have to support. Unfortunately, estimating traffic volumes is an imprecise science. This is particularly true if there is no preexisting network or communications infrastructure. If such an infrastructure existed, it would provide some much-needed clues as to the overall amount of traffic that the new internetwork would have to support.

Absent such a source of information, your next best bet might be to interview users to determine the type of work they do, the locations they need access to, the estimated frequency and duration of their communications with other locations, and an estimate of the bandwidth that will be consumed by each communications session.

When collecting your users' usage volumes, keep in mind that there are actually two traffic volume metrics: maximum traffic volumes and average traffic volumes.

Maximum Traffic Volumes

In reality, actual traffic volume is almost always volatile; it varies with times of day, days of the week, business cycles, seasons, and so on. In other words, you can count on traffic volumes being anything but constant. Given this volatility, it is important to estimate the maximum amount of traffic that could be generated at any given point in time. The *maximum traffic volume* that you expect the network to support is known as the *peak* volume. As its name implies, this is the greatest amount of traffic that you expect the network to have to support.

If you design a WAN without considering peak traffic levels, it is quite likely that your users will experience a degradation of performance, if not an outright service outage, during those times of peak activity.

Average Traffic Volumes

Average volumes are the traffic loads that you can reasonably expect during the course of a business day from any given work location. This type of load is also sometimes referred to as *sustained* volumes.

Establishing these two traffic volumes is critical to the sizing of the WAN's transmission facilities, as well as its routers. If you expect any given location to generate an average traffic load of 100 kbps during the course of a business day, for example, it is clear that a 56 kbps transmission facility will be inadequate.

Performance Delays

Delay is one of the more common metrics that can be used to measure network performance. Delay is the time that elapses between two events. In data communications, these two events are typically the transmission and reception of data. Therefore, delay is the total amount of time that is required by the network to transport a packet from its point of origin to its destination. Given this definition, delay is an aggregate phenomenon with many potential causes. Three of the most common kinds of performance delay are

- *Propagation delays*—Propagation delays are the cumulative amount of time required to transmit, or propagate, the data across each transmission facility in the network path that it must take. The size and quantity of each transmission facility in the network path directly contribute to the aggregate propagation delay of any given transmission. An additional contributor to propagation delay is traffic volumes. The more traffic that is flowing across a given facility, the less bandwidth is available for new transmissions.

- *Satellite uplink/downlink delays*—Some transmission facilities are satellite based. These require the signal to be transmitted up to the satellite and transmitted back down from the satellite. Due to the potentially great distances between the terrestrial transmission facilities and the satellite, these delays can be quite noticeable. Uplink/downlink delays are actually a specific form of propagation delay. For planning purposes, you can safely estimate the round-trip uplink/downlink delay time to be approximately half a second. Due to the lengthiness of this type of delay, however, it is always described separately from terrestrial delays.

- *Forwarding delays*—Forwarding delays in a network are the cumulative amount of time that each physical device needs to receive, buffer, process, and forward data. The difference between forwarding delays and propagation delays is that forwarding delay is measured per device. Propagation delay is measured over the entire network. Forwarding delay is also known as *latency*.

Ideally, you would interview your user community to determine their precise performance requirements, and then select networking technologies and a topology. Practically, this will never happen. Users tend not to know what they need. Their ability to assess a network's performance is usually limited to a reactive, and subjective, opinion. However, users are quite adept at identifying overall levels of performance that are unacceptable! Acceptable levels of performance tend to be a function of habit: Normal network performance is usually defined as whatever they are used to. Obviously, this is a highly subjective way to assess a network's performance. You may find this description of a network's possible sources of delays of little help in designing a WAN. An understanding of them may prove invaluable, however, when trying to figure out why your users aren't thrilled with the performance of an existing network.

Costs of the WAN

Designing a WAN ultimately boils down to a balancing act: The desired performance of the WAN must be reconciled with the cost of providing that performance level. WAN costs include the initial startup costs as well as the monthly recurring expenses. Not surprisingly, the larger and more powerful network components are much more expensive than smaller, less robust components. The greatest source of expense, however, will be the monthly recurring charges you incur for the transmission facilities in your network.

Achieving the balance between performance and cost can be painful. No one wants to design a WAN that will disappoint the users with its performance, but no one wants to design a WAN that blows the budget either! Fortunately, several guidelines can help ensure the design of a WAN that satisfies existing requirements, provides flexibility for future growth, and doesn't exceed the budget.

The capital investments in routers and other network hardware become a fixed part of the network. After they are placed in operation, they must be depreciated over three to five years. You might find yourself stuck with purchased hardware for years after your network outgrows it! Therefore, it might make more sense to buy a larger router, and then add its internal components as you need them. This allows future expansion at modest incremental costs, and little (if any) operational downtime.

Transmission facilities, in comparison to most pieces of internetworking hardware, are relatively easy to replace with other transmission facilities. In theory, they can be replaced as often as your lease agreement with the carrier permits. In practice, swapping out the transmission facilities in your internetwork can be quite disruptive to operations. At a minimum, you will need to carefully plan and coordinate every aspect of such an upgrade. As with physical hardware, your best approach may be overengineering your transmission facilities relative to projected bandwidth requirements.

Applying the wisdom behind these guidelines can help you meet your users' present and future expected requirements within the constraints of your budget. The next step in the planning of your internetwork is the selection of a topology. Topologies can be highly varied. More importantly, they can be customized to fit your particular needs. Therefore, consider the sample topologies presented in the next two sections as information, rather than an actual plan, when building your internetwork.

TOPOLOGIES FOR SIMPLE INTERNETWORKS

The topology of a wide-area internetwork describes the way the transmission facilities are arranged relative to the locations they interconnect. Numerous topologies are possible, each offering a different mix of cost, performance, and scalability. More subtly, some functional specialization may be introduced by topology that has a direct bearing on the transmission facilities.

Some of the more simple topologies are

- Peer-to-peer

- Ring

- Star

- Partial mesh

Each of these is described and illustrated throughout the rest of this section. Their relative cost, performance, scalability, and technology implications are also examined.

Peer-to-Peer Topology

A peer-to-peer WAN can be developed using leased private lines or any other transmission facility. This WAN topology is a relatively simple way of interconnecting a small number of sites.

WANs that consist of just two locations can only be interconnected in this manner. Figure 13-1 depicts a small, peer-to-peer WAN.

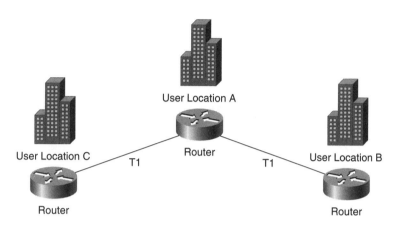

User Location A

Router

User Location C

T1

Router

T1

User Location B

Router

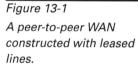

Figure 13-1

A peer-to-peer WAN constructed with leased lines.

This topology represents the least-cost solution for WANs that contain a small number of internetworked locations. Because each location contains, at most, one or two links to the rest of the network, static routing can be used. Static routing can be time intensive to establish but avoids the network overheads of dynamic routing protocols. Given that there aren't any redundant routes to be had in this simple topology, the benefits of dynamic routing are obviated. This fundamental lack of route redundancy must be considered an inescapable limitation of this topology.

Unfortunately, peer-to-peer WANs also suffer from two other limitations. First, they do not scale very well. As additional locations are introduced to the WAN, the number of hops between any given pair of locations remains highly inconsistent and trends upward. This results in varied levels of performance in communications between any given pair of locations. The actual degree to which performance varies depends greatly on many factors, including the following:

- Type and capacity (bandwidth) of transmission facility

- Degree to which the transmission facility is being utilized

- Geographic distances between locations

The degree to which this lack of scalability will affect your internetwork depends directly on how big you expect it could get. If your particular situation is such that it is extremely unlikely that your internetwork will ever grow beyond a handful of locations, this may well be the ideal topology.

The second limitation of this approach is its inherent vulnerability to component failure. There is only a single path between any given pair of locations. Consequently, an equipment or facility failure anywhere in a peer-to-peer WAN can split the WAN. Depending on the actual traffic flows and the type of routing implemented, this can severely disrupt communications in the entire WAN.

Ring Topology

A ring topology can be fairly easily developed from a peer-to-peer network by adding one transmission facility and an extra port on two routers. This minor increment in cost provides route redundancy that can afford small networks the opportunity to implement dynamic routing protocols. Given that the cost of most transmission facilities is mileage sensitive, it would be wise to design the ring to minimize overall distances of those facilities. Figure 13-2 illustrates this WAN topology.

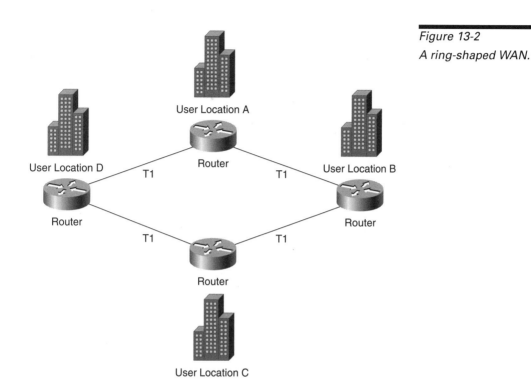

Figure 13-2
A ring-shaped WAN.

User Location A

User Location D

User Location B

Router

T1

Router

Router

T1

T1

T1

Router

User Location C

A ring-shaped WAN constructed with point-to-point transmission facilities can be used to interconnect a small number of sites and provide route redundancy at a potentially minimal incremental cost. The existence of redundant routes through the network means that the use of a dynamic routing protocol affords flexibility not available with static routing. Dynamic routing protocols can automatically detect and recover from adverse changes in the WAN's operating condition by routing around the impacted links.

Rings also have some basic limitations. First, depending on the geographic dispersion of the locations, adding an extra transmission facility to complete the ring may be cost prohibitive. In such cases, Frame Relay may be a viable alternative to dedicated leased lines, provided that its performance limitations are acceptable relative to the projected traffic loads.

A second limitation of rings is that they are not very scalable. Adding new locations to the WAN directly increases the number of hops required to access other locations in the ring. This additive process may also result in having to order new circuits. In Figure 13-2, for example, adding a new location (X) that is in geographic proximity to User Locations C and D would require terminating the circuit from location C to D. Two new circuits would have to be ordered to preserve the integrity of the ring: one running from C to X and the other from D to X.

The final limitation of a ring is its potential hop intensity. Each interior gateway router on a ring is only adjacent to two other interior gateway routers. The number of hops to any other location depends on the way that these locations were interconnected. From a routing perspective, this is not a good way to minimize the number of hops. It does offer route redundancy, but the hop count between any given source and destination address pair can vary widely.

The ring topology, given its limitations, is likely to be of value only in interconnecting very small numbers of locations. It is preferable to the peer-to-peer interconnection of locations only because of its capability to provide a redundant path to the locations within the ring.

Star Network Topology

A variant of the peer-to-peer topology is the star topology, so named for its shape. A star is constructed by homing all locations into a common location. One could argue that this, in essence, creates a two-tiered topology. The distinction between a star and two-tiered topology is that the center router in a star topology may also be used to interconnect the LANs installed at that location with each other as well as the WAN.

In a two-tiered topology, as discussed later in the chapter, the second tier router should be dedicated exclusively to interconnecting the transmission facilities of the other locations. More importantly, a two-tiered topology provides route redundancy by allowing multiple concentration points.

A star topology can be constructed using almost any dedicated transmission facility, including Frame Relay and point-to-point private lines. Figure 13-3 shows an example of a star-shaped WAN.

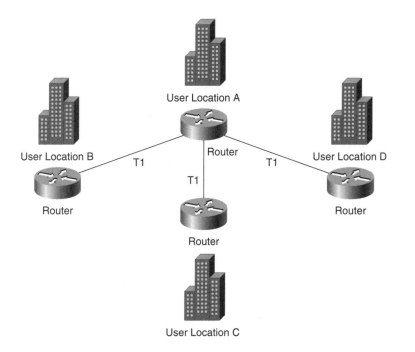

Figure 13-3
A star-shaped WAN.

A star topology WAN with point-to-point transmission facilities is much more scalable than a peer-to-peer or ring network. Adding locations to the star does not require the reengineering of existing transmission facilities. All that is required is to provide a new facility between the concentration router and the router at the new location.

The star topology rectifies the scalability problems of peer-to-peer networks by using a router to interconnect, or concentrate, all the other networked routers. This scalability is afforded at a modest increase in the number of routers, router ports, and transmission facilities compared to a comparably sized peer-to-peer topology. Star topologies may actually be developed with *fewer* facilities than ring topologies, as Figures 13-2 and 13-3 demonstrate. The scalability of this topology would be limited by the number of ports that the router at the center of the star could support. Expansion beyond its capacity requires either a reengineering of the topology into a multitiered topology or the replacement of that router with a much larger unit.

Another benefit of a star topology is improved network performance. Overall network performance in a star topology is, in theory, always better than in either a ring or peer-to-peer network. This is because all network-connected devices are, at most, just three hops away from each other. These three hops are the router at the user's location, the concentrator router, and the router at the destination. This degree of consistency is unique to the star topology.

NOTE

In very small wide-area networks, such as those with only two or three internetworked locations, you may be hard-pressed to perceive any difference between a star topology and a peer-to-peer topology. The benefits of a star topology become increasingly apparent as your network increases in size.

The two drawbacks to this approach are that it creates single points of failure and there is no route redundancy. The existence of a single point of failure means that all WAN communications can be disrupted if the concentrator router experiences a failure. The lack of route redundancy means that if the concentrator router fails, you are out of service until that failure is rectified. Dynamic routing protocols will not be able to calculate new paths through the network because there aren't any!

Of course, this limitation can be compensated for in a variety of ways. Ostensibly, this means a slightly more complex topology, such as the partial mesh, or even splitting the star into two smaller stars that are linked together. In the event of a failure, only half of the remote locations would be affected. Additionally, dial-on-demand technologies, such as ISDN and Switched 56, could be used to reestablish a limited amount of communications.

Partial Mesh Topology

A WAN could also be developed with a partial mesh topology. Partial meshes are highly flexible topologies that can take a variety of very different configurations. The best way to describe a partial mesh topology is that the routers are much more tightly coupled than in any of the basic topologies but are not fully interconnected. Fully interconnected routers form a fully meshed topology. Figure 13-4 shows the partial mesh topology.

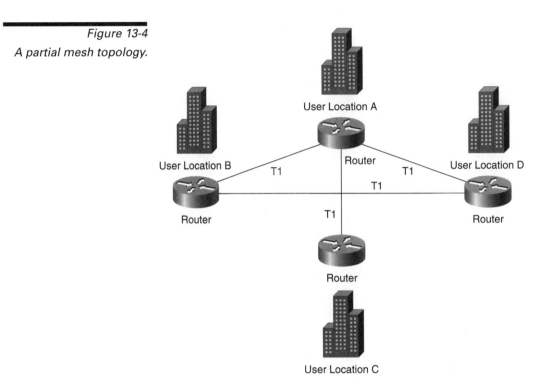

A partially meshed WAN topology is readily identified by the almost complete interconnection of every node with every other node in the network.

Partial meshes offer the capability to minimize hops for the bulk of the WAN's users. Unlike fully meshed networks, a partial mesh can reduce the startup and operational expenses by not interconnecting low-traffic segments of the WAN. This enables the partial mesh network to be somewhat more scalable, and affordable, than a full mesh topology.

TOPOLOGIES FOR LARGE INTERNETWORKS

The preceding survey of sample topologies for simple internetworks should have demonstrated that there are drawbacks to each topology. Many of the topologies in the preceding section suffered from the same limitation: an inherent inability to scale upward. For those of you whose needs transcend the simple topologies, this section presents a sampling of topologies that can only be used in larger, more complex internetworks.

These topologies include the following:

- Full mesh

- Two-tier

- Three-tier

- Hybridized

Full Mesh

At the extreme high end of the reliability spectrum is the full mesh topology. This topology features the ultimate reliability and fault tolerance. Every networked node is directly connected to every other networked node. Therefore, redundant routes to each location are plentiful. In fully meshed networks, static routing is utterly impractical. You are virtually forced into selecting one of the dynamic routing protocols to calculate routes and forward packets in this type of network. Figure 13-5 shows a fully meshed WAN.

This approach absolutely minimizes the number of hops between any two network-connected machines because all locations are directly interconnected. Another benefit is that it can be built with virtually any transmission technology.

Figure 13-5
A fully meshed WAN.

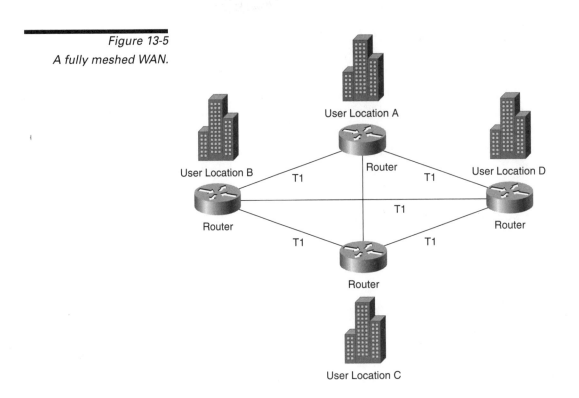

There are, however, some practical limitations inherent in a fully meshed topology. They can be fairly expensive to build, for example. Each router has to be large enough to have a port and transmission facility for each other router in the WAN. This tends to make both startup and monthly recurring operational costs expensive. It also places a finite (although substantial) limit on the scalability of the network. There is a limit on the number of ports a router can support. Therefore, full mesh topologies are more of a utopian ideal with limited practical application.

 NOTE

If you prefer mathematic formulas, for every *n* node in a fully meshed network, you will need to add *n*–1 new ports and transmission facilities every time you add one more node to the network!

One application of a fully meshed topology would be to provide interconnectivity for just those routers or locations that require high network availability. Another potential application is to fully mesh only parts of the WAN, such as the backbone of a multi-tiered WAN or tightly coupled work centers. This approach is described in more detail in the section titled "Hybrid Topologies."

Two-Tiered Topology

A two-tiered topology is a modified version of the basic star topology. Instead of a single concentrator router, two or more routers are used. This rectifies the basic vulnerability of the star topology without compromising its efficiency or scalability.

Figure 13-6 presents a WAN with a typical two-tiered topology. The worst-case hop count increases by one as a result of the extra concentrator (a.k.a. "backbone") router. However, unlike the peer-to-peer network presented in Figure 13-1, the hop count is not adversely affected every time a new location is added to the WAN.

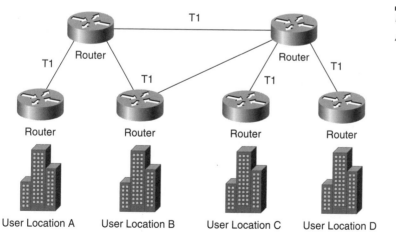

Figure 13-6
A two-tiered WAN.

A two-tiered WAN constructed with dedicated facilities offers improved fault tolerance over the simple star topology without compromising scalability. This topology can be implemented in a number of minor variations primarily by manipulating the number of concentrator routers and the manner with which they are interconnected. Having three or more concentrator routers introduced requires the network designer to select a subtopology for the concentrator tier. These routers can be either fully or partially meshed, or strung together peer to peer.

Regardless of the subtopology selected, hierarchical, multitiered topologies function best when some basic implementation principles are followed. First, the concentration layer of routers should be dedicated to the task. That is, they are not used to directly connect user communities. Second, the user-premises routers should only internetwork with concentrator nodes and not with each other in a peer-to-peer fashion. Third, the interconnection of user-premises routers to concentrator routers should not be done randomly. Some logic should be applied in determining their placement. Depending on the geographic distribution of the users and the transmission facilities used, it may be prudent to place the concentrator nodes to minimize the distances from the user premises. The reason for this is rooted in economics: Most WAN transmission facilities are priced according to their mileage. Longer transmission facilities are more costly than shorter transmission facilities. Therefore, arranging your topology to minimize the distances of transmission facilities will effectively reduce your network's monthly recurring facilities charges.

Given that one or more routers will be dedicated to route aggregation, this topology can be an expensive undertaking. This tends to limit the use of these topologies to larger companies.

Three-Tiered Topology

WANs that need to interconnect a very large number of sites, or are built using smaller routers that can only support a few serial connections, may find the two-tiered architecture insufficiently scalable. Therefore, adding a third tier (or even a fourth or fifth tier) may provide the additional scalability they require. Figure 13-7 illustrates this topology.

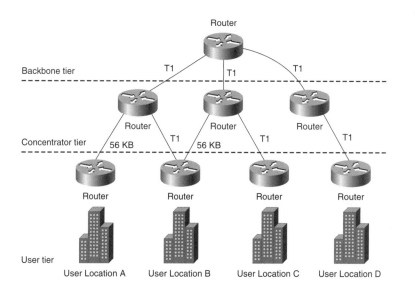

Figure 13-7
The three-tiered WAN topology.

A three-tiered WAN constructed with dedicated facilities offers even greater fault tolerance and scalability than the two-tiered topology. Three-tiered networks are expensive to build, operate, and maintain. They should be used only for interconnecting very large numbers of locations. Given this, it is foolish to develop a WAN of this magnitude and not fully mesh the uppermost, or backbone, tier of routers.

Hybrid Topologies

Hybridization of multiple topologies is useful in larger, more complex networks. It allows the WAN to be tailored to actual traffic patterns instead of trying to force-fit those patterns into a rigid topological model. In other words, the basic topologies presented in this section are examples of constructs intended to stimulate your creative thought. There are no limits on the topological variety that can be introduced to a WAN. The effectiveness of each topology, and subsequent combination of WAN technologies, depends directly on your particular situation and performance requirements.

Multitiered networks, in particular, lend themselves to hybridization. As previously discussed, multitiered WANs can be hybridized by fully or partially meshing the backbone tier of routers. Although there is no right or wrong way to build a hybrid topology, one example of this WAN is illustrated in Figure 13-8.

An effective hybrid topology may be developed in a multitiered WAN by using a fully meshed topology for the backbone nodes only. This affords fault tolerance to the network's backbone and can provide some of the hop-minimization of a full mesh network without experiencing all its costs or incurring its limitations on scalability.

Fully meshing the backbone of a multitiered WAN is just one form of hybridized topology. Other hybrids can also be highly effective. The key is to look for topologies, and subtopologies, that can be used in combination to satisfy your particular networking requirements.

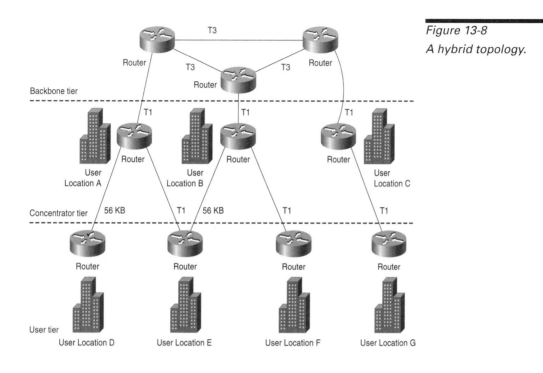

Figure 13-8
A hybrid topology.

BEFORE YOU BUILD THE WAN

After you have collected your users' requirements and evaluated potential topologies, you might be tempted to jump ahead to procurement and implementation. Before you do that, you should address just a few more issues. You must still

- Determine what the aggregate traffic loads will be across your WAN's backbone (if there is a backbone).

- Identify where to place inbound and outbound gateways (such as dial-in modem pools or gateway routers that connect the network to external networks).

- Select the transmission technologies that will be used for each link.

- Identify IP addressing and subnet masking schemes.

- Select which routing protocol(s) will be used.

Determining Backbone Loads

A WAN backbone is a router, or routers, and a series of transmission facilities dedicated to WAN-to-WAN traffic transportation. Not every WAN topology features an organized backbone. In fact, of the topologies presented in this chapter, only a few of the larger, more complex, topologies afford this luxury. Despite this, even the interior gateway routers in small and simple topologies such as peer-to-peer and ring topologies have to function as WAN backbone devices. This capability is needed whenever nonadjacent interior gateway routers need to communicate. For the purposes of this discussion, a WAN's backbone is the collection of routers and transmission facilities used to interconnect nonadjacent interior gateway routers, regardless of whether they also function as interior gateway routers.

Calculating the Load

Given this definition, all traffic routed outside a LAN by an interior gateway router can be considered backbone traffic. This simplification allows you to understand what kind of load you can expect your WAN links to experience. Actually calculating the load on a backbone is difficult, if not impossible, to do proactively. This is especially true in startup scenarios in which there is no historical data on which to base your design. In such cases, you have little choice but to interview users. You should try to do the following:

- Map users' physical locations relative to their desired destinations.

- Identify users' applications and likely transaction types (online transaction processing, ad hoc querying, and so on).

- Identify the quantity of data that will be transmitted, per transaction, for each application and transaction type that users perform.

You should be able to use this information to piece together a rough approximation of the network intensity of their needs. This type of information is invaluable in both sizing the transmission facilities and shaping the WAN's topology.

Fixing Performance Problems

After you establish an internetwork, you can use a great many available tools to track the usage statistics of a network. These are useful in identifying bandwidth-starved hotspots in your WAN. Identifying the problem is the easy part; fixing it may be much more difficult.

There are, generally speaking, two ways to mitigate bandwidth shortages on a WAN backbone:

- Increase the size of the transmission facilities.

- Rearrange the WAN's topology to avoid unnecessary backbone traffic. In other words, base the shape of your WAN on your users' actual traffic patterns. This is, in all likelihood, the lowest-cost approach to improving WAN efficiency.

The typical reaction is to throw more bandwidth at the problem and hope it goes away. This approach only ratchets up the overall cost of the network and is best described as treating a symptom rather than solving a problem. Such an approach may be appropriate if the network is legitimately starved for bandwidth. However, countless new and network-intensive applications are rapidly increasing the demand for bandwidth. The problem might not even be that there isn't enough bandwidth. Instead, the problem might be that there is too much traffic. This can be symptomatic of a poorly designed WAN or evidence of shifting usage patterns. In such cases, the appropriate solution might be to rearrange the WAN's topology. Don't waste time and money blindly chasing after symptoms. Take the time to study the network and identify the nature of the problem. Only with this knowledge can you truly solve the problem.

Placing Gateways

Gateways are any device that enable remote users to enter your internetwork or enable your internal users to access resources outside your network. As such, they are traffic aggregation points. They can funnel traffic in both directions. Therefore, you must understand their effects on your network's traffic patterns and factor them into your design. Much like backbone loads, estimating the magnitude of a gateway's impact on a network can be challenging to calculate proactively. The keys to success lie in understanding the following:

- How many users will be using the gateway

- The application and transaction types that will be performed across the gateway

- How frequently they will use it

After obtaining as much of this information as possible, you can make some educated guesses about where in your network's topology a gateway should be placed. Placement should result in maximum performance of applications across the gateway and minimal impact to the rest of the traffic on your network. This challenge may require you to modify your WAN's topology, upgrade some transmission facilities, migrate to different transmission facility technologies, or any of these scenarios.

Selecting Transmission Technologies

Chapter 6, "Transmission Technologies," includes a survey of the most common LAN and WAN transmission technologies that can be interconnected with routers. One of the critical choices that must be made during the planning of an internetwork is the selection of appropriate transmission technologies for each link in the internetwork.

The WAN Link

The WAN link is the transmission facility that connects the router to another router in the network. As you saw in Chapter 6, a wide range of options is available. Transmission facilities can be packet switched, circuit switched, and even cell switched. Their transmission rate can range from the subrated T-1 (9.6 kbps and up) to 155 Mbps and beyond! Equally varied is the cost of these facilities. Some involve a flat monthly recurring charge based on their geographic length; others incur costs on a usage basis. Selecting the WAN link technology is not a trivial affair. Each of the options must be carefully examined and scrutinized in the context of your performance needs and budgetary constraints.

The LAN Interface

An interior gateway router is responsible for interconnecting the LAN and the WAN. Therefore, it must have at least one interface for each type of network. It is not unusual for a LAN/WAN administrator to just order a router with an interface for whatever LAN architecture is already in use. Therefore, the router becomes, quite literally, just another device in the LAN. Unfortunately, this approach ignores the fact that the router is an aggregation point for both inbound and outbound traffic. In this capacity, it will likely experience a higher amount of traffic than virtually any other LAN-attached device.

This can be a problem if you are using a low-bandwidth, or contention-based LAN architecture such as Ethernet. A 10 Mbps Ethernet may be able to offer eight times the raw bandwidth of a T-1, but its contention-based media access methodology means that you would be hard-pressed to actually use more than 30% or so of this due to collisions. This doesn't mean that Ethernet can't work for you; it just means that you should think before ordering a LAN interface port for your router. You might be better off using either a higher-bandwidth, or more deterministic, LAN architecture for this part of your internetwork.

Selecting Routing Protocols

Part III, "Routing Protocols," provides a detailed examination of some of the most commonly encountered routing protocols. As indicated throughout Part III, not all routing protocols were created equal. Some were designed specifically for use in interior routing, others were designed for exterior gateway routing, and still others function as internetwork border gateway protocols. Selecting a routing protocol, or protocols, for your internetwork requires that you first identify whether your internetwork is strictly a self-contained network, or whether it needs to be interconnected with other external networks.

If the latter is the case, you must examine the routing protocols used on those other networks. It is quite possible that you will either have to select an exterior gateway routing protocol or support a second interior routing protocol for use with that gateway.

After you have identified your gateway router needs (interior, exterior, and/or border), the next step is to choose one of the routing protocols that comprise each category. Routing protocol selection should be based on your needs. Look at the capabilities offered by each one, and compare them with your requirements. Select the one that appears best suited to your needs. Any one of them will most likely work for you. The question you need to answer is "How well will it work in my internetwork?"

AFTER YOU BUILD THE WAN

After you have designed and built your internetwork, there is no time to rest on your laurels. The priority must now shift to maintaining acceptable levels of performance across the internetwork. This requires the collection, and continuous monitoring, of performance metrics.

Many different criteria, or metrics, can be applied to measuring the performance of an existing WAN. Many of these are fairly objective and can be automatically extracted from the network monitoring protocols native to virtually every network device. Others are subjective and can be next to impossible to determine in advance.

Some of the most common metrics are the following:

- Component uptime

- Traffic volumes

- Resource utilization rates

Component Uptime

Each physical component of the WAN can be monitored and measured for its availability using uptime. Uptime is the opposite of downtime: It is the amount of time that the device is functional and in service relative to the users' requirements for its availability. It is quite common for uptime to be statistically overstated by measuring it on a 7×24 (7 days per week, 24 hours per day) basis, even though the users' requirements may only be for 5×12. Remember to tailor this, and every other metric, as closely as possible to your users' stated requirements for network performance.

Electronic devices, although they may be highly reliable, eventually fail. Most manufacturers provide a mean time between failure (MTBF) rating for their equipment as a reassurance of how reliable their products really are. Typically, MTBF ratings are in the tens of thousands of hours. This could, conceivably, translate into years of trouble-free service. Unfortunately, these ratings are statistically derived. The actual time between failures of any given device depends greatly on a number of factors, including the following:

- Ambient temperature ranges of its operating environment

- The cleanliness of the commercial electric power

- How well the device is handled before and during operation

In other words, your mileage *will* vary! Monitoring and tracking uptime of individual components will enable you to demonstrate to your user community how well you are satisfying their requirements for the network's availability.

Component uptime data can also be trended over time to proactively identify potentially problematic components in your network infrastructure. Such trends can provide information about the general reliability of a given type, or brand, of hardware, which can be used to identify individual components that may be at risk of failure.

NOTE

The term *availability* is sometimes used to generically describe aggregate network uptime. It is not, however, a good metric. In theory, network availability provides a quantified synopsis of the network's readiness. In practice, *availability* is so nebulous as to be almost meaningless. To illustrate this point, if a router at a premise location fails, the entire network is unavailable to the users at that location. The network, however, is available to users at every other location. They will not be able to access hosts at the affected location but will not be impeded from accessing every other host in the network. The extent to which the network is available varies greatly by location and by usage requirements. Therefore, quantifying network availability can be more onerous than it is valuable.

Traffic Volumes

Estimated traffic volumes, both maximum and sustained, are important in sizing your network's transmission facilities; they are even more important in measuring the operability of an existing internetwork. Both of these load metrics must be monitored because traffic loads have a nasty habit: They increase over time. Therefore, what was an adequate internetwork at startup can become an underengineered fiasco with the passing of time.

Resource Utilization

The degree to which the various physical resources of the WAN are being utilized is also a good indicator of how well, or how poorly, the WAN is performing relative to the performance requirements. Two main categories of resource utilization rates should be monitored carefully:

- Router resource utilization rates, including CPU and memory

- Transmission facility utilization rates

Router Physical Resources

Routers are one of the most vital components of any WAN. And, unlike the transmission facilities, they are outside the purview of the telecommunications carrier. Therefore, they are distinctly the responsibility of the customer. Fortunately, routers are intelligent devices that contain their own CPU and memory. These physical resources are indispensable in the calculation of WAN routes and the forwarding of packets. They can also be used to monitor the performance of the router.

If either CPU or memory utilization rates approach 100%, performance will suffer. Numerous conditions can result in the utilization rate temporarily spiking upward with consequential performance degradation. One example is a sudden increase in transmissions from the LAN to the WAN. LANs can operate at speeds up to 1 Gbps but usually only operate at either 10, 16, or 100 Mbps. Any of these speeds are a gross mismatch against the typical WAN transmission facility, which offers a paltry 1.544 Mbps of bandwidth. This mismatch in bandwidth must be buffered by the router's memory. It wouldn't take long for a router to become resource constricted during a sustained period of heavy LAN transmissions.

If such situations are rarely experienced, they should be considered aberrations. Aberrations should be monitored, but they shouldn't drive physical upgrades. If these resource constrictions recur or constitute a trend, however, something needs to be done. Usually, this requires an upgrade, either to the next larger router or via an expansion of memory. If a router is chronically at, or near, 100% of capacity with its memory, it is time to purchase additional memory.

Responding to chronically high CPU utilization rates might not be as simple as a memory upgrade. There are really only a few options for improving high CPU utilization rates:

- Upgrade to a more powerful router.

- Identify any specific processes that may be consuming excessive CPU cycles. These may include access control lists (ACLs) and other filtering lists.

- Investigate the WAN's traffic patterns to see whether the load on the problematic router can be reduced.

Manipulating traffic patterns is really only a viable option in larger WANs with complex topologies that afford route redundancy. Even so, if the router in question is a premise-edge vehicle (as opposed to a backbone router), your only option will likely be the forklift upgrade.

NOTE

The term *forklift upgrade* refers to the type of upgrade that requires a completely new device, as opposed to either software or hardware modifications to the existing device.

Transmission Facilities

Transmission facilities can also be monitored for utilization. Typically, this utilization rate is expressed in terms of the percentage of consumed bandwidth. If you are using a T-1, for example, a given sample might indicate that 30% of its 1.544 Mbps of available bandwidth is currently being utilized.

These rates can be tricky to analyze and may even be misleading. It is not uncommon, for example, for network-management software packages to capture utilization data in time intervals. These can be one hour, five minutes, or just about any other interval. The sampling frequency, if set too coarsely, can miss short-duration fluctuations in bandwidth consumption. If the sampling is too frequent, you could find yourself mired in a meaningless morass of data points. The trick is finding the right frequency that provides meaningful data about how the network is performing, relative to the user's expectations.

Beyond merely selecting the sampling rate lies the issue of sampling windows. The sampling window should be determined by the users' requirements for WAN availability. If the utilization samples are spread over a 24-hour day and 7-day week but the users work only 10 hours per day and 5 days per week, the statistical data is not indicative of how well the users' requirements are being met.

Utilization rates are a wonderful statistical tool for monitoring and measuring the status of transmission facilities. They are not, however, the only metric for assessing a network's performance. The network is only successful if it satisfies the users' requirements. Therefore, a combination of performance metrics that provides a multifaceted, composite perspective is likely to provide a better assessment of the network's success.

SUMMARY

Internetworks are complex structures that don't necessarily adhere to any published or open standard. Designing, building, and operating one that consistently satisfies your users' requirements can be a Herculean task. Success lies in understanding the capabilities, limitations, and costs of each WAN component technology. This understanding forms the context for their integration. Each component technology will be well matched with the performance capabilities of each other component and balanced against any budgetary constraints.

CHAPTER 14

Internetworking with Dissimilar Protocols

Many small networks feature a single routing and/or routed protocol. It is a given that each network will require one of each: a routed protocol to encapsulate and transport data to its destination, and a routing protocol to discover, compare, and select optimal routes through the network to that destination. Having one of each protocol greatly simplifies many facets of internetworking, including route calculation and the exchange of routing information between all of its member nodes. Unfortunately, as beneficial as it may be to use just one protocol, it is not always possible or even practical.

In real life, there are countless reasons multiple protocols may be unavoidable in an internetwork. These reasons range from functional necessity to business requirements. Regardless of the actual reason a single routing protocol is inadequate for any given situation, fundamental challenges must be resolved. This chapter identifies some of the more common types of internetworks that necessitate multiple routing protocols, as well as some of the implementation techniques that can be used.

DISSIMILAR ARCHITECTURES

The actual need for supporting two or more routing protocols in an internetwork can come from a variety of sources. Generally speaking, the need derives from architectural dissimilarities between networks that must be internetworked. These dissimilarities can be a result of network administrators' preferences. One network's administrator may prefer Open Shortest Path First (OSPF) and a mixed-vendor environment, for example, whereas the other administrator operates a Cisco-only network and runs Enhanced Interior Gateway Routing Protocol (EIGRP).

Alternatively, dissimilar network architectures could indicate a functional distinction within a network, such as interior and exterior gateway functions. Some of the more common business requirements that could lead to internetworking dissimilar networks include extending an intranet to business partners (which is known as an *extranet*), or even connecting to the Internet. Similarly, mergers and acquisitions can also result in having to internetwork very dissimilar network architectures, or even networks constructed of different vendors' products. Therefore, for a variety of reasons, the purist goal of a singular routing and routed protocol may be impossible.

Regardless of the causes, you might find yourself having to internetwork with dissimilar routing and/or routed protocols. Despite their dissimilarities, you can successfully internetwork such networks using some relatively simple techniques. These techniques vary somewhat, depending on whether the dissimilar protocols are routing or routed protocols, and which particular ones they are.

DISSIMILAR ROUTED PROTOCOLS

Dissimilarity in routing protocols is not the only challenge a network administrator may face. Routed protocols, too, may be problematic. Ideally, an organization selects a single routed protocol such as IP or IPX and implements it broadly. Nevertheless, many of the same circumstances that could result in dissimilar routing protocols can also affect routed protocols. The end result could be multiple dissimilar routed protocols being used in different domains of an internetwork.

There are several options for coping with this incompatibility:

- Supporting redundant routed protocols

- Using protocol conversion gateways

- Tunneling through incompatible network regions

Redundant Routed Protocols

Today's computers, and their network interface cards (NICs), can simultaneously support multiple networking protocols. In theory, each end system in a network could support two or more very different routed protocols, such as IP and IPX, simultaneously. The machine's network interface card doesn't look for these network layer addresses in data frames on its LAN; the NIC looks only at MAC addresses. The routed protocol datagrams are encapsulated in MAC-addressed frames. As the framing is unwrapped by the end system's data link layer protocol, the datagrams are revealed. This allows the data link layer protocol to examine the network layer address and forward the encapsulated data to the appropriate routed protocols for further processing.

The use of multiple network layer protocols is completely transparent to the end systems' NICs, as well as to the various LAN devices. Each of these protocols would, however, have its own address, address architecture, and datagram-forwarding mechanisms. This means that networks would have to support two sets of internetwork addresses—one for each routed protocol. Impacted devices would be routers and Layer 3 switches (if there are any in your network). Fortunately, routers are designed to support multiple routed protocols. Therefore, your network can already simultaneously use dissimilar routed protocols throughout the entire network.

Your options for supporting redundant routing protocols are either full or partial redundancy.

Full Redundancy

A network that uses fully redundant routed protocols requires each networking device to simultaneously run both routed protocols. Consider, for example, the case of a networked environment that is in the midst of a transition from Apple-based computers and networking to Microsoft's Windows NT. The original networked environment used the AppleTalk protocol suite. The new network operating system, NT, will be used with IP. In such a scenario, a reasonable migration path might be to run both protocols on all devices simultaneously. Such a scenario could be temporary, until a migration can be completed. Alternatively, such a solution could be permanent, as would be the case with monitoring the IPv4-addressed management ports of older Ethernet hubs in an IPv6 network.

Figure 14-1 demonstrates fully redundant routed protocols in a small network.

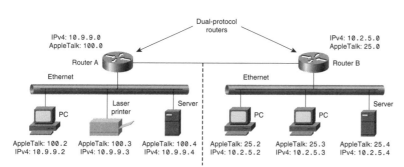

Figure 14-1

*Fully redundant routed
protocols.*

In this scenario, any device could communicate with any other
end system using either AppleTalk or IP addresses. Ostensibly,
each end-system's applications would be configured to use one or
the other protocol. As the transition progresses, support for
AppleTalk could be phased out.

Partial Redundancy

Another approach to using redundant routed protocols is to
install the redundant protocol only where it is needed. In such
cases, some end systems would have two routed protocols
installed and configured. Others would rely on just one. Figure
14-2 demonstrates such partial routed protocol redundancy in a
small network.

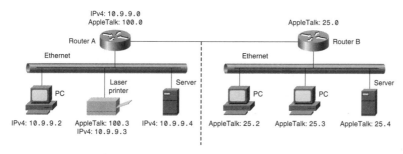

Figure 14-2

*Partially redundant routed
protocols.*

In this example, the laser printer has been given an address in both routed protocols. Therefore, users on both networks can use it. However, this is the only resource that can be accessed universally. All the other end systems have just one routed protocol and, consequently, can only communicate with other end systems on their LAN.

The benefit of this approach is that end systems that don't need the second protocol are spared the overhead of running it. Additionally, the network's administrator is spared the bother of installing and supporting extra protocols on devices that do not require them. The one drawback is that devices that only use one protocol can only communicate with other devices that run that same protocol. In other words, an AppleTalk-only end system cannot communicate with any IP-only end systems. This drawback, however, can be eliminated through proper planning and identification of users' needs.

One of the most important benefits of the separation of a network's layered functions is that two or more network protocols can simultaneously operate over the same LAN. Therefore, there is no need to rewire or add another network to support dual protocols.

Gateways

One way to avoid using redundant protocols on end systems is to use a gateway. *Gateway* is a generic term for any device that provides a translation function between two dissimilar networking, or computing, mechanisms. In the case of a routed protocol, a single device could be installed in the network that can communicate with other end systems, regardless of which routed protocol they use. An IP-only end system that needed to communicate with an IPX-only host, for example, would forward its datagrams to the gateway. The gateway would convert the IP datagram to IPX, complete with addressing, and forward the new datagram to its destination. Responses from the host to the end system would function in a similar manner, albeit in reverse.

Figure 14-3 demonstrates use of a protocol-converting gateway in a small network. In this illustration, both protocols are used simultaneously in the same LAN environment, but each LAN-attached device is only configured for one of the protocols.

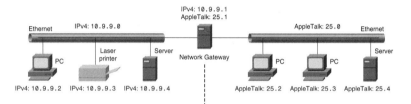

Figure 14-3

Using a gateway to translate between dissimilar routed protocols.

Gateways can be almost any type of computer. The only criterion is that the gateway device be capable of translating between the two protocols' address architectures and data structures. This requires that the gateway computer have the necessary NICs, device drivers, and conversion software to function as a gateway. Of course, it would also be beneficial if this computer also had the processing power needed to accommodate the loads that will be placed on it!

Tunnels

The third way to overcome the barriers caused by dissimilar routed protocols is to use tunnels. *Tunnels* are relatively simple constructs that can be used to pass data through an otherwise incompatible network region. Datagrams that are to traverse this dissimilar network region must be encapsulated in the packet structure of the dissimilar network protocol. This allows the original datagram to be forwarded through the otherwise incompatible section of the network en route to its destination. The original framing and formatting is retained but treated as data by the encapsulating protocol.

Upon reaching the end of the tunnel, the encapsulating protocol "wrapper" is removed and discarded. This restores the datagram to its original format, complete with its original internetwork addressing. Implied in this description of tunneling is that both the source and destination machines use the same routed protocol, but that some portion of the network interconnecting them uses a different protocol. The tunnel would be constructed between the two routers that form the boundaries between the dissimilar regions. As such, they would be capable of using both routed protocols. These routers, in theory, would be the ones in the network that are closest to both the source and destination machines.

This type of mechanism is used as a transitional device between the two versions of IP: IP Version 4 (IPv4) and IP Version 6 (IPv6).

Figure 14-4 illustrates the tunneling of IPv4 packets through an IPv6 network region. Because of the inherent difference in the length of these two protocols' addresses, they are not directly compatible. To overcome this incompatibility, IPv4 packets are wrapped in IPv6 by Router A for transmission through an IPv6 WAN. Router B removes the IPv6 wrapper and presents the restored IPv4 packet to the destination host in the form that it can recognize.

This same process works in reverse: IPv6 datagrams can be wrapped in IPv4 packets for delivery through an IPv4-only network.

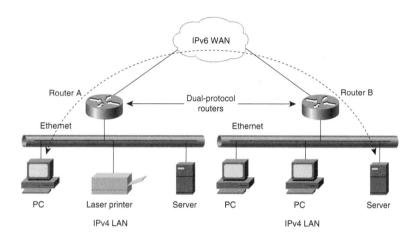

Figure 14-4
Tunneling IPv4 packets
through an IPv6 region.

DISSIMILAR ROUTING PROTOCOLS

Routers use routing protocols to calculate routes, share network topology information, and identify optimal next-hops for any given datagram. These protocols are completely transparent to the end systems in a network. Therefore, solving incompatibilities between them may not be as large or vexing a challenge as with routed protocols.

Internetworking two (or more) networks that use dissimilar routing protocols may be accomplished in three different ways:

- Integrated routing protocols
- Redundant routing protocols
- Redistributing route information

The merits and implications of each of these potential solutions are examined throughout the remainder of this chapter.

Integrated Routing Protocols

One approach to supporting multiple routing protocols is to use a single, integrated routing protocol. An *integrated protocol* is simultaneously capable of routing two different protocols and addresses. Examples of this form of routing protocol are the emerging series of *ng* protocols that are designed to facilitate the migration between IPv4 and IPv6. Specific examples of integrated protocols are OSPFng and RIPng and RIP Version 2 (RIP-2). RIP-2 was designed to be fully backward compatible with RIP Version 1. Therefore, it qualifies as an integrated routing protocol.

Using an integrated routing protocol provides a seamless integration of different routing protocols. The one drawback to this approach is that there are so few integrated routing protocols! Most (if not all) such protocols are nothing more than advanced versions of routing protocols that are backward compatible with their earlier versions. As such, they are transitional mechanisms that facilitate a graceful migration from one version of a routing protocol to the next. In theory, the entire network will eventually be converted to using the newest version of the protocol. After the transition is complete, therefore, the integration features of the routing protocol become moot. However, the network benefits from the expanded capability set of the new version of the protocol.

Figure 14-5 demonstrates a small RIP network that is being upgraded, in sections, to RIP-2. Portions of the network are still using RIP. The migration began with upgrading the gateway router to RIP-2. Each of the subnetworks can then be upgraded to RIP-2 without disrupting service across the network.

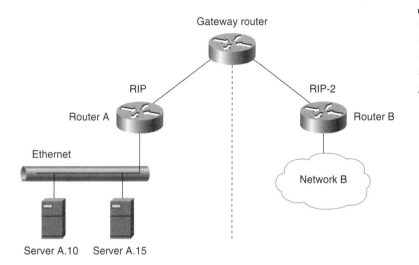

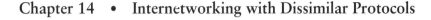

Figure 14-5

Networks with multiple routing protocols may use an integrated routing protocol, such as RIP-2.

Networks using an integrated routing protocol, unlike networks using any of the other mechanisms for supporting dual routing protocols, function as a *single* network. There is no need to convert datagrams, translate addresses, or redistribute routing information between the old protocol and the new, integrated protocol. Interoperability between RIP and RIP-2, for example, is a native function of RIP-2. The only functional limitation is that routers still running the older version of the RIP cannot benefit from any of the features added to RIP-2.

Other integrated protocols exist, too. Some examples include IS-IS, which can carry both DECnet and IP, and Cisco's EIGRP, which can share routing information with IGRP networks. Selecting an integrated routing protocol is a matter of understanding your particular requirements. You may find one that fits your needs perfectly, or you may discover that none of the available integrated protocols will work in your particular situation.

Redundant Routing Protocols

One way to work around incompatibilities in routing protocols is to implement them redundantly. This approach can be implemented in varying degrees, depending on your needs. On one extreme, for example, you could implement two routing protocols on every router in your internetwork. This would result in each router

- Having two sets of routing tables

- Performing two sets of table updates

- Converging twice after topology changes

In other words, each router would have twice the work to do in addition to the usual responsibility of forwarding datagrams on behalf of end systems. Therefore, using redundant routing protocols is unavoidably resource intensive! The router's internal resources, including CPU cycles and memory, are consumed at prodigious rates. The network can also suffer as bandwidth consumption on the network increases. The extent to which each of these resources will be taxed depends directly on

- The size of the internetwork using redundant protocols

- The protocols used

- The actual metrics or settings implemented

Given these variables, it may not be easy or feasible to assess the actual effects of using redundant routing protocols. Nevertheless, these factors adversely affect the network's performance. Unlike with routed protocols, however, it doesn't make sense to use fully redundant routing protocols. Each protocol would be capable of calculating routes through the network to any given destination, so there is nothing to be gained from full routing protocol redundancy.

A more sensible approach is to partition off just the pieces of the internetwork that require redundant protocols and use a single protocol everywhere else. This would improve the operational efficiency of the routers, as well as the overall network. You may elect, for example, to create stub networks within your internetwork. Each stub could use a simple, distance-vector protocol such as RIP or RIP-2. The remainder of the network would use a more robust protocol such as OSPF or EIGRP. In such a scenario, only the border routers between the two network regions would have to support both protocols. Figure 14-6 illustrates this.

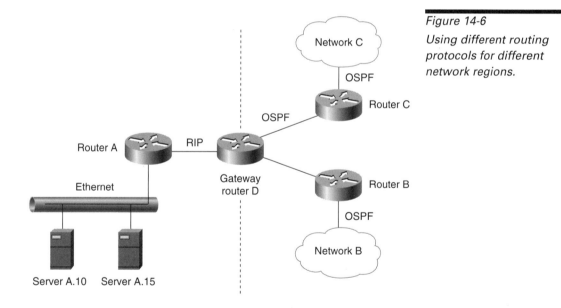

Figure 14-6

Using different routing protocols for different network regions.

In the network depicted in Figure 14-6, the use of different routing protocols for different parts of the network improves overall network performance. Specifically, topological change wouldn't trigger a networkwide convergence. Each network region need only track the topology of its own region. Therefore, the change were to occur within the OSPF region, only the OSPF routers would have to converge on a new understanding of the network's topology. Similarly, if the change were to occur within the RIP region, the OSPF routers wouldn't need to know about the new topology.

The OSPF routers would, however, need to know whether the change meant that entries in their routing tables were now invalid. This information would be gained via the exchange of routing information with RIP nodes. Although it is quite normal for routers with the same routing protocol to exchange routing information, a logistical challenge arises when two neighboring routers actually use different routing protocols. The term that describes the exchange of routing information between dissimilar routing protocol nodes is *route redistribution*. In the example presented in Figure 14-6, the border router(s) must redistribute routing information from the RIP network into the OSPF network and vice versa.

Redistributing Routing Information

Routers that function as the border gateway between network regions that use different routing protocols must redistribute routing information between the two regions. Route redistribution is just the summarization and forwarding of a network's routing information to a router or routers in another network.

Route redistribution must be configured on each border gateway router. Therefore, it is possible to configure (or not configure, as the case may be) a pair of border gateway routers to redistribute routes in one of three different manners:

- From Network A to Network B

- From Network B to Network A

- Bidirectionally

These forms of redistribution can be used either between networks with different routing protocols or between different networks that use the same routing protocol. Both of these permutations are examined in the following sections.

NOTE

The network names A and B were arbitrarily selected to demonstrate the two one-way relationships that can exist between any pair of bordering networks. In a real-world network, these networks would have IP addresses.

Redistribution from Network A to Network B

Using the network shown in Figure 14-6, Figure 14-7 demonstrates the redistribution of RIP routing information into the OSPF network. In this example, OSPF routing information is not redistributed to the RIP network. This would result in the end systems of the RIP network not being able to establish communications with end systems in the OSPF network. The end systems in the OSPF network, however, could establish communications with the end systems in the RIP network. Given that an IP-based communications session is inherently bidirectional, the RIP router would have to have a default route configured so that response packets could be forwarded to the OSPF network.

Although such a situation may sound odd, it could be quite useful. In an extranet, for example, the two networks would belong to two different companies. Ostensibly, their business processes are interrelated, and they have linked their networks together to facilitate their mutual business. However, the administrators of the

OSPF network might need to provide their user community with access to end systems, yet not want to compromise the security of their own network. In such cases, it might be necessary to add security mechanisms such as a firewall or even to use a router's access control list to prevent unwanted ingress.

A less glamorous possibility is that this configuration could be accidental. That is, the two networks should have established bidirectional route redistribution, but the OSPF network administrators may have neglected to configure their border gateway router to do so.

This one-way route redistribution is illustrated in Figure 14-7.

Figure 14-7
RIP routing information is
redistributed to the OSPF
network.

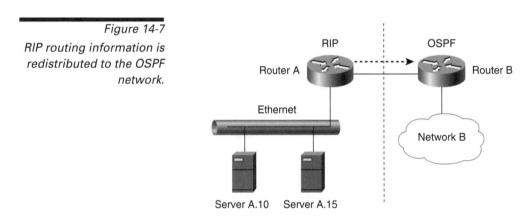

Redistribution from Network B to Network A

The scenario presented in Figure 14-7 could work in reverse: The OSPF network could redistribute its routing information into the RIP network without receiving the RIP network's routes in return. Figure 14-8 illustrates this other one-way route redistribution.

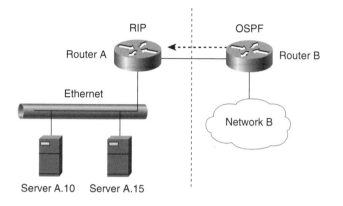

Figure 14-8
OSPF routing information
is redistributed to the RIP
network.

This arrangement offers the same types of benefits and uses as the preceding one-way arrangement. The only difference is direction. As with the preceding example, some means of supporting bidirectional communications must be established. Again, this can be either a static or default route.

Mutual Redistribution

Finally, route redistribution can be configured on both of the border gateway routers. Therefore, routes are redistributed bidirectionally, or mutually. This scenario enables end systems in both networks to establish communications with each other. Figure 14-9 demonstrates mutual route redistribution.

Redistribution Between Same-Protocol Networks

Although route redistribution is almost always associated with internetworking between networks that use dissimilar routing protocols, that is not its only use. Route redistribution can be an effective way of compartmentalizing networks that use the same

routing protocol. For example, a large IGRP network can be logically configured as two separate IGRP networks with routes redistributed between them. This would simulate the function of OSPF
areas: Convergence becomes much more rapid, without compromising interconnectivity between any given pair of end systems.

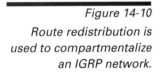

Figure 14-9
Routing information is
redistributed
bidirectionally between
the RIP and OSPF
networks.

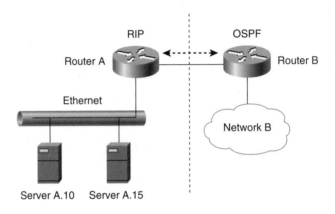

Figure 14-10 illustrates this form of route redistribution.

Figure 14-10
Route redistribution is
used to compartmentalize
an IGRP network.

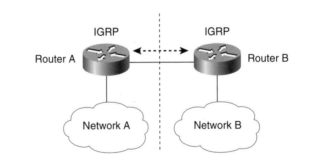

The Mechanics of Route Redistribution

Route redistribution is one of the more powerful, yet complex, of a router's capabilities. In essence, route redistribution is a fairly simple concept. The gateway routers participate in route calculation and convergence for the networks of which they are members. Routing information for that network is summarized and shipped to a neighboring network (albeit one that runs a different routing protocol). In practice, configuring a route redistribution scheme is fairly complicated.

One of the main reasons for the complexity of route redistribution is the fundamental differences that can exist between the various routing protocols. As demonstrated throughout Part III, "Routing Protocols," such protocols can make their routing decisions using very different algorithms (distance-vector versus link-state) as well as a surprising variety of actual routing metrics.

Routing information can only be distributed if it is expressed in a form that is understood by the receiving network's routing protocol. Attempting to ship IGRP composite metrics to a RIP network would not be very productive. RIP uses only a single metric: hop count. A RIP network wouldn't understand the IGRP metrics or any other protocol's metrics. Routing information that is to be redistributed to a RIP network must, therefore, be expressed in terms of hop count. Therefore, route redistribution requires the use of a metric common to both networks' routing protocols. In other words, redistributing routing information is a least-common-denominator exercise.

You must specify a default metric that will be used to express a route's cost. Routes redistributed to external networks use this default metric to calculate routes and make routing decisions. It is imperative, therefore, that you understand the routing protocols that you will be redistributing information to (and from) before you select a default metric. If you understand the routing protocols and their respective metrics, you shouldn't have any problem with configuring a default metric.

Problems with Route Redistribution

Given the disparity of logic and routing metrics that exists between the various routing protocols, several innate problems arise from redistributing routes:

- No common routing metric

- Dissimilar convergence mechanisms

- The existence of redundant gateways in a network

Each of these factors is quite normal in a network or routing protocol—yet within the context of a route redistribution scenario, they pose interesting challenges that must be addressed.

No Common Routing Metric

Perhaps the most obvious problem inherent in route redistribution is the lack of any common routing metrics between the two routing protocols being internetworked. One such example is redistributing routing information from RIP *into* IGRP. As shown in the chapters of Part III, "Routing Protocols," IGRP is alone in its use of a composite routing metric. Because RIP is limited to the single, dimensionless metric hop count, it lacks the mechanisms to develop a mathematically derived composite perspective of a network's routing information. In fairness, other protocols also have nothing in common with IGRP. OSPF, for instance, uses link-state routing information to calculate its routes. Therefore, it suffers from no direct equivalent metric.

How then do other routing protocols redistribute their routing information to IGRP? The answer is simple: IGRP is configured to apply a fictitious composite metric to such external routes. This default value creates stability, but it does not necessarily enable IGRP to make optimal decisions between two comparable external routes to the same destination.

Configuring an IGRP Default Metric

Route redistribution between two networks that use different and dissimilar routing protocols is one of the more complicated tasks a network administrator will face. The single most commonly made mistake in configuring such a mutual redistribution is a failure to actually configure the default metric! Consequently, it is necessary to deviate from this book's customary aversion to syntax and to present you with the correct syntactical string. The following command sets the default metric for external routes to common composite value:

```
router igrp n
        default-metric 10000 100 255 1 1500
```

In this command sequence, bandwidth is set to 10000, delay to 100, reliability to 255, loading to 1, and MTU to 1500. The resulting value should avoid routing problems in most networks, although you may need to manipulate one or more of the individual settings to accommodate your particular network needs. In any case, using a default metric value to represent all external routes will solve the problem of not having comparable metrics.

Dissimilar Convergence Mechanisms

Another potentially devastating problem with route redistribution is that different routing protocols use different convergence mechanisms. Convergence, by its very nature, creates a temporary instability in a network. For example, OSPF and RIP use very different convergence mechanisms. A topological change can be quickly detected and accommodated in an OSPF network. RIP, however, must endure the elapse of several timing mechanisms before routes can be invalidated. Therefore, redistribution between RIP and OSPF may work well until the network's topology changes. When such a change occurs, the dissimilarity of the two convergence mechanisms will create a disparity in consensus and lead to further instability in the network.

In a network that uses both RIP and OSPF and redistributes routes bidirectionally, the result of a failure in the RIP network may well be detected first by the OSPF routers. These routers might not know what the new topology is, but they agree that the affected routes are unreachable. It may take several minutes before RIP nodes detect the failure and attempt corrective action. This time disparity creates the opportunity for host- and application-level problems within the OSPF network.

Specifically, during this brief period of instability, it wouldn't be surprising if an IP datagram's time-to-live (TTL) expired. Upon expiration, the IP internal protocol Internet Control Message Protocol (ICMP) would transmit an error message to that datagram's source. This message would notify that source machine of the TTL's expiration. Most applications interpret this message as indicative of the destination's unavailability. Consequently, these applications will cease trying to communicate with that device.

Unfortunately, there aren't any good countermeasures against such instability. Fortunately, the period of instability is relatively short, and the damage easily rectified after the networks converge. Recovery is often as simple as re-initiating a communications session or just restarting the application.

Unauthorized Gateways

In large networks, particularly those operated by multiple network administrators, it is not uncommon to find unauthorized, or *backdoor*, interconnections between network regions. These backdoors are usually implemented as a result of an informal agreement between two or more network administrators, or could even be the result of a mistake or misunderstanding. Indeed, it is quite possible for even network administrators to be unaware of the existence of such backdoors.

They rationalize that a little deviation from the standard network topology is warranted because of localized needs. The existence of such a gateway may or may not be made known explicitly to the rest of the network's administrators. This sets the stage for routing loops during convergence. This can be particularly problematic for networks that redistribute routing information.

The solution is for all administrators of the network to agree on using a particular gateway for redistributing routes. Alternatives may exist for route redundancy, but there should be no informal, unadvertised backdoors between the two networks. Such policies are easily enforced using access control lists with `permit` and `deny` options explicitly identifying gateways for redistributing routes. Properly configured, these permissions would prevent the distribution of false routing information (made possible by dissimilar convergence mechanisms) from creating loops during convergence.

SUMMARY

Different routing protocols offer different combinations of capabilities. These sets of capabilities may be highly beneficial when used properly. Therefore, even within an autonomous system, it may be to your advantage to use multiple routing and routed protocols. In other circumstances, you may find yourself without much choice: You may be forced to support a second routing protocol.

Regardless of the reasons driving the use of multiple protocols, a solid knowledge of each protocol's capabilities, limitations, features, and data structures is essential. Armed with this knowledge, you can develop a solid strategy that enhances rather than impedes the network's functionality and capabilities.

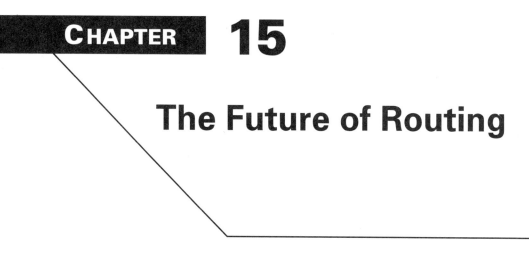

The Future of Routing

As technologies go, routing is ancient. The need for routing goes back to the dawn of internetworking. Many of a router's component technologies date back more than 20 years! During this time, many substantial innovations and advances have been made in networking, computing, and even transmission technologies. It doesn't take much of an imagination to see that some of these innovations, including IP switches and software-based routing engines, appear to be designed to eliminate the need for a hardware-based router in a LAN. In fact, during the emergence of LAN switching several years ago, some of the proponents of this technology even proclaimed routing to be dead while drumming up support for their new technology.

A fair question to ask is, "Does routing have a future, or are its days numbered?" This chapter answers that question by examining some of the key trends and technological developments that have affected routing.

The key technological advances that directly affect routing include

- Development of routing software that can run on low-end computers

- Multilayer switching

- Next-generation routing protocols

463

Each of these has affected traditional, hardware-based routing in different ways, and to different extents. Examining the affects (or potential) of these technologies provides an indication of the future of routing.

COMPUTER-BASED ROUTERS

Traditional, standalone routers are hardware specific: You purchase a specialized physical platform, including a chassis, sheet metal, power supply, CPU, memory, I/O ports, and a motherboard together with the routing engine. These components are described in Chapter 4, "Routers and WANs."

In a standalone router, the routing engine is an integral part of the unit. It is not separable, nor portable, from the standalone router. In a computer-based router, the routing engine is executable software designed to run on a general-purpose computer rather than a highly specialized device. In fairness, this isn't a new trend. In fact, the earliest routers were really UNIX-based computers that calculated routes using one of the myriad primitive RIP-like protocols described in Chapter 8, "Routing Information Protocol." This early form of software-based routing was, subsequently, almost completely supplanted by the various generations of hardware-based routers that emerged.

Figure 15-1 illustrates a typical, but now obsolete, configuration for using a computer-based router to calculate routes in the pre-PC era of computing.

In Figure 15-1, dumb terminals are hardwired to a UNIX server. This server, in addition to its application base, hosts a Routing Information Protocol (RIP) routing engine. This engine was the first generation of computer-based routing. It was used by the terminals and the server to access other internetworked devices.

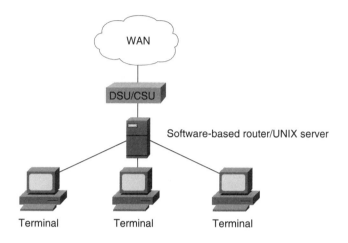

Figure 15-1
An early computer-based
router.

The appearance of the specialized standalone routers brought some substantial benefits relative to computer-based routing:

- A processing platform dedicated to route calculation and packet forwarding

- Placement of the routing function at the boundary between the LAN and WAN rather than at the LAN's periphery

- Support for more advanced routing protocols

- Potential for sharing a WAN access facility across a greater base of users

- A more reliable platform that had fewer moving parts than an end system

These benefits resulted in the dominance of the standalone router. Over time, routers became increasingly more powerful and feature rich. These developments enabled standalone routers to expand their presence in internetworks. Specifically, they began to be used in nontraditional ways, such as to construct LAN backbones.

Today's Products

Today, the amount of computational power available at the desktop is greater than that of mainframes 20 years ago. Also, more sophisticated routing protocols than RIP are available in executable software. Therefore, it seems logical that today's powerful computers should be used to provide sophisticated route calculation at the network's periphery.

On the surface, this would appear to be a direct threat to the traditional standalone router. In theory, you wouldn't need a standalone router anymore. After all, its real value lies in its routing engine rather than its physical components. All you would need is a peripheral computer with a routing engine, an appropriate network interface card, and transmission facilities. Beyond the surface, it is easy to see that this is not the case. Instead, the re-emergence of computer-based routing is complementary to, rather than competitive with, standalone routers.

The New Uses of Computer-Based Routing

The computer-based router's flexible platform and multitasking capabilities enable it to perform many more different functions than a standalone router. The key to benefiting from a computer-based router is to take advantage of these features, which cannot be duplicated on a standalone router.

A computer-based router can be used to authenticate dial-in users, for example, before granting them access to an internal, and secured, internetwork. Figure 15-2 demonstrates how a computer-based router can be used in this fashion. It is important to note that, in this figure, a standalone router is still required to support traditional WAN access.

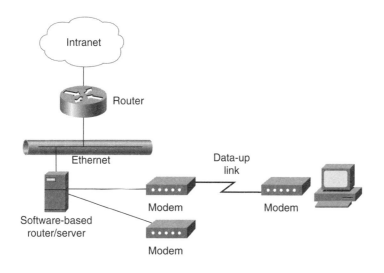

Figure 15-2
A computer-based router can be used to augment a network's capabilities.

This example demonstrates that a computer-based router is not a replacement for traditional standalone routers. Similarly, a general-purpose computer running Windows NT Server can interconnect two different LANs and provide a routed interface between them. Obviously, that NT device needs to have two network interface cards (NICs), but is another example of the flexibility of computer-based routing. All such devices must be considered a complementary service that enhances the usefulness of routing technologies in a network. The specific benefits of the configuration illustrated in Figure 15-2 include the following:

- The ability to use a general-purpose computer rather than a specialized, and possibly more expensive, standalone router

- Support for dial-on-demand transmission technologies (POTS, Switched 56, ISDN)

- VPN tunnel construction

- Management of router via client/server administrative infrastructure rather than through a fully separate network management infrastructure

MULTILAYER SWITCHES

Another interesting development that potentially affects routing is the multilayer switch. Multilayer switches operate much like LAN switches (such as Ethernet switches), except that they are designed to forward datagrams based on their IP addresses rather than MAC addresses. This capability, at least superficially, appears to position a multilayer switch as a potential replacement for stand-alone routers in a LAN. Closer examination, however, reveals that this technology cannot completely supplant traditional standalone routing in a LAN because there are several fundamental limitations of multilayer switching. The best way to understand these limitations is to examine how a multilayer switch operates and its uses.

NOTE

Multilayer switches are more commonly known as IP switches, or even Layer 3 switches, because IP has become the dominant routed protocol.

A multilayer switch operates in much the same way that a bridge or LAN switch operates, even though its functionality more closely approximates a router's capabilities. This type of switch builds tables that correlate I/O port with known addresses. Framed data is received through any of the switch's I/O ports and buffered just long enough to identify the destination IP address of the datagram embedded within the frame. The switch compares this address with its routing table to determine where to forward that datagram. Layer 3 switches use routing protocols, such as OSPF or RIP, to calculate routes and build routing tables.

Although this process may appear identical to how a standalone router forwards datagrams, there are physical differences between multilayer switches and standalone routers that dictate different uses. Multilayer switches are designed for intrapremises communications only, for example. This is evident in the types of I/O ports that they can be configured with. The vast majority of today's multilayer switches only support LAN architectures, usually just Ethernet interfaces (10 and 100 Mbps versions).

This effectively limits the use of multilayer switches to just an intrapremises communications role. In other words, it can only be used for LAN-to-LAN communications. Chapter 3, "Routers and LANs," examines some of the ways traditional standalone routers could be used to improve the efficiency of LANs. One particular method is described as the *collapsed backbone*. In a collapsed backbone LAN, a router is used to segment LANs to improve the performance of each, while simultaneously providing WAN access (if needed). The multilayer switch has some interesting attributes that can be used to further improve LAN-to-LAN communications, by using it to construct a modified form of the collapsed backbone LAN topology. This is explained further in the next section.

Benefits and Uses of Multilayer Switches

The multilayer switch is both faster and less expensive than a standalone router. These attributes make multilayer switches an attractive way to supplement a premise-edge router. Its best use is as a front end to an interior gateway router in a modified form of collapsed backbone LAN. Figure 15-3 illustrates this.

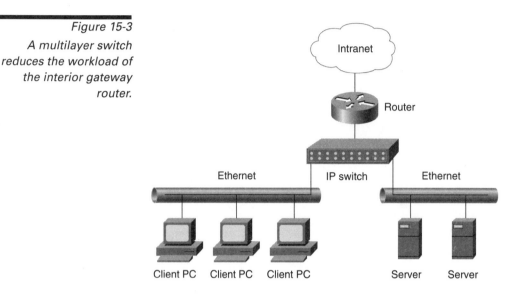

This arrangement features the following division of responsibilities:

- The hardware-based router is used as a gateway between the LAN and the internetwork beyond.

- The less-expensive IP switch helps reduce the workload of that interior gateway router by functioning as a collapsed backbone switch.

In this arrangement, the only datagrams that would be passed from the IP switch to the router would be those addressed to destinations that lie beyond the local LAN. All communications between clients and servers (which reside on separate LAN segments) would be spared the hop through the standalone router. There are three main benefits to using this configuration:

- The efficiency of the standalone router is greatly increased because its workload is limited to just WAN access functions.

- The cost per-port of LAN switches tends to be substantially less than the cost of a comparable router port. Reducing the router's workload may also enable the use of a smaller, less-expensive router.

- The efficiency of LAN-to-LAN communication is also increased, because the multilayer switch operates much faster than a traditional router in a collapsed backbone LAN.

After examining the benefits and limitations of multilayer switches, there can only be one conclusion: They are a wonderful complement to a standalone router in very large LAN environments.

NEXT-GENERATION ROUTING

Communications protocols are always evolving; there seems to be no end to the variety of features and functions that can be developed. Many of the most significant emerging communications protocols are related to the IETF's "IP: The Next Generation" (IPng) project. IP Version 6 (IPv6) is designed to be a simple, forward-compatible upgrade to the existing version of IP. This upgrade is also intended to resolve all the weaknesses that IP Version 4 (IPv4) is currently manifesting. From the perspective of an end user, these weaknesses include the following:

NOTE

The IETF working group that was commissioned to study and design the IPng was called the IPng working group. Ostensibly, this name stood for "IP: The Next Generation." The name was probably inspired by science fiction. As the specification was being developed, it was named *IP Version 6* (IPv6). Many people fail to appreciate the distinction between the working group and its product. Consequently, they refer to the new protocol as IPng.

- The inability to accommodate time-sensitive traffic (known as *isochronous services*)

- The lack of network layer security, including both authentication and encryption services

IPv4 also suffers from other limitations that users might not appreciate. These include

- The shortage of available IPv4 addresses

- The limitations that its two-level address imposes on the global scalability of the Internet and other large IP networks

For all of these reasons, the IETF launched a working group to develop the next generation IP: IPv6.

The Effects of IPv6

When finally completed and supported in commercial products, IPv6 will have a profound effect on internetworking. It will affect routers in four distinct ways:

- Individual routing table entries will increase in size.

- The overall size of routing tables will decrease due to the way routes are aggregated.

- Next-generation routing protocols will emerge that can work with the new address architectures.

- Routers will have to support many services that are not currently available at the network layer.

Many of these changes are either self-explanatory or have been adequately examined in the context of their address architectures. The one exception is the myriad network-layer services that routers will soon be supporting. These services fall predominantly into one of two categories: security or isochronous services. The security protocols are embedded in a new suite of protocols known as *IP Security* (IPSec). Isochronous protocols are a bit less well organized, and do not enjoy the architectural context of a protocol suite such as IPSec. Nevertheless, the various emerging *Voice over IP* (VoIP) technologies will benefit tremendously from IPv6's isochronous capabilities, including its capability to deliver a specific quality of service (QoS).

NOTE

Although these services may have emanated, either directly or indirectly, from the development of IPv6, you won't have to wait for IPv6 to use them. This is because IPv4 continues to grow and evolve, concurrent with the development of the specifications for IPv6. Therefore, IPSec will be supported by both versions of IP, as will many of the isochronous service protocols.

IPSec

The IETF has developed the IPSec architectural framework for securing transmissions over an IP network. IPSec features network layer support for authentication of the originator, encryption of transmitted data, and even protection of the header information of transmitted packets through a process known as *encapsulation*. These services enable end-to-end security of data through an IP network. Although this may not seem significant, remember that IP was designed to provide best-effort delivery of data through a routed and connectionless network environment. Connectionless means that virtually every packet could take a different route through the network. Therefore, the challenge was to develop a series of mechanisms that would allow each router in an internetwork to support the end-to-end security of the data in transit.

The solution developed by the IETF is known as a *security association* (SA). An SA is a logical, simplex "path" between a source and a destination machine. This path is considered logical rather than physical because it remains possible for each transmitted packet to take a different route through the network. The SA itself is a relatively simple construct. It consists of a security parameter index (SPI), the security protocol being used, and the destination IP address. This construct can be supported in both IPv4 and IPv6. Its fields are added to the datagram after the IP header, but before the TCP or UDP header.

Placing these fields at the beginning of the IP datagram's payload is a relatively easy way of enabling end-to-end protection of the IP data, despite its passage through an otherwise unsecured network. Equally as important, this technique does not encumber the routers in the network. They can forward IPSec-compliant datagrams just as they would any other IP datagram. Thus, they can contribute to the end-to-end security of an IPSec-compliant session without having to do anything but forward datagrams! This preserves their previous level of operational efficiency, while adding substantial network layer security.

SAs can be used to support two IPSec security protocols: Authentication Header (AH) and Encapsulating Security Payload (ESP). It is important to note that IPSec only permits one SA per service! Therefore, if you want to perform both encapsulation and authentication, you would need two SAs. SAs, however, are simplex in nature. That is, they only work in one direction. To illustrate this point, consider Figure 15-4. This figure illustrates a simplex authentication SA. The source machine is authenticated to the destination machine, but any datagrams generated in response are not similarly authenticated. In other words, the destination machine is assumed to be legitimate and no authentication is performed.

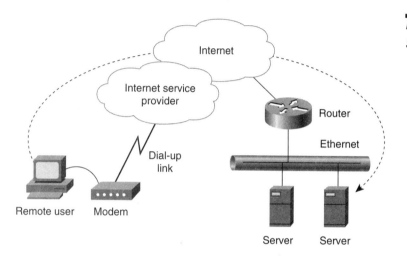

Figure 15-4
Simplex authentication.

Assuming that the destination machine is legitimate can be a dangerous assumption. Providing bidirectional authentication is just a matter of using two unidirectional authentication SAs:

- One authenticates the source machine to the destination machine.

- The other authenticates the destination machine to the source machine.

Figure 15-5 depicts this bidirectional authentication.

ESP headers work the same way. They are simplex, but can be paired to provide bidirectional encapsulation. The important thing to remember is that multiple SAs are permitted, per connection. Providing bidirectional authentication and bidirectional encapsulation on a connection would require the definition of four SAs. This flexibility enables a network administrator to customize the degree of security according to the users' needs.

Figure 15-5
*Bidirectional
authentication.*

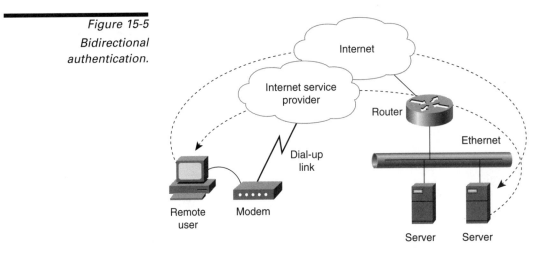

SAs are little more than the mechanisms that enable IPSec to function. The actual security protocols, AH and ESH, warrant further examination.

Authentication Header

IPSec AH is the protocol that enables two communicating machines to verify that they are, in fact, who they purport to be. Authentication is important for several reasons—not the least of these is that IP addresses are so easily spoofed. Previously, the only other form of network layer security was the access control lists that routers provided. These lists provide a modicum of security by allowing administrators to specify which addresses (or ranges of addresses) could access which other addresses. The fundamental flaw in access control lists was that the router assumed that the source IP address in the datagram's header was legitimate.

Therefore, anyone could gain illicit access to networked destinations just by spoofing the source IP address in the datagrams he or she transmitted.

Authentication is a means of ensuring that the machines (and/or their users) are who and what they purport to be. A sequence of data is passed between the two machines. This sequence, known as a *key*, is then run through an algorithm that is known only to both communicating parties. If the expected output is not received, the datagram is assumed to be from a spurious source and is discarded.

The IETF sought to improve network layer security by adding source authentication to the router's existing, but limited, set of security mechanisms. Rather than re-create existing functionality, the IETF sought to leverage the capabilities of myriad existing authentication technologies. Therefore, they developed a modular architecture that enabled users to select specific component technologies. The result is that IPSec's AH can support many of today's more popular authentication mechanisms, including Internet Key Exchange (IKE), Kerberos, SKIP, and many others. AH can also support either manual or automatic distribution of keys.

If AH is used in conjunction with ESP, AH would function similarly regardless of which ESP options are used. This is important because ESP supports two very different forms of transmission protection, known as *modes*.

Encapsulating Security Payload

The Encapsulating Security Payload protocol was designed to ensure that the transmitted data cannot be intercepted. Ostensibly, this is most useful when sensitive data must be transmitted over a network that is either not secured or not trusted.

Two implementation options can be used:

- Transport mode

- Tunnel mode

These two modes are named for the manner in which they protect transmitted data. Transport mode protects only the payload of data being transported. The remainder of the datagram, including all its header fields, are transmitted in the clear. This mode, because of its modest amount of overhead, offers a clear transmission performance advantage over Tunnel mode. It is not perfect, however; it leaves destination addresses exposed, which can promote unwanted types of attention.

Tunnel-mode ESP goes a step beyond by creating a tunnel for the data to pass safely through. The tunnel is, essentially, an IP datagram within an IP datagram. This tunnel can then be used to protect (through encryption) the payload and header fields of the "inside" datagram, but not the "outside" datagram's header fields. Implicit in this description is that some sacrificial machine must be used as the other end of the tunnel. The sacrificial machine forms a gateway between the trusted and untrusted network domains. It receives the tunneled datagrams, performs any required authentication, and then strips off the outer datagram to reveal the encrypted datagram that was tunneled inside it. After decrypting this datagram, it is placed on the trusted network where it can be forwarded to its ultimate destination.

TIP

The performance overheads of tunneling can be substantial. Although tunnel-mode ESP provides a maximum degree of protection, its performance might not be acceptable to your users. Understand its actual performance impact before you commit to using it.

Encryption

Modularity of protocol specification enables customization of the encryption engine. *Encryption* is a systematic scrambling of data in such a way that only the intended recipient(s) can restore the data to its original state. There are many different techniques for encrypting data. The differences between them can be fairly subtle, such as different algorithms applied to the data. They can also be fairly obvious, such as using different-sized encoding sequences (also known as keys) to scramble the data. Generally speaking, the larger the encoding sequence, the more possible permutations that data can take. The greater the number of possible permutations, the more difficult it is for unintended recipients to decode.

Within the IPSec architecture, encryption can only be used with the ESP security protocol, although it can be used in either Transport mode or Tunnel mode. The IETF designed IPSec to afford maximum flexibility for implementation. Its modular architecture treats encryption as a separate function that is not dependent or interrelated with any of the mechanics of the ESP. Therefore, you are free to select your own encryption engine, including the use of whatever-sized encoding sequence may best fit your needs. The actual encryption engine may be a software module that is loaded on to a computer or it may be a physical device that plugs in to the network.

Isochronous Services

Isochronous services are another group of next-generation functions that are rapidly being developed for the network layer. An *isochronous service* is one that is time sensitive. Examples include real-time voice over IP, videoconferencing, or streaming voice and video transmissions. Isochronous data types are the antithesis of what IP networks were designed for! Today's data networks and their various networking protocols were designed to deliver data. In many cases, the higher-layer protocols were explicitly designed to guarantee successful delivery regardless of how much time or how many retries were needed. These technologies are direct descendants of the very first data networks that were challenged by noisy electromagnetic switching and the lack of fiber-optic transmission facilities. Consequently, they have ample mechanisms that detect and correct transmission errors. The applications from this early era also required only that the data eventually be delivered intact so that it could be reconstructed into its original, pretransmitted state. The amount of time it took to receive good data was almost irrelevant when weighed against the need to receive good data.

Isochronous communications reverse this paradigm. Data that is received late, or even out of sequence, is discarded! The reason for this is simple: It minimizes the damage. To further explain this point, consider what would happen if the datagram contained a video frame in a live videoconferencing session. This application type is highly isochronous. Video frames are played virtually as they arrive. If the datagram containing video frame number 3,862 in the series arrived after 3,863, it would be discarded. The reason is that skipping the frame can produce a mild form of distortion in the video sequence that might not even be noticed by the viewers. Datagrams that arrive late are automatically skipped by this application type. Reinserting them out of sequence after they arrive creates a second distortion in the sequence being viewed. Therefore, dropping the datagram reduces application errors by half—quite a difference from the traditional application types!

Retrofitting data networks to accommodate time-sensitive data and their applications is not a trivial undertaking. Numerous proposals have been made over the years, each with a slightly different twist on how to improve the quality of service that can be guaranteed for different types of applications. Somewhat predictably, and very unlike network layer security mechanisms, there is no single architectural framework for the development or deployment of open standard isochronous services. Instead, there are a series of competing proposals for open standardization.

Without forcing you to endure an exhaustive review of competing proposals, suffice it to say that these proposals tend to work in one of two ways: They either reserve bandwidth or tag packets. These two approaches attempt to resolve the same problem, albeit in very different ways. To date, neither approach has garnered enough mindshare (for lack of a better word) to be considered as the preferred approach.

Bandwidth Reservation

One way to ensure that isochronous applications receive the bandwidth that they need through a network is to reserve that bandwidth in advance. This technique, although it provides a means of satisfying time-sensitive applications, comes with a couple of steep costs.

The first cost incurred with bandwidth reservation is one of opportunity. By definition, bandwidth reserved is not available for use by other users or applications. To illustrate the significance of this point, consider the following example. A pair of users require 256 kbps of bandwidth for a live videoconference between their respective workstations. They are approximately 3,000 miles apart and are interconnected by their company's intranet. To ensure that their videoconference performs acceptably, they use a bandwidth reserving protocol (such as RSVP).

This protocol then negotiates a path through the intranet between their end systems and reserves the needed bandwidth. The routers in this path must ensure that traffic from other sources does not infringe on this reserved bandwidth. Obviously, for sporadic and/or limited use, bandwidth reservation does not pose a problem. However, this approach does not scale upward very gracefully. Even just a few such sessions over a single transmission facility can result in noticeably degraded throughputs for the remainder of the intranet's user community.

A second, more subtle implication of reserving bandwidth is the loss of flexibility. Routers excel at calculating paths and automatically detecting and accommodating unexpected changes in a network's topology. Bandwidth reservation runs contrary to this fundamental capability. If a topological change adversely impacts a link that is used by a bandwidth-reserving communications protocol, the result may well be a failure of that communications session!

Packet Tagging

The second approach to recognizing the very different performance requirements of isochronous applications is packet tagging. This approach is much simpler and inherently more efficient. Datagrams created by isochronous applications are identified through new header fields made possible by extending basic packet header formats. Routers in an internetwork recognize the significance of the field and treat the datagrams accordingly.

These datagrams are forwarded in much the same way as datagrams from conventional applications, with one exception. When the time-to-live (TTL) of an isochronous datagram expires, the datagram is just dropped from the application's stream. Packet tagging improves the efficiency of an internetwork by enabling routers to determine whether a datagram can be discarded. Demonstrating the potential degree of the effectiveness of packet tagging requires a quick examination of routing time-sensitive datagrams without this mechanism.

Without packet tagging, all the routers in an internetwork would be obligated to deliver the datagram to its intended destination, regardless of how much time this took or how many retransmission attempts were needed. Datagrams that arrived late, or out of sequence, would just be discarded by the recipient despite the effort put into delivery by the network's routers. Tagging packets with a high time value spares the routers this wasteful activity.

The drawback to this simple scheme is that packet tagging stops short of guaranteeing the level of performance that might be needed by isochronous applications. Therefore, packet tagging must be viewed as a compromise approach with an inherent bias toward the operational efficiency of an internetwork, as opposed to being a true enabler of multimedia communications.

SUMMARY

Recent trends and technological developments have reinforced the criticality of routing in future networks. Routing, as a function, is maturing. Rather than this maturation being evidenced by a decline in its usefulness, routing's maturity is characterized by an increase in its use! Specifically, many of the new technologies being developed take the basic concept of routing, enhance it in some way, and then proliferate routing even further throughout the network. Today, routing technologies are being used to do things that were beyond the capabilities of traditional hardware-based routers.

These specialized routing products include multilayer switches, increasingly powerful and feature-rich hardware-based routers, and an endless series of sophisticated routing protocols. All these developments further the proliferation of routing technologies throughout networks. The end result is a more powerful, more efficient, and more feature-rich internetwork than would have been possible with traditional routing technologies.

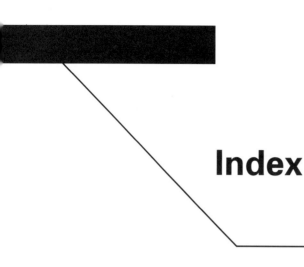

Index